# Food Lovers' London

## by Jenny Linford

## Photography by Chris Windsor

**Food Lovers' London**
Written by Jenny Linford
Photography by Chris Windsor
Edited by Andrew Kershman
Illustrations designed by Lesley Gilmour
Book design by Susi Koch and Lesley Gilmour

First published in Great Britain 1991 by Macmillan, updated editions
published in 1995, 1999, 2003 and 2005 by Metro Publications Ltd.

Published in 2010 by
**Metro Publications, PO Box 6336, London, N1 6PY**

**Printed and bound in India by Imprint Digital**
Produced using paper from registered sustainable and managed sources.
Suppliers have provided both LEI and MUTU certification.

© 2010 Jenny Linford
Photography ©2010 Chris Windsor

British Library Cataloguing in Publication Data.
A catalogue record for this book is available from the British Library.

ISBN 978-1-902910-35-2

for Mummy, Daddy, Chris and Ben
and in memory of Harry Greenwald
who believed in me.

# About the Author

**Jenny Linford** is a freelance food writer based in London and a member of the Guild of Food Writers. She is the author of several books including The London Cookbook (Metro Publications), a celebration of London's gastronomy past and present and Great British Cheeses (Dorling Kindersley), a reference book detailing over 300 British and Irish cheeses. Her work has ranged from research and writing for the British Library's Food Stories website to food writing for newspapers including The Financial Times.

An inveterate food shopper, Jenny founded the highly successful Gastro-Soho Tours in 1994. The personal guided tours offer a unique exploration of Soho's culinary treasures from bustling Chinese supermarkets to vintage Italian delis. www.jennylinford.co.uk

**Chris Windsor** is a freelance, professional photographer, based in London. Chris's work has ranged from advertising campaigns and company reports to books including *Food Lovers' London* and *The London Cookbook*. www.chriswindsor.com

# Contents

# Introduction

When I was a child my family moved from London to Florence and English food took on an especial importance. Visitors were entreated to bring packets of 'ordinary' tea, cheese and onion crisps and Walls' sausages. One small shop near the Duomo, Ye Olde English Store, sold a quaint mixture of English food: tinned asparagus, lemon puffs and Gentleman's Relish. Small jars of Marmite cost a few thousand lire more than they should have, but were savoured nevertheless. When I returned to London, in a culinary reversal, I found myself shopping for fresh pasta, basil and chunks of Parmesan cheese to try to recreate the sunny tastes of Tuscany. My own childhood experience brought home to me how much food means for expatriate communities, for whom it takes on a new significance and importance as a source of identity.

This book started out of personal nostalgia but turned into an enjoyable and fascinating journey of discovery. London, where I have lived for so many years, suddenly revealed glimpses into new and varied worlds: the aesthetic delight of a Japanese fish counter, dainty, pistachio-dusted, baklava from a Turkish patisserie,

the hustle and bustle of Brixton Market, freshly baked bagels in a busy Jewish bakery in Golders Green, being offered a free soft drink in Southall to commemorate a Sikh martyr who had preached tolerance to all. Encounters have been, on the whole, enjoyable (although one Iranian shop-owner accused me, only half-jokingly, of being a tax inspector!). Waiting in a Polish bakery to talk to the baker while three old ladies brought their rye bread and sausages chatting away in Polish, I gathered, from their sideways glances to me standing notebook in hand, that they were wondering what I was doing there. As one opened her purse to pay the baker, she suddenly broke into English "Daylight robbery!" she exclaimed, and shot a wicked, amused glance in my direction.

We are so much creatures of habit that new things are avoided almost automatically and this is certainly true with food. One of the great pleasures for me in writing this book has been the discovery of new ingredients and dishes. I had, for example, walked down Drummond Street many times to buy some fudge-like barfi from the Ambala Sweet Centre, but had never stopped to look at the unusual Asian vegetables on sale outside the grocers on the same street. Now I know a little more about them and have enjoyed cooking and eating vegetables such as tindola and dudi.

Since I first wrote Food Lovers' London in 1991, food shopping in Britain has changed enormously. In those days, if I wanted mascarpone cheese or lemon grass, I had to visit an Italian delicatessen or a shop in Chinatown. Today, my nearest supermarket stocks these and many other foodstuffs alongside them. Supermarkets, however, cannot offer everything or keep it in the best conditions, especially, it seems, fresh produce. Tired-looking rambutans or rock-hard mangoes in a supermarket compare badly with the excellent quality and good value fruit on offer in Gerrard Street, Asian greengrocers or West Indian markets.

One of the pleasures of shopping for food is to visit a shop where the staff know what they are doing and take pride in what they're selling. My local weekly fruit and veg market has a fish stall, run with cheery friendliness by Rita and her husband Alan, which sells a small selection of wonderfully fresh fish. Visiting this stall has become a satisfying weekly ritual. There's always a queue, predominantly made up of pensioners who obviously care about

the freshness of the fish they eat, waiting patiently while Rita and Alan skilfully gut, fillet or skin the fish as requested. I get a similar satisfaction from visiting I Camisa, an Italian delicatessen in Soho, where the Parma ham or mortadella is expertly sliced to the right thickness and they'll know how much pasta I need when I ask for "fresh white tagliatelle, to serve two for a main course". A trip to Neal's Yard Dairy to buy cheese is another heartening reminder of how great independent food shops can be; the friendly staff are happy to offer freshly-cut tastings of cheeses such as savoury Stichelton or delicate St Tola, make recommendations and share their enthusiasm for the farmhouse cheeses on the counter.

As I've travelled around this vast city researching this book, I've come to realise how lucky we Londoners are to have such an incredible variety of food shopping experiences available to us. With regard to food markets, Londoners can hunt for bargains at down-to-earth Queens Market in Newham, marvel at the Caribbean cornucopia of Brixton Market, enjoy seasonal food at one of London's many farmers' markets or stroll around Borough Market, with its many fine food stalls. Our city is home to grand, historic shops such as the venerable wine merchants

Berry Bros ("older than my country," as a visiting American friend observed when I took her there) and Fortnum and Mason's, revamped for its 300th anniversary. There are also new, imaginatively-conceived shops, such as Unpackaged in Islington, campaigning against wasteful food packaging. Greensmiths, near Waterloo, is another novel addition to London's food scene offering several top-notch, high street food shops under one roof.

Sadly, however, the picture is not entirely rosy. When I first wrote Food Lovers' London in the early 1990s, I wrote about the sadness of witnessing small food shops being forced to close down, hit hard by steeply rising rents and rates and competition from supermarkets. These problems continue today, joined by the congestion charge and the difficulty and expense of parking a car. Of the six or so Italian delicatessens which were in Soho when I first researched Food Lovers' London, only two remain. London has many gastronomic riches to offer, but they are under threat on many fronts. As food shoppers, however, we are not totally powerless. Over the years I've met an increasing number of people who, instead of automatically shopping at a supermarket, make a point of using markets or their local, independent shops. I myself set up my

Gastro Soho Tours to highlight the wonderful, historic food shops we have in the West End and to encourage people to use them. Food shopping doesn't have to be an impersonal slog around a vast supermarket; instead it can be a sociable, enjoyable experience. If we all make a point of shopping in independent shops, we really can help them to survive. This book offers a very personal guide to London's cosmopolitan food scene; I hope it will help you to discover your own favourite shops and explore the culinary diversity the capital has to offer.

Jenny Linford

# Price key

Prices are approximate, average prices per head for a meal without wine

£     £5-£10
££    £15-£25
£££   £25-£45
££££  £45-£65
£££££ £65 plus

# Soho

## ● Shops

## ● Eateries

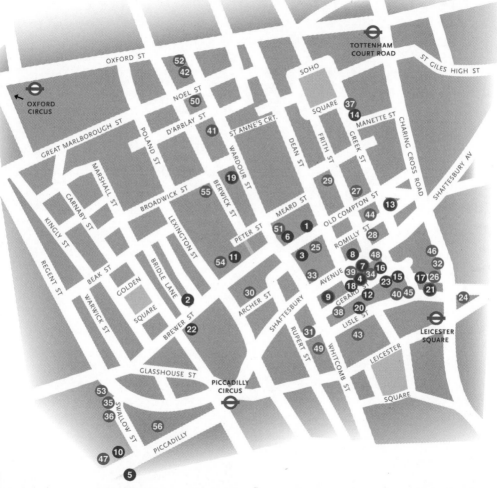

# Marylebone

## ● Shops

## ● Eateries

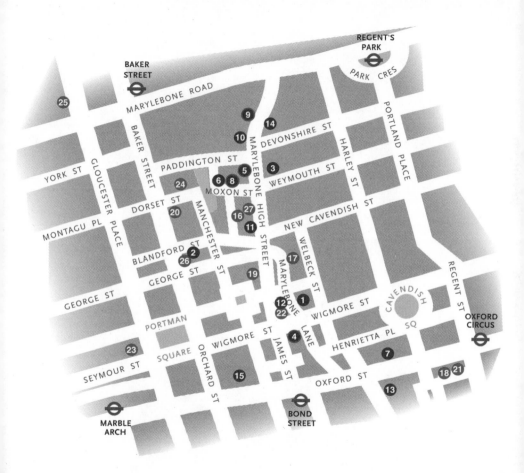

# Notting Hill

## ● Shops

1) **Artisan du Chocolat** (chocolate) p.43
2) **Athenian Grocery** (Greek) p.181
3) **Books for Cooks** (bookshop) p.322
4) **Daylesford Organic** (health food) p.72
5) **Gail's** (bakers & patisserie) p.19
6) **Garcia R. & Sons** (Spanish) p.293
7) **Golborne Fisheries** (fishmongers) p.62
8) **Hummingbird Bakery** p.301
9) **Impress Food Oriental Supermarket** (Chinese) p.276
10) **James Knight of Mayfair** (fishmonger) p.63
11) **Kalinka** (Russian) p.308
12) **Kingsland Edwardian Butchers** p.28
13) **Le Marrakech** (Morrocan) p.244
14) **Lisboa Delicatessen** (Portuguese) p.293
15) **Melt** (Chocolate) p.43
16) **Mr Christians** (deli) p.50
17) **Negozio Classica** (Italian) p.194
18) **Oriental City Supermarket** (Chinese) p.148
19) **Ottolenghi** (Mediterranean deli) p.48
20) **Planet Organic** (health food) p.72
21) **Portobello Market** p.77
22) **Notting Hill Farmers' Market** p.79
23) **Sara Super Market** (Iranian) p.245
24) **Spice Shop** p.81
25) **Tavola** (Italian deli) p.194
26) **Tawana** (Thai) p.277
27) **The Grocer on Elgin** (deli) p.49

## ● Eateries

28) **Alounak** (Middle Eastern) p.251
29) **Assaggi** (Italian) p.199
30) **Café Garcia** (Spanish) p.297
31) **Café Oporto** (Portuguese) p.297
32) **Fresco** (Lebanese) p.251
33) **Galicia** (Spanish) p.297
34) **Hafez** (Iranian) p.251
35) **Lisboa Patisserie** (Portuguese) p.298
36) **Mandarin Kitchen** (Chinese) p.154
37) **Moroccan Tagine** (Morrocan) p.252
38) **Oddono's Gelati** (gelateria) p.203
19) **Ottolenghi** (Mediterranean deli) p.48
39) **Royal China** (Chinese) p.155
40) **Taqueria** (Mexican) p.307
26) **Tawana** (Thai) p.277

# Chiswick / Turnham Green

## ● Shops

## ● Eateries

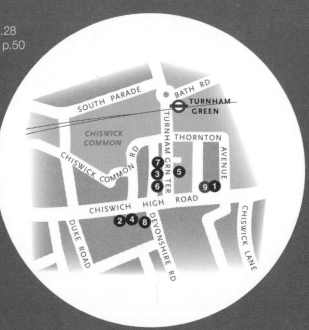

# Northcote Road

## ● Shops

1) **A. Dove & Son** (Butcher) p.30
2) **Dandelion Foods** (Health Food) p.73
3) **Gail's** (Bakery) p.21
4) **Hamish Johnston** (Cheese) p.38
5) **Hennessy's** (Butcher) p.30
6) **Hive Honey Shop** (Honey) p.93
7) **La Cuisiniere** (Kitchenware) p.315
8) **Northcote Road Market** p.77
9) **Philglass & Swiggot** (Wines & Spirits) p.91
10) **Recipease** (Deli & Cookery school) p.52
11) **Salumeria Napoli** (Italian) p.195
12) **Whole Foods Market** (Health Food) p.73

## ● Eateries

13) **Donna Margherita** (Italian) p.200
14) **Lola Rojo** (Spanish) p.298

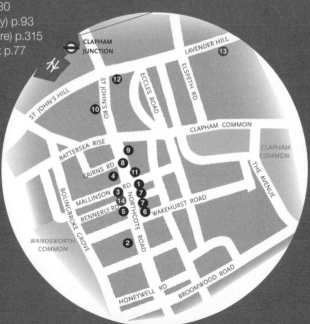

# General Foodshops

Bakers & Patisseries

Princi

During the 1990s pioneering bakeries such as Clarke's and De Gustibus showed just how delicious real bread could be. Recent years have seen several new craft bakers setting up business in London, selling through stalls at farmers' markets round the capital and opening shops offering artisan breads such as focaccia, sourdough and rye breads alongside tempting cakes and pastries.

# Central

## Baker & Spice

- 54-56 Elizabeth Street, SW1
- 020 7730 3033
- www.bakerandspice.uk.com
- Sloane Square LU, Victoria LU/Rail
- Mon-Sat 8am-7pm

This Belgravia branch of an acclaimed chain is an attractive café-cum-shop. It offers an appetising range of Baker & Spice's own-baked cakes, pastries and breads.

## Cocomaya

- *12 Connaught Street, W2*
- *020 7706 2770*
- *www.cocomaya.co.uk*
- *Marble Arch*
- *Mon-Fri 7am-7pm, Sat 8am-7pm, Sun 8am-4pm*

Decked out in light wood panels, this artisanal bakery and tea-room offers tempting, freshly-baked cakes and patisserie – from light blueberry muffins and cinnamon rolls to luxurious cakes and flans. They also run the delectable chocolate shop next door (see page 40).

## De Gustibus

- *4 Suffolk Street, SE1*
- *020 7407 3625*
- *www.degustibus.co.uk*
- *London Bridge LU/Rail*
- *Mon-Fri 7am-5pm, Sat 7am-4pm*

In a prime position backing onto Borough Market, this is a London outlet for artisanal baker Dan Schickentanz. It offers a range of his breads such as Six Day Sour (made with a sourdough starter) and Milwaukee Rye. The lunchtime trade is catered for with superior sandwiches.
*Branch at: 53 Blandford Street, W1 (020 7486 6608)*

## Konditor & Cook

- *46 Gray's Inn Road, WC1*
- *020 7404 6300*
- *www.konditorandcook.com*
- *Mon-Fri 7.30am-6.30pm*
- *Chancery Lane LU*

A branch of the popular bakery, noted for its quality cakes and pastries.

## Paul

🏠 *29 Bedford Street, WC2*
☎ *020 7836 3304*
🖃 *www.paul-uk.com*
🚌 *Covent Garden LU*
🕐 *Mon-Fri 7.30am-9pm*
   *Sat and Sun 9am-9pm*

This smart shop is the first London branch of a French chain now well-established here. It offers an attractive range of pastries and cakes and French-style breads, all baked on the premises. This thoroughly Gallic enterprise attracts patient queues both for the bakery and the back-room salon du thé, (see also French London).
*Branches throughout London (see website).*

## Le Pain Quotidien

🏠 *72-75 Marylebone High Street, W1*
☎ *020 7486 6154*
🖃 *www.lepainquotidien.com*
🚌 *Baker Street LU*
🕐 *Mon-Fri 7am-7pm, Sat 8am-6pm,*
   *Sun 9am-6pm*

London's first branch of this bakery-cum-café chain (founded in Brussels in 1990), is a spacious, stylishly rustic affair. There is a range of sourdough breads available made from organic stone-ground flour. You can sample the breads in the busy café area with moreish jams and good quality tea or coffee.
*Branches throughout London (see website).*

## Poilâne

🏠 *46 Elizabeth Street, SW1*
☎ *020 7808 4910*
🖃 *www.poilane.fr*
🚌 *Sloane Square LU, Victoria LU/Rail*
🕐 *Mon-Fri 7.30am-7pm; Sat 7.30am-6pm*

This dainty shop is a lovingly recreated replica of a famous Parisian bakery, complete with a wood-fired oven in the basement. Regulars return for Poilâne's huge, round sourdough loaves, with their distinctive tang. They are sold whole, halved, quartered or simply by the slice, (see also French London).

## Princi

🏠 *135 Wardour Street, W1*
☎ *020 7478 8888*
🖃 *www.princi.co.uk*
🚌 *Leicester Square LU*
   *Oxford Circus LU Piccadilly Circus LU,*
🕐 *Mon-Sat 7am-12midnight, Sun 9am-10pm*

This glamorous addition to London's baking scene combines a pasticceria, bakery and café. It serves up its own-made Italian breads, cakes and pastries, displayed in a long glass counter which stretches the length of the shop. Highlights include pizza and focaccia – freshly baked in a wood-fired oven – and brought warm to the counter. The food here tastes as good as it looks. Princi are also featured in the Italian London section (see p.191).

## St John

🖥 *26 St John Street, EC1*

☎ *020 7251 0848*

✎ *www.stjohnrestaurant.co.uk*

🚌 *Farringdon LU/Rail*

🕐 *Bread sold from 7am Mon-Sat*

This much-applauded Clerkenwell restaurant is famous for chef Fergus Henderson's appreciative approach towards offal. Less well know is its side-line trade in bread baked on the premises. The St John sourdough is particularly popular. *Branch at: 94-96 Commercial Street, E1 (020 7251 0848)*

## William Curley

🖥 *198 Ebury Street, SW1*

☎ *020 7730 5522*

✎ *www.williamcurley.co.uk*

🚌 *Sloane Square LU*

🕐 *Mon-Sat 9.30am-6.30pm Sun 10.30am-6pm*

This distinctly chic establishment offers a selection of William Curley's acclaimed patisserie, which can be enjoyed in the café area or bought to take away. *Branch at: 10 Paved Court, Richmond, Surrey, TW9 (see page 21)*

# North

## Dunn's

🖥 *6 The Broadway, Crouch End, N8*

☎ *020 8340 1614*

🕐 *Mon-Sat 6am-6pm, Sun 9am-5pm*

🚌 *Finsbury Park LU/Rail, then bus W7*

This family-run bakery has a loyal local following and sells an extensive range of freshly-baked breads, cakes and pastries.

## Euphorium

🖥 *202 Upper Street, N1*

☎ *020 7704 6705*

✎ *www.euphoriumbakery.com*

🚌 *Angel, Highbury and Islington*

🕐 *Mon-Fri 7.30am-11am, Sat 8am-9pm, Sun 9am-11pm*

A popular North London bakery and café offering breads, pastries and cakes.

## Gail's

🖥 *64 Hampstead High St, NW3*

☎ *020 7794 5700*

✎ *www.gailsbread.co.uk*

🕐 *Mon-Fri 7am-8pm, Sat-Sun 8am-8pm*

🚌 *Hampstead LU*

This small but popular café-cum-shop offers Gail's trademark range of high-quality breads, cakes and pastries. They look great and taste delicious!

## Peyton and Byrne

- 11, The Undercroft
  St Pancras Station, NW1
- 020 7278 6707
- www.peytonandbyrne.com
- Mon-Fri 7.30am-8pm,
  Sat-Sun 9am-8pm

This pretty bakery-cum-café specialises in British baking. It offers treats such as fairy cakes, Chelsea buns, scones and biscuits, to be taken away or enjoyed in the café with a cup of tea. Savoury snacks include upmarket sandwiches, excellent Scotch eggs and hearty pies.

## Victoria Bakery

- 83 High Street, Barnet, EN5
- 020 8449 0790
- High Barnet LU
- Mon-Sat 7.30am-5pm

This small, traditional English bakery offers a range of excellent, freshly baked white, brown and soda breads. Other specialities include scones and currant buns, with the cheese straws and iced ring doughnuts going down a storm with local schoolchildren.

# North-West

## Gail's

- 5 Circus Road, NW8
- 020 7722 0983
- www.gailsbread.co.uk
- St John's Wood
- Mon-Fri 7am-8pm, Sat-Sun 8am-8pm

A café-cum-shop branch of this established bakery offering a great selection of freshly made artisanal breads and some very fine patisserie which can be enjoyed at home or in their comfy café.

# West

## & Clarke's

🏠 *122 Kensington Church Street, W8*
☎ *020 7229 2190*
🚌 *High Street Kensington LU*
   *Notting Hill LU*
🕐 *Mon-Fri 8am-8pm, Sat 8am-4pm,*
   *Sun 10am-4pm*

An elegantly rustic shop next door to Sally Clarke's restaurant, that sells her famous selection of breads including a delicious rosemary and sea-salt loaf. Other own-baked treats range from savoury pizzas to sweet tarts, including fresh fruit, chocolate and (at Thanksgiving) pumpkin. The discerningly selected stock features own-made treats such as delectable chocolate truffles, puff pastry made with French unsalted butter, and chutneys.

## Baker & Spice

🏠 *20 Clifton Road, W9*
☎ *020 7266 1122*
🖱 *www.bakerandspice.uk.com*
🚌 *Warwick Avenue*
🕐 *Mon-Sat 7am-7pm, Sun 8am-6pm*

An attractive café-cum-shop branch of the established bakery.

## Exeter Street Bakery

🏠 *1B Argyll Road, W8*
☎ *020 7937 8484*
🚌 *High Street Kensington LU*
🕐 *Mon-Sat 8am-7pm, Sun 9am-6pm*

This small shop sells traditionally-made Italian breads, such as ciabatta or pane Pugliese.

## Gail's

🏠 *138 Portobello Road, W11*
☎ *020 7460 0766*
🖱 *www.gailsbread.co.uk*
🚌 *Notting Hill*
🕐 *Mon-Fri 7am-7pm, Sat 7am-7.30pm,*
   *Sun 8am-7.30pm*

A popular café and shop branch of Gail's, offering excellent in-house baked breads and patisserie. This is a great place to relax and replenish your batteries before embarking on an exploration of Portobello Market on a busy Saturday.

# South

## Konditor & Cook

- 22 Cornwall Road, SE1
- 020 7261 0456
- www.konditorandcook.com
- Waterloo LU/Rail
- Mon-Fri 7.30am-6.30pm,
  Sat 8.30am-3pm

Gerhard Jenne's bakery is noted for its creative hand-made cakes and pastries, from wildly colourful 'magic cakes' to imaginatively personalised birthday cakes (much in demand with celebrity clients). One reason for Gerhard's success is that he firmly believes everything should taste as good as it looks.

## Konditor & Cook

- 63 Stamford Street. SE1
- 020 7921 9200
- www.konditorandcook.com
- Waterloo LU/rail
- Mon-Fri 7.30am-6.30pm
  Sat 9.30am-4.30pm

A South Bank branch of this well-established bakery, noted for its quality cakes and pastries.

## Konditor & Cook

- 10 Stoney Street, SE1
- 020 7407 5100
- www.konditorandcook.com
- London Bridge LU/rail
- Mon-Fri 7.30am-6pm, Sat 8.30am-5pm

Right by Borough Market, this small branch of Konditor & Cook does a roaring trade in sandwiches, cakes and pastries.

# South-West

## Baker & Spice

- 47 Denyer Street, SW3
- 020 7589 4734
- www.bakerandspice.uk.com
- Knightsbridge LU, South Kensington LU
- Mon-Sat 7am-7pm, Sun 8am-6pm

A smart branch of this established bakery.

## K & S Bakery

- 247 Old Brompton Road, SW5
- 020 7373 8338
- Tues-Sat 7am-7pm, Sun 10am-5pm
- www.ksbakery.co.uk
- Earl's Court

This bakery offers Londoners a rare chance to sample freshly baked German breads, cakes and pastries. Germanic specialities include rye bread, multigrain bread, pretzels and classic Apple Strudel.

## Gail's

- 64 Northcote Road, SW11
- ☎ 020 7924 6330
- www.gailsbread.co.uk
- Clapham Junction rail
- Mon-Fri 7am-7.30pm
  Sat-Sun 8am-7pm

A roomy café-cum-shop, offering Gail's tempting range of in-house baked goods, from breads to pastries.

## Old Post Office Bakery

- 76 Landor Road, SW9
- ☎ 020 7326 4408
- Clapham North LU
- Mon, Wed, Thur 7am-7pm,
  Tue 7am-5.30pm, Fri 7am-6pm,
  Sat 7am-5.30pm, Sun 9am-2pm

Founded in 1982, London's first organic bakery is still going strong, though no longer housed in the 'old post office' which was its first home. Loyal customers return for the handmade breads (including sourdough rye and three seed wholewheat) and the excellent pastries. All the goods here are freshly baked on the premises by Richard Scroggs and John Dungevel and the prices are still very reasonable.

## Newens: the Original Maids of Honour

- 288 Kew Road, TW9
- ☎ 020 8940 2752
- www.theoriginalmaidsofhonour.co.uk
- Kew Gardens LU
- Mon 9.30am-1pm,
  Tue-Sat 9.30am-6pm

The Newens family have been baking Maids of Honour cakes (traditional almond tarts) in the Richmond area since 1850. The recipe continues to be a closely guarded family secret. Their Tudor-style bakery-cum-tea room is just by Kew Gardens. Classic British treats on offer include custard tarts, scones, tea cakes and Maids of Honour as well as truly splendid steak and salmon pies.

## William Curley

- 10 Paved Court, TW9
- ☎ 020 8332 3002
- www.williamcurley.co.uk
- Richmond LU/Rail
- Tue-Sat 10am-5.30pm, Sun 11am-4pm

William Curley's minimalist shop, discreetly located on a historic Richmond side-street, showcases William's exquisite patisserie, all freshly baked on the premises.

# South-East

## East Dulwich Deli

🏠 *15-17 Lordship Lane, SE22*

☎ *020 8693 2525*

🚉 *East Dulwich Rail*

🕐 *Mon-Thur 9am-7pm, Fri 9am-8pm,
Sat 8.30am-6pm, Sun 10am-4pm*

This large, smart delicatessen showcases freshly baked breads from Born & Bread, their own wholesale bakery. The bread is organic, made from stone-ground flour and baked in a splendid wood-fired oven. Born & Bread's crunchy baguette is a popular choice. For their deli review see p.36.

# East

## De Gustibus

🏠 *53-55 Carter Lane, EC4*

☎ *020 7236 0056*

🖋 *www.degustibus.co.uk*

🚉 *St Paul's LU*

🕐 *Mon-Fri 7am-5pm*

A City-based café outlet for De Gustibus breads, with diners being able to mix and match breads and fillings.

## Konditor & Cook

🏠 *The Gherkin, 30 St Mary Axe, EC3*

☎ *0845 262 3030*

🖋 *www.konditorandcook.com*

🚉 *Aldgate LU*

🕐 *Mon-Fri 7.30am-6.30pm*

A stylish shop-cum-café branch of the popular bakery, noted for its quality cakes and pastries.

## Loafing

🏠 *79 Lauriston Road, E9*

☎ *020 8986 0777*

🚉 *London Fields rail*

🕐 *Mon-Fri 7.30am-6pm, Sat 8am-6pm,
Sun 9am-6pm*

An attractive bakery-cum-café, offering a well-chosen range of breads and cakes from suppliers including Clarke's, Flour Power and Jade Boulangerie. Locals pop in for Monmouth coffee and a slice of carrot cake, to be enjoyed either inside or in the small courtyard.

## The Spence Bakery

🏠 *161 Stoke Newington Church Street,*

☎ *020 7249 4927*

🖋 *www.thespence.co.uk*

🚉 *Stoke Newington rail*

🕐 *Mon-Sat 8am-6pm. Sun 9am-6pm*

This small, friendly bakery sells its own hand-made breads, freshly baked on the premises.

Butchers

*Allens of Mayfair*

Even the most basic high-street butcher's is a fast-vanishing breed, while a really decent one is extremely hard to find. Encouragingly, in the years since the BSE crisis those butchers who put the emphasis on providing quality, plant-fed, free-range or organic meat have seen sales improve. Many customers now realise the value of buying meat from a trustworthy, traceable source.

# Central

## Allens of Mayfair

- 117 Mount Street, W1
- 020 7499 5831
- www.allensofmayfair.co.uk
- Bond Street LU
- Mon-Fri 6am-5.30pm,
  Sat 6am-2pm

With its beautiful tiles and huge wooden chopping blocks, this venerable butchers is a Mayfair institution with customers ranging from film stars to famous chefs. Game is a particular forte of Allens, which is noted both for the quality and range of game it carries. During the game season the shop has a wonderful display of feathered and furred game. Its aged, prime Scotch beef is another speciality.

## Biggles

- 66 Marylebone Lane, W1
- 020 7224 5937
- www.ebiggles.co.uk
- Bond Street LU
- Mon 10am-4.30pm
  Tue-Sat 10am-6pm

Tucked away down a charming side-street, Biggles is a sausage specialist. The sausages are made-on-the-premises with a high-meat content and lots of varieties, from Toulouse to Greek.

## The Ginger Pig

- 8-10 Moxon Street, W1
- 020 7935 7788
- www.thegingerpig.co.uk
- Bond Street LU
- Mon-Thur 9am-6pm
  Fri-Sat 9am-6.30pm, Sun 10am-2.30pm

This handsome shop showcases Tim Wilson's own-reared meat from his farm in the Yorkshire Dales. Here can be found flavourful, well-hung beef from long horn cattle, prime pork from rare breed pigs, and lamb and mutton from the Swaledale sheep that graze on the hills behind the farm. There is also a splendid charcuterie counter laden with their own-made pork pies, sausage rolls, terrines and pâtés.

## Jack O'Shea's

- *11 Montpelier Street, SW7*
- *020 7581 7771*
- *www.jackoshea.com*
- *Knightsbridge LU*
- *Mon-Fri 8am-7pm, Sat 8am-5pm*

As befits its Knightsbridge location, this is a smart-looking shop, a London outlet for an Irish family butchers business established in 1790. Free-range and organic meat is on offer including grass-fed Irish veal, prime Irish Black Angus beef and Shetland Island, seaweed-fed lamb. Their own dry-cured bacon is a rare treat. The eponymous Jack O'Shea works behind the counter, happy to offer advice and cooking tips. An appetising, savoury smell comes from meat roasting in the shop's ovens – the shop does a brisk trade in roast beef sandwiches.

## McKenna

- *21 Theobald's Road, WC1*
- *020 7242 7740*
- *Holborn*
- *Mon-Fri 6am-5.30pm, Sat 6am-2.30pm*

This small, down-to-earth Bloomsbury butchers shop is well-known for both the range and quality of its meat and the competitiveness of its pricing. It consequently has a loyal local following – expect to queue! Game is a particular forte here and the helpful staff are happy to order anything they don't stock.

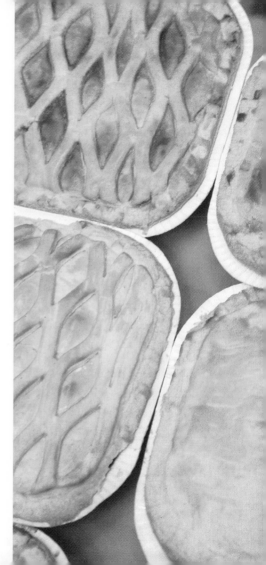

## Wyndham House

⌧ *39 Tachbrook Street, SW1*
☎ *020 7821 6341*
🚌 *Pimlico LU*
🕐 *Tue-Fri 9am-5pm, Sat 9am-4.30pm*

This smart contemporary butcher has an excellent range of free-range meat and poultry. The chicken here is excellent. Popular Christmas purchases are the three-bird roasts and Norfolk bronze turkeys.

# North

## B & M Seafoods

⌧ *258 Kentish Town Road, NW5*
☎ *020 7485 0346*
🚌 *Kentish Town LU/Rail*
🕐 *Mon-Sat 7.30am-5.30pm*

Despite its name, this friendly, down-to-earth shop offers not only fish but an excellent range of organic meat and poultry. The meat is carefully sourced from small-scale, organic suppliers and the quality is very high.

## Baldwins

⌧ *469 Green Lanes, N4*
☎ *020 8340 5934*
🖱 *www.baldwinsfoods.com*
🚌 *Manor House LU
then bus 29, 141, 341*
🕐 *Mon-Sat 8am-6.30pm, Sun 8am-4pm*

Attractively spick and span, this smart corner shop with friendly staff, offers an excellent selection of meat and poultry. Their produce includes more unusual meats such as rabbit and venison and at Christmas they do a roaring trade in free-range bronze turkeys.

## James Elliott

⌧ *96 Essex Road, N1*
☎ *020 7226 3658*
🚌 *Angel LU*
🕐 *Mon-Thurs 8am-5pm, Fri 8am-6pm,
Sat 8am-5pm*

A well-established shop, that sells excellent, well-hung, free-range meat and poultry, plus a discerningly chosen selection of cheeses. Elliot's is particularly known for its prime Scotch beef and its own-cooked hams. It attracts a steady steam of regulars, who enjoy the butcher's banter as he expertly cuts their meat to order.

## Frank Godfrey Ltd

- *7 Highbury Park, N5*
- *020 7226 2425*
- *www.fgodfrey.co.uk*
- *Arsenal LU*
- *Mon-Fri 8am-6pm, Sat 8am-5pm*

This down-to-earth family butcher's – now run by fourth generation brothers Chris and Jeremy Godfrey – has a loyal and devoted following who know good meat when they see it. All the meat sold here is free-range and very good quality, from the English corn-fed chickens to the plant-fed pork and Orkney Island beef. The brothers work closely with their suppliers to ensure high feed and welfare standards, and the results are reflected in the quality of the meat.

## Highland Organics

- *14 Bittacy Hill, NW7*
- *020 8346 1055*
- *www.organicbutcher.net*
- *Mill Hill LU*
- *Mon-Sat 8am-6pm*

As the name suggests, organic meats are the thing here, from Welsh Black beef steaks to huge plump home-made sausages. Customers can also stock up on basic organic groceries – from fresh bread to baked beans.

## Midhurst

- *2 Midhurst Parade, N10*
- *020 8883 5303*
- *East Finchley LU, then the 102 bus*
- *Mon-Thur 8am-4.45pm, Fri 7am-4.45pm, Sat 7am-4pm*

Tucked away in a little parade of shops between Muswell Hill and East Finchley, this small shop offers decent meat (some organic) with fresh fruit and veg outside.

## Moore & Sons

- *25 Greenhill Parade, Great North Road, EN5*
- *020 8449 9649*
- *www.mooreandsonsbutchers.co.uk*
- *High Barnet LU*
- *Mon-Thur 8am-530pm, Fri 7am-5.30pm, Sat 7am-4pm*

A small, traditional, well-established butcher with friendly staff. Specialities include Scotch beef, own-made sausages and a fine display of game.

### Morley Butchers

- 23 Broadway Parade, N8
- 020 8340 2436
- Finsbury Park LU/Rail
  then bus W3 or W7
- Mon-Fri 8.30am-5pm, Sat 8.30am-4pm

This small, friendly Crouch End butcher has a loyal local following. Customers return for the Scotch beef, English lamb, pork and poultry and a good range of furred and feathered game during the season.

# West

### Kingsland Edwardian Butchers

- 140 Portobello Road, W11
- 020 7727 6067
- Notting Hill Gate LU
- Mon-Sat 9am-5.30pm

A bright red frontage marks out this attractive, old-fashioned butcher's shop. There is a good range of meat, from their own dry-cured bacon to Orkney Aberdeen Angus beef. Their speciality is rare breeds meat, from Gloucester Old Spot pork to seaweed-fed North Ronaldsay lamb from Orkney. The staff are friendly and helpful.

### C. Lidgate

- 110 Holland Park Avenue, W11
- 020 7727 8243
- www.lidgates.com
- Holland Park LU
- Mon-Fri 7am-7pm, Sat 6.30am-6.30pm

A grand old butcher's established in 1850, which specialises in high-quality, naturally-grown and fed meat and poultry. Run with great expertise and commitment by David Lidgate, the shop's stock includes organic meat from Highgrove (The Prince of Wales' estate), free-range bronze turkeys and geese. In addition, this family-run business sells award-winning home-made pies and own-cooked hams.

### Macken Bros

- 44 Turnham Green Terrace, W4
- 020 8994 2646
- www.mackenbros.co.uk
- Turnham Green LU
- Mon-Fri 7am-6pm, Sat 7am-5.30pm

A seemingly perpetual queue testifies to this well-established shop's popularity. Staff are helpful and friendly and the range of meat and poultry is extensive while the quality remains very high.

## Meat Like It Used To Be

☐ *50 Cannon Lane, HA5*

☏ *020 8866 4611*

🚇 *Pinner LU*

🕒 *Mon-Thur 8am-5.30pm, Fri 7.30am-6pm, Sat 7.30am-5pm Sun 9am-1pm*

The name says it all. This friendly, well-run butcher's stocks an impressive range of fully-traceable free-range meat and poultry. Stock includes certified Aberdeen Angus beef, Kelly Bronze turkeys and a good selection of game.

## Richardsons

☐ *88 Northfield Avenue, W13*

☏ *020 8567 1064*

🚇 *Northfield LU*

🕒 *Mon-Fri 8am-5.30pm, Sat 8am-4.30pm*

This down-to-earth, busy butcher's attracts a loyal clientele, drawn back by the quality of the meat on offer. Richardsons has a well established reputation for its excellent beef and award-winning sausages.

## Sheepdrove Organic Farm Family Butcher

☐ *5 Clifton Road, W9*

☏ *020 7266 3838*

🖱 *www.sheepdrove.com*

🚇 *Maida Vale LU*

🕒 *Mon-Fri 9am-7pm, Sat 9am-5pm, Sun10am-4pm*

On a peaceful Maida Vale street, this small, smart butchers shop comes with impeccable organic credentials with all meat coming from Sheepdrove Organic Farm. The counter is filled with good-looking meat and poultry, from Aberdeen Angus steaks (hung for 4 weeks) to organic chickens and dry-cured bacon. Commendably, the butcher also focuses on thriftier cuts, such as chicken wings, pork belly and pig's trotters.

## H. G. Walter

☐ *51 Palliser Road, W14*

☏ *020 7385 6466*

🖱 *www.hgwalter.com*

🚇 *Baron's Court LU*

🕒 *Mon-Fri 8am-7pm, Sat 8am-5pm*

This small, immaculate blue-and-white tiled butcher's shop has a notable reputation. They proudly display their award as 'Best Small Butchers' Shop in Great Britain' on the window. A family business, it is run with friendly efficiency and an eye for detail by brother-and-sister team Adam and Clare Heanen. All the meat is free-range or organic and their Scotch beef, dry-aged for 28 days in a purpose-built cool room, is a source of particular pride. Also on offer is a range of seasonal game (including rarities such as grey partridge), Plantation Pig pork, luxuriously expensive Wagyu beef and home-made burgers and sausages. Thanksgiving and Christmas sees the shop doing a roaring trade in free-range and organic turkeys and geese, but throughout the year they are busy with loyal customers prepared to go out of their way to find quality meat.

# South-West

## The Butcher & Grill

39-41 Parkgate Road, SW11
020 7924 3999
www.thebutcherandgrill.com
Clapham Junction Rail
Mon-Sat 8am-9pm, Sun 9am-4pm

A smart contemporary outfit, enterprisingly combining an upmarket butchers with a spacious restaurant. The emphasis is on quality meat, using suppliers such as Highfields Farm in East Sussex. In addition, the shop also offers a usefully range of fresh fruit and vegetables and some delicatessen stock items too.

## A. Dove & Son

71 Northcote Road, SW11
020 7223 5191
www.doveandson.co.uk
Clapham Junction Rail
Mon 8am-4pm, Tue-Sat 8am-5pm

This characterful butcher's shop, run with passion by Bob Dove, has a loyal clientele. Highlights include the well-hung beef, popular meat pies and excellent bronze turkeys. This is a shop well worth a visit, particularly on a Saturday when Northcote Road Market is in full swing.

## Hennessy's

80 Northcote Road, SW11
020 7228 0894
Clapham Junction Rail
Tue-Sat 9.30am-6pm, Sun 9.30am-1pm

This down-to-earth, established butcher's shop offers organic and free-range meats and home-made sausages.

## M. Moen & Sons

24 The Pavement, SW4
020 7622 1624
www.moen.co.uk
Clapham Common LU
Mon-Fri 8.30am-6pm, Sat 8am-5pm

This well-established butcher's offers a distinctly upmarket stock. The meat is good quality – from home-made sausages to a range of in-season game.  Additional delights include wild mushrooms and seasonal produce like sea-kale.

## Pether

🖼 *16 Station Parade, Kew Gardens, TW9*
☎ *020 8940 0163*
🚉 *Kew Gardens LU*
🕐 *Mon-Fri 7.30am-6pm, Sat 7.30am-5pm*

An appetising smell of spit-roasted chicken wafts out from this old-fashioned butcher's. All the meat here is free-range and the shop does a roaring trade in home-made pies. A real Kew institution and worth visiting.

## Randalls

🖼 *113 Wandsworth Bridge Road, SW6*
☎ *020 7736 3426*
🚉 *Fulham Broadway LU*
🕐 *Mon-Fri 8.30am-5.30pm, Sat 8am-4pm*

This fine butchers offers top-notch, free-range and organic meat.  Attractively presented, the meat  both looks and tastes good.  The marinaded meats and own-made sausages are particularly popular.

## Wyndham House

🖼 *339 Fulham Road, SW10*
☎ *020 7352 7888*
🚉 *Fulham Broadway LU*
🕐 *Mon-Sat 7.30am-6pm*

This small, smart shop offers a cracking range of attractively presented, free-range meat and poultry.  Stock includes Label Anglaise chickens, lamb, pork and Welsh Black beef.  This is also a very good place to source game during the season.

# South-East

## I. M Butchers

🖼 *147 Evelina Road, SE15*
☎ *020 7732 2820*
🚉 *Nunhead Rail*
🕐 *Mon-Fri 8am-5pm, Sat 8am-4pm*

A small, friendly butchers shop offering free-range chickens in addition to beef, lamb and pork.  Another great feature of the store is the selection of deli meats including some very fine shop-prepared hams.

## K. Libretto

🖼 *112 Wood Vale, SE23*
☎ *020 8693 3175*
🚉 *Forest Hill rail*
🕐 *Tue & Thur 10am-5pm, Wed 10am-1pm, Fri 10am-6pm, Sat 8.30am-2pm*

Established over 26 years, this traditional butchers shop is run with amiable care by Kim Lebretto.  Customers range from regulars who have shopped here for years to new arrivals to the area.  Kim is happy to offer advice on which cuts of meat to buy and has lots of great cooking tips.

## William Rose

126 Lordship Lane, SE22
020 8693 9191
www.williamrosebutchers.com
East Dulwich rail
Tue-Fri 8am-5.30pm, Sat 8am-5pm

Having moved from Vauxhall to Lordship Lane in 2005, this upmarket, family butchers has been greeted with enthusiasm by the local community. On offer is an fine range of free-range and organic meat and poultry, as well as game.

## William Rose

75 East Dulwich Grove, SE22
020 8693 7733
www.williamrosebutchers.com
East Dulwich rail
Tue-Fri 8am-5pm, Sat 8am-4pm

William Rose's flagship shop offers his hallmark free-range and organic meat. Of particular note is the Longhorn and Red Poll beef and the excellent Gloucester Old Spot pork sausages. The chicken and other poultry is also of a very high standard.

# East

## The Ginger Pig

99 Lauriston Road, E9
020 8986 6911
London Fields rail
www.thegingerpig.co.uk
Tue 9am-5.30pm, Wed-Fri 9am-6.30pm, Sat 9am-6pm, Sun 9am-3pm

A smart new, Hackney branch of this excellent butchers. This store has really gained in popularity, helped by the growing popularity of Lauriston as a foodie enclave including Bottle Apostle, Loafing and Jonathan Norris fishmongers.

Neal's Yard Dairy, Borough

Cheese Shops

If you enjoy eating cheese, then it is well worth finding a good cheesemonger to shop at. Looking after artisanally-made cheese so that it can be eaten and enjoyed at its best, requires skill, care and attention. The best cheesemongers not only pride themselves on the quality of the cheeses that they stock, but also enjoy sharing their knowledge and enthusiasm for cheese. Visiting such a store is a great experience.

# Central

## Cheese at Leadenhall

4-5 Leadenhall Market, EC3
020 7929 1697
Liverpool Street LU/Rail
www.cheeseatleadenhall.co.uk
Mon-Wed 9am-5pm, Thur-Fri 9am-8pm

Housed in a long narrow space, formerly a butcher's shop, Cheese at Leadenhall is run with panache by Sue Cloke. On offer is a carefully selected range of British, Irish and French cheeses as well as around 50 wines, chosen to complement cheese. In addition to buying cheese, customers can sit and sample the wares at the bar, enjoying a cheese platter and glass of wine. Dishes on offer change seasonally and include 'proper' Croque Monsieur, raclette, tartiflette and grilled goat's cheese with salad.

## La Cave du Fromage

24-25 Cromwell Place SW7
0845 1088 222
South Kensington LU
www.la-cave.co.uk
Tue-Wed 10am—7pm
Thur-Sat 10am-9pm, Sun 11am-5pm

This smart cheese shop comes with impressive credentials – set up by Eric Charriaux and Amnon Paldi who run a company supplying farmhouse cheeses to top restaurants. On offer in the shop is an extensive range of 160 cheeses from Britain, France, Italy and Spain, matured in-house and varying seasonally. Bestsellers include Fourme au Maury, Tartufette and Epoisse. The cave also contains a select range of charcuterie, freshly baked bread and wines. Not surprisingly, the shop has been embraced by the local French community, who appreciate the well-chosen stock and helpful, informed service. Customers can sit and sample cheese platters and also take part in regular wine and cheese-tastings.

## La Fromagerie

2-4 Moxon Street, W1
020 7935 0341
Baker Street LU
www.lafromagerie.co.uk
Mon-Fri 8am-7.30pm,
Sat 9am-7pm, Sun 10am-6pm

Just off Marylebone High Street, this spacious, attractive shop is an alluring destination for cheese-lovers, with its temperature-controlled cheese room very much at the heart of the shop. Owner Patricia Michelson, whose passionate enthusiasm for cheese is genuine and infectious, carefully sources her artisanal cheeses direct from the producers and also matures them. The shop stocks between 150-200 seasonal farmhouse cheeses, featuring both classics such as Beaufort Chalet d'Alpage to Corsican ewe's milk brocciu and Austrian St Theodor.

## Neal's Yard Dairy

- *17 Shorts Gardens, WC2*
- *020 7240 5700*
- *www.nealsyarddairy.co.uk*
- *Covent Garden LU*
- *Mon-Sat 10am-7pm*

A pioneering champion of British farmhouse cheeses, this small shop has an impressive range of traditionally-made farmhouse cheeses including classics such as Appleby's Cheshire, Montgomery's Cheddar and Kirkham's Lancashire. Other produce includes good-quality breads, pickles and chutneys and farmhouse butter. Customers are encouraged to taste before buying – one of the joys of artisanal-made cheese being that they vary in flavour from batch to batch.

## Paxton & Whitfield

- *93 Jermyn Street, SW1*
- *020 7930 0259*
- *www.paxtonandwhitfield.co.uk*
- *Piccadilly Circus LU*
- *Mon-Sat 9.30am-6pm*

This picturesque, vintage shop, established in 1797, is a grand old name in cheese-selling and prides itself on the broad range of around 100 British and continental cheeses stocked. While bestsellers include Cheddar and Cropwell Bishop Stilton, specialities include own-imported mozzarella, sold within 24 hours of making. A partnership with Androuet in Paris means that there's an impressive range of French cheese. There's also biscuits, chutneys and relishes.

## Rippon Cheese Stores

- 26 Upper Tachbrook Street, SW1
- *020 7931 0628*
- *www.ripponcheese.com*
- *Pimlico LU, Victoria LU/Rail*
- *Mon-Fri 8am-5.30pm*
  *Sat 8.30am-5pm*

Well-known for their wholesale cheese business, Karen and Philip Rippon stock an astonishing assortment of around 550 European cheeses in this cool, neat shop. Karen, Philip and their helpful staff are very happy to offer advice and guidance to their extensive range of cheeses.

# North

## Cheeses

*11 Fortis Green Road, N10*
*020 8444 9141*
*www.cheesesonline.co.uk*
*East Finchley LU, Bus 134*
*Mon-Sat 9.30am-6pm*

Tucked away in an old-fashioned parade of
shops just off Muswell Hill Broadway, this tiny
shop offers an excellent array of European
cheeses, served by friendly and helpful staff.

## La Fromagerie

*30 Highbury Park, N5*
*020 7937 8004*
*www.lafromagerie.co.uk*
*Highbury & Islington LU/Rail*
*Mon 10.30am-7pm, Tue-Fri 9am-7pm,*
*Sat 9am-7pm, Sun 10am-5pm*

Patricia Michelson's Islington shop
features a cool backroom, filled with
a carefully sourced range of between
200-250 seasonal farmhouse cheeses.
Complementing the cheeses is a delicious
range of breads and patisserie.

# West

## Jeroboams

- 96 Holland Park, W11
- 020 7727 9359
- www.jeroboams.co.uk
- Holland Park LU
- Mon-Fri 8am-8pm, Sat 8.30am-7pm, Sun 10am-6pm

This noted wine merchant also offers an impressive range of artisanal European cheeses, with an emphasis on French cheeses such as 22 months-old, aged Mimolette. Jeroboams does its own affinage; for example, buying in fresh chèvre and maturing them. The Pave d'Affinois is matured to perfection and other bestsellers include Italian burrata, Vacherin and Stilton.

# South

## Neal's Yard Dairy

- 6 Park Street, SE1
- 020 7367 0799
- www.nealsyarddairy.co.uk
- London Bridge LU/Rail
- Mon-Fri 9am-6pm, Sat 8am-5pm

With its eye-catching display of cloth-wrapped Cheddar cheeses and impressive long counter display of artisanal British and Irish cheeses, this spacious shop is a real treat for cheese-lovers. On offer here is a carefully-chosen selection, ranging from traditional cheeses such as Cheddar, Stilton and Wensleydale to contemporary cheeses such as Stichelton (a blue-veined cheese made from unpasteurised organic cow's milk), delicate Perroche (a soft goat's cheese) and Gubbeen (a rich, Irish, washed-rind cheese). Tastings are offered by the staff, who are happy to offer advice and suggestions. Additional stock ranges from dairy produce to fine olive oils. The autumn months see boxes of rare apples and pears from Brogdale Trust appear on display.

## Hamish Johnston

*48 Northcote Road, SW11*
*020 7738 0741*
*www.hamishjohnston.com*
*Clapham Junction Rail*
*Mon-Sat 9am-6pm, Sun 11am-4pm*

This dapper shop has a loyal following, drawn by the selection of cheeses, numbering around 150 – depending on the time of year. Preference is given to small-scale cheese producers, with delights on offer ranging from Golden Cross to Picos de Europa. The shop also sells an excellent range of deli items, from olive oils and vinegars to top quality bacon and hams. The staff are also friendly and helpful.

# South-East

## The Cheese Block

*69 Lordship Lane, SE22*
*020 8299 3636*
*East Dulwich Rail*
*Mon-Fri 9.30am-6.30pm, Sat 9am-6pm*

This small, down-to-earth shop stocks around 260 cheeses from Britain and Europe. The stock ranges from classics to more obscure cheeses which you can try before you buy.

## The Cheeseboard

*26 Royal Hill, SE10*
*020 8305 0401*
*www.cheese-board.co.uk*
*Greenwich DLR/rail*
*Mon-Wed & Fri 9am-5pm,*
*Thur 9am-1pm, Sat 8.30am-4.30pm*

This small, friendly cheesemongers stocks around 100 British and continental cheeses. Stock ranges from classics such as Italian Parmesan or buffalo mozzarella to Spanish Payoyo and French Boulette d'Avesnes.

*Rococo*

Nowadays London is home to a number of talented chocolatiers, many of whom have set up their own shops. The emphasis is on hand-made chocolates using quality ingredients and imaginative flavourings.

# Central

## Artisan du Chocolat

- 89 Lower Sloane Street, SW1
- 020 7824 8365
- www.artisanduchocolat.com
- Sloane Square LU
- Mon-Sat 10am-7pm, Sun 12noon-5pm

This austerely smart shop showcases the considerable talents of chocolatier Gerard Coleman and his partner Anne Weyns. Here one can buy Gerard's elegant ganache-filled chocolates, with their distinctive flavourings such as sea-salted caramel, lemon and thyme or green cardamom.

## Charbonnel et Walker

- 1 The Royal Arcade, 28 Old Bond St, W1
- 020 7491 0939
- www.charbonnel.co.uk
- Piccadilly Circus LU
- Mon-Sat 10am-6pm

An elegant chocolatiers established in 1875. It has a reputation for high quality chocolates and smartly-packaged chocolate gifts.

## Cocomaya

- 35 Connaught Street, W2
- 020 7706 2770
- www.cocomaya.co.uk
- Marble Arch LU
- Mon-Sat 11am-7pm

Positioned in a peaceful side-street, this delightfully decorative chocolate shop offers a range of delectable chocolates, all hand-made on the premises by chocolatier Jonathan Deddis. A long table displays a range of beautiful dishes, each enticingly filled with gorgeously colourful, jewel-like chocolates. Flavours change seasonally, with Christmas seeing the range of truffles (raspberry caramel, tarte tatin, pomegranate) extend to include flavours such as eggnog, whisky, and chestnut. Assorted chocolate-coated nuts are another tempting treat on offer.

## La Maison du Chocolat

- 45-46 Piccadilly, W1
- 020 7287 8500
- www.lamaisonduchocolat.co.uk
- Piccadilly LU
- Mon-Sat 10am-7pm, Sun 12noon-6pm

Seriously elegant, La Maison du Chocolat, with its marble and wood fittings and phalanx of suited staff, brings chocolate-shopping à la Parisienne to London. The hand-made French chocolates are created by Robert

Linxe, a famous chocolatier who opened his first chocolate 'boutique' in Paris in 1977. Seasonal treats range from sophisticated ice creams in flavours such as salted caramel during the summer, to plump marrons glace in the winter. A café area allows customers to sit and enjoy exquisite in-house pastries.

## Paul A Young

- 20 Royal Exchange, EC3
- 020 7929 7007
- www.paulayoung.co.uk
- Bank LU
- Mon-Wed & Fri 10am-6.30pm,
  Thur 10am-7pm

A petite branch of the eponymous choco-latier's business. It offers his trademark elegant, contemporary chocolates.

## Prestat

- 14 Princes Arcade, SW1
- 020 7494 3372
- www.prestat.co.uk
- Green Park/Piccadilly Circus LU
- Mon-Fri 9.30am-6pm, Sat 10am-5pm

A small, gaudy shop selling Prestat's chocolates from bars to artisan truffles. All the chocolates are packaged in Prestat's trademark vibrant colours.

## Rococo

- 45 Marylebone High Street, W1
- 020 7935 7780
- www.rococochocolates.com
- Baker Street LU
- Tue-Sat 10am-6.30pm,
  Sun-Mon 12noon-5pm

Chantal Coady's second distinctly chic shop offers Rococo's delicious blend of beautiful, quality chocolate treats. Flavours include salted caramel ravioli, quality chocolate bars, flavoured chocolate wafers and dainty hand-made truffles.

## Rococo

- 5 Motcomb Street, SW1
- 020 7245 0993
- www.rococochocolates.com
- Sloane Square/South Kensington
- Tue-Sat 10am-6.30pm,
  Sun-Mon 12noon-5pm

Hidden down a peaceful Belgravia side-street, this stylish shop-cum-café showcases Rococo's range of elegant chocolates, from hand-painted chocolate figurines to flavoured wafers and bars. Rococo's master chocolatier, Laurent Couchaux, works downstairs in his glass-walled kitchen, creating an innovative range of hand-made truffles. This branch has a pretty, Moroccan-themed garden.

Chocolate Shops

*Rococo*

### William Curley

198 Ebury Street, Orange Square, SW1
020 7730 5522
www.williamcurley.co.uk
Mon-Sat 9.30am-6.30pm, Sun 10am-6pm

This immaculate establishment, with its white walls and caramel-coloured seating, celebrates the eponymous William Curley's talents as both chocolatier and patissier. Customers can sit in comfort and try William's exquisite pastry creations, such as a gold-flecked Madagascan Chocolate or buy his chocolates and pastries to take away.

# North

### Paul A Young

33 Camden Passage, N1
020 7424 5750
www.paulayoung.co.uk
Angel LU
Tue-Thur 11am-6pm, Fri 11am-7pm, Sat 11am-6pm, Sun 12noon-5pm

This dapper shop showcases talented chocolatier Paul A Young's creations from signature marmite truffles and award-winning sea salt caramels to seriously rich brownies, all freshly hand-made on the premises. As well as offering beloved favourites, there are seasonal creations, such as bergamot and maya honey in the summer or moreish Christmas pudding truffles and brownies in the winter.

# West

## Artisan du Chocolat

- 81 Westbourne Grove, W2
- 0845 2706 996
- www.artisanduchocolat.com
- Notting Hill/Queensway LU
- Mon-Thur 10am-7pm,
  Fri-Sat 10am-8pm, Sun 11am-5pm

This funky-looking shop and 'chocolateria' not only offers Artisan's distinctive chocolates but also has a café area with treats such as salted caramel tart.

## Melt

- 59 Ledbury Road, W11
- 020 7727 5030
- www.meltchocolates.com
- Notting Hill LU
- Mon-Sat 10am-6.30pm,
  Sun 11am-4pm

This distinctly chic chocolate boutique with its cool, white interior and minimal styling sells a witty and stylish range of chocolate. Creations range from popular Love Bars (milk chocolate and feuillantine) to fresh flavoured olive caramel bonbons. All the chocolates are hand-made on the premises in the backroom kitchen by Chika Watanabe.

## Theobroma Cacao

- 43 Turnham Green Terrace, W4
- 020 8996 0431
- Turnham Green LU
- Mon-Tue & Sat 10am-6pm, Wed-Fri
  10am-7.30pm, Sun 10am-5.30pm

This pretty little shop, complete with a cocoa bar, is filled to brimming with own-made chocolate treats. Stock ranges from chilli chocolate shards to unusual chocolate incense sticks.

# South

## Demarquette Fine Chocolates

- 285 Fulham Road, SW10
- 020 7351 5467
- www.demarquette.com
- Tue-Thur 11am-6pm, Fri-Sat 11am-7pm
- South Kensington LU

This chic chocolate shop-cum-café offers a chance to sample noted chocolatier Marc Demarquette's elegant creations. Unusual flavours include tea flavoured chocolates inspired in partnership with England's first tea estate – Tregothnan in Cornwall.

## The Melange

- 184 Bellenden Road, SE15
- ☎ 007722 650711
- www.themelange.com
- Peckham Rye rail
- 🕐 Wed-Fri 12noon-7pm,
  Sat-Sun 10am-6pm

Isabel Alaya's pretty chocolate boutique offers a range of Isabel's own hand-made chocolate bars and truffles. She pairs flavourings together, with spices a particular favourite, in combinations such as five spice and lemon grass, coffee and aniseed and orange and chilli. Customers can also sit and savour her hot chocolate or chocolate sorbet.

## Rococo

- 321 King's Road, SW3
- ☎ 020 7352 5857
- www.rococochocolates.com
- Sloane Square LU,
  then the 11, 19 or 22 bus
- 🕐 Tue-Sat 10am-6.30pm, Sun 12noon-5pm

Chocolate lover Chantal Coady set up this pretty shop in 1983. On offer here are Rococo's stylish in-house chocolates, from hand-made truffles to flavoured bars.

## William Curley

- 10 Paved Court, Richmond, TW9
- ☎ 020 8332 3002
- Richmond LU/Rail
- 🕐 Mon-Sat 9.30am-6.30pm,
  Sun 10.30am-6pm

William Curley's elegant shop showcases not only William's eye-catching patisserie, freshly prepared upstairs, but his own acclaimed hand-made chocolates.

# East

## Montezuma

- 51 Brushfield Street, E1
- ☎ 020 7539 9208
- www.montezumas.co.uk
- Liverpool Street LU/Rail
- 🕐 Mon-11am-4pm, Tue- Sun 10am-6pm

A London outlet for the West Sussex-based chocolate company, noted for its funky range of chocolates.

Delicatessens

L'Eau à la Bouche

Londons's delicatessens range from small, cosy, family-run shops which have carved out a loyal, local following in their neighbourhoods to larger-scale, distinctly smart establishments aimed at the affluent. With rents and rates so high, many of London's delicatessens increasingly offer a café in addition to a food shopping experience.

# Central

## Kennards Good Foods

- 57 Lambs Conduit Street. WC1
- 020 7404 4030
- www.kennardsgoodfoods.com
- Holborn, Russell Square, WC1
- Mon-Fri 8.30am-7pm,
  Sat 9.30am-5pm, Sun 11am-5pm

On this charming Bloomsbury street, Marc Kennard's cheerful 'modern grocers' is very much a community shop, offering good things to eat to appreciative locals. Despite its small size, the shop punches above its weight with a discriminatingly chosen range of delicious foods, from excellent bacon and cheese to treats such as Toffee Shop fudge. The café element, offers good quality meals and coffee and adds to the buzzy atmosphere.

## Paul Rothe & Son

- 35 Marylebone Lane, W1
- 020 7935 6783
- Bond Street LU
- Mon-Fri 8am-6pm,
  Sat 11.30am-5.30pm

This charming, old-fashioned delicatessen-cum-sandwich bar was established by Paul Rothe in 1900. It remains a family business to this day, run with affable courtesy by his grandson Paul Rothe. The shelves are neatly lined with a huge range of jams and jellies– such as medlar and mulberry – chutneys and pickles. The sandwich bar does a roaring lunch-time trade with fillings such as home-made liptauer or kummel and Paul's home-made soup.

## Villandry

- 170 Great Portland Street, W1
- 020 7631 3131
- www.villandry.com
- Great Portland Street LU
- Mon-Sat 8am-10pm, Sun 9am-4pm

A pioneer of the deli-cum-diner concept, Villandry nowadays focuses more on diners than food shoppers. This store offers a small, select range of foodstuffs, with breads and pastries dominating.

# North

## Flavours

- 10 Campdale Road, N7
- ☎ 020 7281 6565
- ✎ www.delibelly.com
- 🚇 Tufnell Park
- 🕐 Mon 10am-5pm, Tue-Fri 9.30am-6pm, Sat 10am-6pm, Sun 10am-2pm

Having won BBC MasterChef, Julie Friend opened this small, friendly deli. The home-made cakes, quiches and sausages rolls are particularly popular, with deli stock ranging from jams and condiments to Monmouth Coffee and Garafalo pasta. Flavours' café is next door.

*Branch:*
*91 Torriano Avenue, NW5 (020 7485 2266)*

## Niven's Fine Food and Provisions

- 157 King's Cross Road, WC1
- ☎ 020 7837 3717
- ✎ www.nivensfinefood.com
- 🚇 King's Cross LU/Rail
- 🕐 Mon-Fri 7am-7pm, Sat 10am-3pm

A short stroll from King's Cross station, Niven Garland's small, bright café-cum-deli offers an appetising mixture of own-made food (salads, freshly-baked quiches, fishcakes and sandwiches) and a small, choice range of deli items.

## Melbury & Appleton

- 271 Muswell Hill Broadway, N10
- ☎ 020 8442 0558
- ✎ www.melburyandappleton.co.uk
- 🚇 Highgate LU, then bus 134
- 🕐 Tue-Fri 9am-6pm, Sat 9.30am-6pm, Sun 11.30am-5.30pm

This small but well-stocked delicatessen offers a wide range of good things to eat and drink, from cheeses and charcuterie to jams, condiments and sweets. Customers can sample the wares in the cosy café.

## Melrose & Morgan

- 42 Gloucester Avenue, NW1
- ☎ 020 7722 0011
- ✎ www.melroseandmorgan.com
- 🚇 Chalk Farm LU
- 🕐 Mon-Sat 9am-8pm, Sun 10am-6pm

Strikingly housed in a large, high-ceilinged, modern space, Ian James's and Nick Selby's contemporary grocer's includes an open-plan kitchen, with chefs busy cooking up predominantly British fare. Dishes range from serious sausage rolls to fish pie, served up on a magnificent long table which stretches down the centre of the shop. In addition, there is a carefully selected range of both fresh and store-cupboard, fine quality foodstuffs. Treats include Regent's Park honey, Toffee Shop Fudge, British cheeses and excellent bacon.

## Ottolenghi

- 287 Upper Street, N1
- 020 7288 1454
- www.ottolenghi.co.uk
- Angel, Highbury & Islington LU
- Mon-Sat 8am-11pm, Sun 9am-7pm

An alluring display of beautiful sweet and savoury food attracts a steady stream of customers to this elegant, flag-ship branch of Ottolenghi's. The shop offers both food to go and an airy restaurant in which to sit and eat. Since opening his first branch, Chef Yotam Ottonlenghi and his team have built up a dedicated clientele for their delicious seasonal salads and scrumptious cakes.

## Rosslyn Delicatessen

- www.rosslyndeli.net
- 56 Rosslyn Hill, NW3
- 020 7794 9210
- Hampstead LU
- Daily 8.30am-8.30pm

Very much a Hampstead institution, this spacious, well-established delicatessen offers upmarket foodstuffs, including traiteur dishes, cheeses, charcuterie and store cupboard staples. Hampstead Heath picnickers are catered for with a smart range of hampers. Rosslyn's is well worth a visit, but also runs a well organised and efficient delivery service.

## Sourced Market

- St Pancras International
  Pancras Road, NW1
- 020 7833 9352
- www.sourcedmarket.com
- Mon-Fri 7am-9pm
  Sat 8am-8pm, Sun 10am-8pm

Part of St Pancras International's handsome redevelopment is this smart food shop offering a range of fine quality foodstuffs and tipples. Stock includes Neal's Yard Dairy cheeses, Flour Power City breads, Laverstoke Park Farm meats, Brindisa charcuterie, wines and beers.

# West

## Chegworth Farm Shop

- 221 Kensington Church Street W8
- 020 7229 3016
- www.chegworth.com
- Notting Hill LU
- Mon-Sat 8am-8pm, Sun 9am-6pm

This rustic shop showcases organic produce from Chegworth Farm in Kent and other small British producers. Boxes of seasonal fresh fruit and vegetables fill the front room, with Chegworth's apple and pear juices eye-catchingly displayed behind the till. Customers return for ingredients including Chegworth's apples , excellent organic steaks, bacon and Hurdlebrook yoghurts.

## The Grocer on Elgin

*6 Elgin Crescent, W11*

*020 7221 3844*

*www.thegroceron.com*

*Ladbroke Grove LU*
*Notting Hill Gate LU*

*Mon-Fri 8am-8pm,*
*Sat-Sun 8am-6pm*

This large, sophisticated shop, with a café area at the back, specialises in traiteur meals, vacuum-packed in stylish microwavable bags. On offer are dishes such as cassoulet, braised beef and upmarket mashed potato, flavoured with ingredients such as mustard, black truffle or chestnuts.

## Jeroboams

*96 Holland Park, W11*

*020 7727 9359*

*www.jeroboams.co.uk*

*Holland Park LU*

*Mon-Fri 8am-8pm*
*Sat 9am-7pm, Sun 10am-6pm*

In additions to its noted range of wines, this branch of Jeroboams offers a fine and extensive cheese counter and an impressive, wide-ranging selection of deli foods. Stock ranges from sweet and savoury biscuits, oils and vinegars to smoked salmon, blinis and sea urchin caviar.

Ottolenghi

## Mortimer & Bennett

*33 Turnham Green Terrace, W4*
*020 8995 4145*
*www.mortimerandbennett.co.uk*
*Turnham Green LU*
*Mon-Fri 8.30am-6pm, Sat 8.30am-5.30pm (also Sundays in December)*

Dan Mortimer's small, well-established shop is crammed with goodies, including 80-100 British and European farmhouse cheeses (many sourced directly), charcuterie, jams and olive oils. Chocolate, confectionary and biscuits are also well-represented, with Dan keeping an eagle eye out for new, speciality treats to stock.

## Mr Christians

*11 Elgin Crescent*
*020 7229 0501*
*www.mrchristians.co.uk*
*Notting Hill Gate LU*
*Mon-Fri 7am-7pm,*
*Sat 7am-6.30pm, Sun 8am-5pm*

Now owned by Jeroboam's, who have a smart wine shop next door, this well-established delicatessen does a roaring business. Mr Christians is particularly renowned for its traiteur dishes such as soups and quiches as well as breads, cheeses, cold meats and a host of treats.

## Raoul's

*8-10 Clifton Road, W9*
*020 7289 6649*
*www.raoulsgourmet.com*
*Warwick Avenue LU*
*Mon-Fri 7.30am-8.30pm*
*Sat 7.30am-8pm, Sun 8.30am-6pm*

Run with flair by Geraldine Leventis this attractive delicatessen, linked to the popular café, has a loyal local following. Spread over two rooms, Raoul's offers an interesting range of good things to eat, both savoury and sweet. The traiteur side is very popular, with customers returning for dishes such as salads, soups and pasta dishes, cheeses and own-made desserts such as tiramisu.

## Tavola

*155 Westbourne Grove, W11*
*020 7229 0571*
*Notting Hill Gate LU*
*Mon-Fri 10am-7.30pm, Sat 10am-6pm*

Chef Alistair Little and his wife Sharon have created a delicious food shop, with dishes freshly cooked on the premises, ready to be taken home and enjoyed traiteur-style. The menu is seasonal, so summer brings gazpacho and crab cakes, while winter months see hearty Italian bean soups and pasta sauces. "We're all about taste," explains Sharon. A range of tableware adds to the appeal of this little gem.

# South-West

## Bluebird Epicerie

  350 King's Road, SW3
  020 7559 1140
  www.bluebird-restaurant.com
  Sloane Square LU, then 11, 19, 22, 49 bus
  Mon-Fri 8am-8pm, Sat 9am-7pm,
  Sun 9am-5pm

Linked to the elegant Bluebird restaurant, this stylish food shop sells own-baked breads and freshly made traiteur dishes as well as a select range of deli stock.

## Elizabeth King

  34 New King's Road, SW6
  020 7736 2826
  www.elizabethking.com
  Parsons Green LU
  Mon-Sat 9am-8pm, Sun 9am-6pm (butchers Mon-Sat 9am-5.30pm)

In a residential part of Fulham, this well-stocked, upmarket food shop offers a one-stop shop, carrying an extensive range of groceries, from basics to indulgences. Stock includes meat and fresh fish from Cornwall, fresh fruit and vegetables, 150 cheeses and charcuterie.

## MacFarlane's

  48 Abbeville Road, SW4
  020 8673 5373
  Clapham Common LU
  Clapham South LU
  Mon-Fri 10am-7pm
  Sat 9am-6pm, Sun 10am-5pm

Tucked away on a residential Clapham side-street MacFarlane's has been described as "South London's best-kept secret." Despite its discreet location, the shop has built up a loyal local following. Run with friendliness and enthusiasm by Angus MacFarlane Wood and Angie Laycock, MacFarlane's is a textbook example of what a neighbourhood deli should be. Pride of place goes to the cheese counter, which carries up to 110 farmhouse cheeses from Britain, Ireland, France and Italy. Unique to the shop is the olive oil, sourced from a Pescara co-operative through a family connection. The deli counter stocks freshly made salads, dips and olives, while frozen treats include butter puff pastry and upmarket ice cream. Angus's Scottish roots proudly manifest themselves in the presence of Macsween's haggis, Scottish smoked fish and black and white pudding.

## Partridges

*2-5 Duke of York Square*
*King's Road, SW3*
*020 7730 0651*
*www.partridges.co.uk*
*Sloane Square LU*
*Daily 8am-10pm*

Distinctly upmarket, as befits a business which has a Royal Warrant as Grocers to the Queen. This smart, spacious shop comes complete with a café and wine bar. Partridges offers an extensive range of stock, from grocery staples to luxuries, traiteur dishes and Christmas hampers. Saturdays sees the Partridges Food Market in the square outside the shop. ( See page 77)

## Partridges

*17-21 Gloucester Road, SW7*
*020 7581 0535*
*www.partridges.co.uk*
*Gloucester Road LU*
*Daily 8am-11pm*

A smaller branch of the King's Road establishment, with a particular focus on American foodstuffs.

## The North Street Deli

*26 North Street, SW4*
*020 7978 1555*
*Clapham Common LU*
*Mon-Sat 10am-4pm*

Relaxed and welcoming, the North Street deli, run by Maddalena Bonino and her partner Nathan Middlemiss, does a roaring trade in home-made sandwiches, salads and coffees. Maddalena cooks a daily-changing range of dishes in the small kitchen downstairs, including delicious soups and salads. Foodstuffs include top-notch breads, a carefully chosen range of charcuterie and cheeses as well as groceries including dried pasta, olives and vinegars. The fresh fruit and vegetables are bought daily for Maddalena's use but are also on sale until they are used up.

## Recipease

*48-50 St John's Road, SW11*
*020 3006 0001*
*Clapham Junction LU*
*Mon-Fri 9am-9pm, Sat 8am-8pm*
*Sun 9am-6pm*

TV chef Jamie Oliver is behind this spacious, characteristically enterprising venture, which combines a cookery school, meal-assembly points and food and kitchenware shops. Customers can pop in for ready-made meals, prepared in the on-site kitchen or try some of the freshly made bread.

## LA FROMAGERIE

Stylish and unconventional LA FROMAGERIE is recognised as being one of the best cheese shops in England. Both shops & Tasting Cafés are open everyday serving **Breakfast, Lunch & Afternoon Tea**

www.lafromagerie.co.uk
www.twitter.com/LaFromagerieUK

**LA FROMAGERIE**
2-6 Moxon St, Marylebone,
London, W1U 4EW
Tel: 020 7935 0341
moxon@lafromagerie.co.uk

**LA FROMAGERIE**
No 30 Highbury Park,
London, N5 2AA
Tel: 020 7359 7440
highbury@lafromagerie.co.uk

- ON SITE MATURING ROOMS
- WALK IN CHEESE ROOM
- TASTING CAFÉ
- TUTORED CHEESE & WINE TASTINGS
- REGIONAL TASTING SUPPERS
- AVAILABLE FOR PRIVATE HIRE
- BESPOKE WHOLESALE SUPPLYING SOME OF THE BEST RESTAURANTS IN AND AROUND LONDON

## Rippon Food Market

- 12 Upper Tachbrook Street, SW1
- 020 7931 0628
- www.ripponcheese.com
- Pimlico LU, Victoria LU/Rail
- Mon-Sat 9am-5pm

Rippon Cheese Stores from down the road have set up this food shop offering good things to eat including pâtés and hams.

## Rosie's Deli Café

- 14e Market Row, SW9
- www.rosiedelicafe.com
- Brixton LU
- Mon-Sat 9.30am-5.30pm

This small, jauntily decorated, mellow café-cum-deli in the heart of Brixton Market has carved out a loyal following. Regulars come by to sample the fresh simple food, or to buy stock from fresh bread to quality chorizo. The café is run with fun and generosity by the wonderful Rosie who also has made room for a few Cookbooks including her own inspirational book, 'Spooning With Rosie'.

## Trinity Stores

- 5-6 Balham Station Road, SW12
- 020 8673 3773
- Balham LU/Rail
- Mon-Fri 9am-8pm,
  Sat 9.30am-5.30pm, Sun 10am-5pm

Handily positioned for commuters by Balham Station, this spacious and friendly deli-cum-café does a roaring trade. Customers pop in to enjoy a coffee and own-made cake or a light lunch. Food shoppers are well served, with stock ranging from quality fresh produce such as Secretts Farm salad and a well-chosen range of cheese and charcuterie. Larder items include spices, condiments and tinned seafood.

## Wild Caper

- 11A-13 Market Row, SW9
- 020 7737 4410
- Brixton LU
- Mon-Sat 10am-5pm

In a Brixton Market arcade, this austerely stylish deli-cum café has been set up by Bridget Hugo and Giuseppe Mascol, founders of acclaimed pizzeria Franco Manca, a few doors down. On offer here are a discerningly-chosen, range of good things to eat and drink. Treats include Wild Caper's flavourful, own-baked sourdough breads, excellent Sicillian olive oil and fine Italian wines.

# South-East

## Beamish & McGlue

- 461 Norwood Road, SE27
- 020 8761 8099
- www.beamishandmcglue.com
- Mon-Fri 9am-7pm,
  Sat 9.30am-5.30pm, Sun 10am-4pm

An exuberant bright blue façade marks this cheerful, unpretentious corner shop, run with friendly hospitality by Antonia Beamish and Casey McGlue. 'A delicious food shop' is Antonia's own description and indeed Beamish & McGlue is crammed with good things to eat; crates of organic fruit and vegetables, artisanal breads, decent bacon, salamis and cheeses. Customers pop in for a chat along with a slice of home-made cake or a sandwich all accompanied by the store's delicious coffee.

## East Dulwich Deli

- 15-17 Lordship Lane, SE22
- 020 8693 2525
- East Dulwich Rail
- Mon-Thur 9am-7pm, Fri 9am-8pm
  Sat 8.30am-6pm, Sun 10am-4pm

This spacious shop, run by Tony Zuccola, houses an impressive range of foods, from basics to luxuries. Bread is from Born and Bread, the wholesale bakery set up by Tony Zuccola and Tracey Woodward.

## Franklin's Farm Shop

- 155 Lordship Lane, East Dulwich, SE22
- 020 8693 3992
- www.frankinsrestaurant.com/farmshop
- East Dulwich (Rail)
- Mon-Sat 9am-6pm, Sun 10am-5pm

This farm shop is an offshoot of Franklins restaurant next door and sells the same ingredients used in the kitchen such as fresh fruit and veg from Kent farms, fine English cheeses and delicious artisanal cakes. The farm shop also offers ready meals prepared in the restaurant.

## Frog on the Green

- 119 Consort Road, SE15
- 020 7732 2525
- www.frogonthegreen.com
- Peckham Rye Rail
- Mon-Sat 8.30am-7.30pm, Sun 9am-6.30pm

John Gionleka's pretty, café-cum-deli, attractively housed in a bright white corner shop, has a loyal local following. Customers can sit inside or in the front courtyard enjoying coffee and sampling cakes, pastries or savoury dishes such as spinach feta pie. All the food is freshly made in the kitchen downstairs and generously served. Also on offer are a well-chosen range of keenly-priced deli foods, including excellent olive oils, charcuterie and dried pasta.

## Mimosa

- 16 Half Moon Lane, SE24
- 020 7733 8838
- Herne Hill Rail
- Mon-Fri 9am-6pm,
  Sat 9am-5.30pm, Sun 9.30am-2.30pm

This pretty delicatessen-cum-traiteur also has a small café area in which to enjoy a coffee and snack. The place is popular with a loyal local following who enjoy the emphasis is on French food, with a Moroccan twist. This interesting combination means that French charcuterie and cheeses sit in the counter alongside own-made Moroccan dishes such as humous, tchachouka and baba ghanoush.

## Romeo Jones

- 80 Dulwich Village, SE21
- 020-8299 1900
- North Dulwich rail
- Mon-Fri 8am-5pm, Sat-Sun 9am-6pm

As befits its Dulwich Village location, this is a snazzy boutique food shop-cum-café, specialising in artisanal foods from Britain and Italy. Stock ranges from Rhug meats to fresh pasta with the ready-meals such as Boeuf Bourguignon proving very popular. Opened in 2008, this place has proved popular with the locals who often enjoy a coffee or glass of wine while stocking up on a few delicious treats.

# East

## A. Gold

- 42 Brushfield Street. E1
- 020 7247 2487
- www.agoldshop.com
- Mon-Fri 8am-4pm, Sat-Sun 10am-6pm

Atmospherically housed in 18th-century premises, this charming shop-cum-cafe is now run by Philip Cundall. The store still offers an appetising mix of home-made foods to go, such as soup and sandwiches, as well as a carefully-chosen range of traditional British foods, from Toffee Shop Fudge to fine English farmhouse cheeses.

## Albion

- 2-4 Boundary Street. E2
- 020 7229 1051
- www.albioncaff.co.uk
- Liverpool Street, Old Street, LU/Rail
- Daily 8am-midnight

Located in a Terence Conran restaurant complex, this small, smart shop offers a select range of British foodstuffs. On the shelves can be found an appealing range of breads, cakes, biscuits and pastries – all baked on-site.

## The Deli Downstairs

- 99 Lauriston Road, E9
- 020 8985 7515
- London Fields Rail
- Tue 9am-5.30pm, Wed-Fri 9am-6.30pm, Sat 9am-6pm, Sun 9am-3pm

In the basement of The Ginger Pig's butchers shop, this small, friendly delicatessen has a 'village shop' ethos. It offers a small but carefully chosen range of good things to eat and drink, including ever-popular Ginger Pig sausage rolls.

## L'Eau à la Bouche

- 36-37 Broadway Market, E8
- 020 7923 0600
- London Fields Rail
- Mon-Fri 8.30am-7pm, Sat 8.30am-5pm, Sun 9.30am-5pm

In a prime position on this picturesque street, Stephane Cusset's handsome delicatessen-cum-café is hugely popular with locals. Saturdays see it thronging with customers drawn by the market on its doorstep. La Bouche stocks a range of carefully chosen deli foods, including charcuterie and cheeses. The café corner offers good quality coffee and snacks and is always busy.

A. Gold

Delicatessens

## Food Hall

☐ *374-378 Old Street, EC1*
☎ *020 7729 6005*
🚌 *Old Street LU*
🕐 *Mon-Fri 8.30am-7.15pm*
 *Sat-Sun 9.30am-5.15pm*

Housed in a tiled former dairy, Food Hall stocks an expansive range of foods, with the emphasis on quality names such as Daylesford, Ginger Pig, and L'Artisan du Chocolat. A separate room houses British and European cheeses and charcuterie, while a café area caters to hungry customers.

## Leila's

☐ *15-17 Calvert Avenue, E2*
☎ *020 7729 9789*
🚌 *Old Street LU/Rail*
🕐 *Wed-Sat 10am-6pm, Sun 10am-5pm*

Just by Arnold Circus, Leila's relaxed and individualistic shop is a quiet oasis just a minutes walk from the traffic of Shoreditch High Street. It's spread over two premises. Number 15 was once a fruiterers and now offers stock such as fresh fruit, apple juice, pulses and great bread. Next door, at Number 17, customers can sit at communal tables enjoying excellent coffee and simple dishes such as fried eggs with sage. Leila is the owner of the store and her enthusiasm is on of the reasons this is such a great place.

## Verde & Co.

☐ *40 Brushfield Street, E1*
☎ *020 7247 1924*
🌐 *www.verde-and-company-ltd.co.uk*
🚌 *Liverpool Street LU/Rail*
🕐 *Mon-Fri 8am-5pm,*
 *Sat 11am-6pm, Sun 10am-5pm*

Just by Spitalfields Market, housed in a beautifully restored late 18th century building owned by novelist Jeanette Winterson, Verde's evokes a different era. Boxes of lovingly arranged fruit and vegetables are on display outside and there is a cosy seating area by a stove inside its atmospheric interior. The shop is run with flair and enthusiasm by chef Harvey Cabaniss, who stocks a wide range of delicious treats from handmade chocolates to top-notch Italian staples such as dried pasta and fresh pesto. The home-made sandwiches, salads and a daily-changing range of soups, such as rabbit with barley, are hugely popular.

Fishmongers

F.C. Soper

Nowadays, a fishmongers or 'wet fish shop' is an all too rare sight on London's high streets. This is such a shame, as fishmongers are essential for the enjoyment of fresh fish and seafood. Only a skilled fishmonger can ensure fresh stock as well as fillet and prepare it to your requirements. If you are lucky enough to have a good fishmonger near your work or home, make sure you use them – you'll taste the difference.

# Central

## Fishworks

- 89 Marylebone High Street, W1
- 020-7935 9796
- Baker Street LU
- Daily 10am-10.30pm

Alongside its contemporary fish restaurant, Fishworks offers a small fishmongers stocking a limited selection of upmarket fish and seafood.

## Moxon's

- 17 Bute Street, SW7
- 020 7591 0050
- South Kensington LU
- Tue-Fri 8.30am-7.30pm
  Sat 8.30am-5.30pm
- www.moxonsfreshfish.com

A smart South Kensington outlet for this respected fishmongers, noted for the quality and freshness of its fish and seafood.

# North

## B & M Seafoods

- 258 Kentish Town Road, NW5
- 020 7485 0346
- Kentish Town LU/Rail
- Tue-Sat 9am-6pm

This friendly, well-established shop, unusually combines a fishmonger's with a butcher's. It has an excellent range of carefully sourced, choice fish. Stock ranges from basics like herring and mackerel to upmarket fish such as turbot, wild sea bass and prime smoked salmon.

## France Fresh Fish

- 99 Stroud Green Road, N4
- 020 7263 9767
- Finsbury Park LU/Rail
- Mon-Sat 9am-7pm, Sun 11am-5pm

An eye-catching window display of brightly coloured tropical fish is an attractive feature of this long-established fish-shop. It is owned by the same Mauritian family who run the Chez Liline restaurant next door. Staff are friendly and happy to offer advice on the exotic stock.

## Hampstead Seafoods

🔲 *78 Hampstead High Street, NW3*
☎ *020 7435 3966*
🚇 *Hampstead LU*
🕐 *Tue-Fri 7.30am-5pm, Sat 7.30am-4pm*

Tucked away off the High Street, this small shop offers a good range of quality seafood.

## Steve Hatt

🔲 *88-90 Essex Road, N1*
☎ *020 7226 3963*
🚇 *Angel LU*
🕐 *Tue-Thur 8am-5pm, Fri-Sat 7am-5pm*

An Islington institution, this popular fishmonger, knowledgeably run by Steve Hatt. There's an excellent range of fish with everything from herring to swordfish and the shop is known for its own-smoked fish.

## La Petite Poissonnerie

🔲 *75 Gloucester Avenue, NW1*
☎ *020 7387 6101*
🚇 *Chalk Farm LU*
🕐 *Tue-Sat 9.30am-7.30pm,*
    *Sun 10.30am-5.30pm*
🖱 *www.lapetitepoissonnerie.com*

This upmarket fishmongers has an eye-catching boat-shaped display-case and offers a fine selection of prime fish. The fish is sourced by chef Nic Rascle with an eye to sustainability. Plans are afoot to include French wine and traiteur dishes.

## Poisson

🔲 *7 Station Parade*
    *Cockfosters Road, EN4*
☎ *020 8449 0335*
🚇 *Cockfosters LU*
🕐 *Tue-Sat 8am-5pm*

A smart fishmonger's with an excellent assortment of fish and seafood, including luxuries such as monkfish, raw clams and scallops. Staff are helpful and are happy to take orders in advance.

## Walter Purkis & Sons

🔲 *17 The Broadway, N8*
☎ *020 8340 6281*
🚇 *Finsbury Park LU/Rail, then the W7 bus*
🕐 *Tue-Sat 8am-5pm*

Right in the middle of Crouch End's bustling Broadway, this friendly shop sells a good range of fish, from herring to salmon.

## A. Scott & Son

🔲 *94 High Road, N2*
☎ *020 8444 7606*
🚇 *East Finchley LU*
🕐 *Tue-Thur 8.30am-5.30pm,*
    *Fri 8.30am-6pm, Sat 8.30am-5pm*

This small, friendly fishmonger's has an excellent range of fresh fish and seafood. Luxury items include clams, raw tiger prawns and frozen crab meat.

# West

## Copes Seafood Company

- 700 Fulham Road, SW6
- ☎ 020 7371 7300
- Fulham Broadway LU
- Mon-Sat 9am-7.30pm,
  Sun 12noon-6pm

The sheer quality of the fresh,
Cornish-caught fish on offer here
has gained this fishmonger a notable
reputation and loyal local following.

## Covent Garden Fishmongers

- 37 Turnham Green Terrace, W4
- ☎ 020 8995 9273
- Turnham Green LU
- Tue, Wed & Fri 8am-5.30pm
  Thur & Sat 8am-5pm

Despite small premises, veteran fishmonger
Phil Diamond's shop stocks an impressive
range of seafood, from fresh wild Scotch
salmon to Pallourde clams and langoustines.

## The Fish Shop

- 201 Kensington Church Street, W8
- ☎ 020 7243 6626
- Notting Hill LU
- Tue-Fri 9am-7pm, Sat 9am-5pm

This small, sleek annexe to the Kensington
Place restaurant sells a select range of
north sea fish, plus tuna and swordfish.

The majority of the fish on sale is
delivered from Cornwall fresh and whole,
before being filleted on the premises.

## Fishworks

- 13-19 The Market Square,
  Richmond TW9
- ☎ 020 8948 5965
- Richmond LU/Rail
- Daily 9am-10pm

This branch of Fishworks combines
a small fishmonger's at the front of a
contemporary fish restaurant. Stock
is select, with the emphasis very much
on prime, spanking fresh fish and
seafood, such as Fine du Claire oysters
and Megrim sole. The restaurant
connection is apparent in the own-made
fish cakes and classy taramasalata,
made to an Elizabeth David recipe.

## Golborne Fisheries

- 75 Golborne Road, W10
- ☎ 020 8960 3100
- Ladbroke Grove LU
- Tue-Sat 8am-6pm

George's bustling fish shop is a local
institution, always busy with customers.
The range of stock is enormous, from
live eels and octopus to tropical fish such
as barracuda and parrot fish. They also
have an excellent range of shellfish.

## James Knight of Mayfair

🏠 *67 Notting Hill Gate, W11*
☎ *020 7221 6177*
🚇 *Notting Hill LU*
🕐 *Mon-Sat 9am-6pm*

This smart fishmonger has an eye-catching display of fish on a marble counter. It opened in 1985 as a retail outlet for a well-respected wholesale fish supplier to the catering trade, whose past customers included the famous chef Escoffier. It prides itself both on the range of its fish including high-grade yellow fin tuna and also for the emphasis on sustainability. Staff are knowledgeable and helpful, as you would expect of a company baring two Royal Warrants as fishmonger to both Her Majesty the Queen and HRH The Prince of Wales.

## La Maree

🏠 *76 Sloane Avenue, SW3*
☎ *020 7589 8067*
🚇 *South Kensington LU*
🕐 *Mon-Sat 8am-6pm*

This tiny annexe of the Poisonnerie restaurant sells a small but select range of seafood. Rarities include both scallops in their shells and wild salmon. Prices are high but so is the quality and the staff are very willing to offer advice and prepare the fish exactly to your requirements.

# South-West

## Moxon's

🏠 *Westbury Parade, Nightingale Lane, SW4*
☎ *020 8675 2468*
🌐 *www.moxonsfreshfish.com*
🚇 *Clapham South LU*
🕐 *Tue-Fri 9am-8pm, Sat 9am-6pm*

Right by Clapham South tube, Robin Moxon's immaculate, white-tiled fishmongers, much appreciated by locals, sells an excellent range of carefully sourced fish. Stock ranges from sardines and mackerel to rod-and-line-caught sea bass, 'unsoaked scallops', razor clams and oysters. Additional treats include sea salt, crevettes gris and Elvas plums.

## Sandys

🏠 *56 King Street, TW1*
☎ *020 8892 5788*
🚇 *Twickenham Rail*
🕐 *Mon-Wed & Sat 8am-6pm, Thur 8am-8pm, Fri 8am-7pm, Sun 9am-12noon*

This large fishmonger impresses with its range of stock. The shop's ethos is summed up by a tiled sign on the walls which reads, 'Welcome to Sandys where only the best is good enough'. Halibut, sea bass and raw langoustines sit alongside jellied eels and cod roes. Sandys also offers a range of poultry.

# South-East

## Moxon's

- 149 Lordshop Lane, SE22
- 020 8299 1559
- www.moxonsfreshfish.com
- East Dulwich Rail
- Tue-Sat 9am-5.30pm

An attractive shop with impressively fresh fish and helpful staff. Robin Moxon sources prime fish and seafood caught around the British coast, from mackerel to plump crabs.

## F.C. Soper

- 141 Evelina Road, SE15
- 020 7639 9729
- Nunhead Rail
- Tue-Fri 9am-5.30pm
  Sat 8.30am-5.30pm, Sun 9am-2pm

This well-established fishmonger has a loyal South London following. A fine range of prime fresh fish is the draw, carefully sourced and knowledgeably sold. Stock ranges from bargain fish heads for stock to upmarket sea bass and scollops. Staff are friendly and happy to offer advice and cooking suggestions.

# East

## Fin and Flounder

- 71 Broadway Market, E8
- 0783 8018395
- www.finandflounder.com
- London Fields rail
- Tue-Fri 10am-6.30pm. Sat 9am-5pm

In a prime spot on Broadway Market, this friendly, contemporary fishmongers prides itself on offering sustainably-sourced fish and seafood. Among the fish on display are ling, red gurnard and red mullet – all bought direct from Cornish day boats. Advice and recipe suggestions are happily offered.

## Jonathan Norris of Pimlico

- 207 Victoria Park Road, E9
- 020 8525 8999
- London Fields rail
- Tue-Fri 10am-7pm, Sat 9am-5pm
  Sun 12am-4pm

Warmly welcomed by local residents, Jonathan's smart new fishmongers offers an excellent range of fish and seafood, with the focus on fish sourced direct from Cornwall. Stock ranges from pollack, hake, skate wings and gurnard to luxuries such as lobsters, crabs, clams and sea urchins. In a nod to his East End location, Jonathan also stocks jellied eels, cockles and winkles – particularly popular with Sunday shoppers.

Foodhalls

*Fortnum & Mason*

L ondon's food halls range from grand, vintage establishments such as Fortnum and Mason to the elegant, contemporary setting of Harvey Nichols. An interesting newcomer is Greensmiths, just by Waterloo Station, which aims to offer a quality, traditional high street food shopping experience under one roof.

# Central

## Fortnum & Mason
181 Piccadilly, W1
020 7734 8040
Piccadilly Circus LU
Mon-Sat 10am-8pm, Sun 12noon-6pm
Established in 1707, this grand, spacious store, has long been noted for its upmarket foods and delicacies. It has recently undergone a smart refurbishment to celebrate its tercentenary. An extensive range of foods is still carried, from prime fresh meat in the basement to treats such as chocolates, biscuits and jams on the ground floor. The beautifully packaged stock is attractively displayed making Fortnum & Mason's a real shopping experience. The in-house eateries range from a wine bar to a tea-room, offering shoppers a chance to sit and revive themselves.

## Greensmiths
27 Lower Marsh, SE1
020 7921 2970
Waterloo LU
Mon-Fri 8am-8pm, Sat 8am-6pm
Handsomely housed in a corner site, just a short distance from Waterloo Station, Greensmiths is an ambitious project. It sets out to offer the convenience of a supermarket combined with the quality and service of an old-fashioned high street. Owner Chris Smith has gathered together an impressive range of partners under one roof including butchers Ginger Pig, The Old Post Office Baker, Antica Coffee, fresh produce wholesalers Solstice and Waterloo Wine – all spaciously represented here. General grocery stock and a café serving up food freshly prepared on the premises complete the picture.

## Harrods

🗺 *87 Brompton Road, SW1*
☎ *020 7730 1234*
🚇 *Knightsbridge LU*
🕐 *Mon-Sat 10am-8pm, Sun 11.30am-6pm*

The beautiful food halls – some complete with vintage tiling – recall Harrods' roots as a tea merchant's. As one would expect, the range of foodstuffs stocked is enormous: from the eye-catching fresh fish display to exotic fruits and vegetables. Highlights include the extensive charcuterie and cheese counters. There is an extensive selection of packaged foods with many exclusive brands including Harrods own label. As well as whole white truffles for a small fortune there are plenty of affordable treats to be found.

## Harvey Nichols Food Hall

🗺 *Knightsbridge, SW1*
☎ *020 7235 5000*
🚇 *Knightsbridge LU*
🕐 *Mon-Sat 10am-8pm, Sun 12noon-6pm*

This stylish food hall, with its high-tech marketplace feel offers an upmarket range of good things to eat and drink. The adjourning restaurant completes the experience.

## John Lewis

🗺 *Oxford Street. W1*
☎ *020 7629 7711*
🚇 *Oxford Circus*
🕐 *Mon-Fri 9.30am-8pm, Sat 9.30am-7pm, Sun 12noon-6pm*

Housed in the basement, this roomy Waitrose foodhall offers a useful range of foodstuffs, including fresh fish, meat and poultry and fruit and vegetables. Particularly appealing elements include the range of breads and pastries and the walk-in cheese room.

## Selfridges

🗺 *400 Oxford Street, W1*
☎ *0800 123 400*
🚇 *Bond Street LU Marble Arch LU*
🕐 *Mon-Wed, & Sat 9.30am-8pm, Thur-Fri 9.30am-9pm, Sun 12noon-6pm*

Immaculate and gleaming, the food hall at Selfridges reflects its cosmopolitan clientele with an impressively international range including Middle Eastern, Japanese and Italian ingredients and ready-made foods. From seafood and cheeses to meat and bread, the quality of the food is very high and includes indulgent treats such as Pierre Herme's acclaimed macarons.

Unpackaged

Nowadays health foods and organic foods have become mainstream. London's health food shop scene features both veteran independents, such as the Haelan Centre in Crouch End to major retail chains such as Planet Organic and Daylesford Organic. Increasingly these stores act as alternative supermarkets, offering the opportunity for customers to do all their grocery shopping under one roof.

# Central

## Alara Wholefoods
- 58-60 Marchmont Street, WC1
- 020 7837 1172
- www.alarashop.com
- Russell Square LU
- Mon-Fri 8am-8pm, Sat 10am-6pm
  Sun 11am-5pm

Tucked away on a Bloomsbury side-street, this well-established shop-cum-café offers an excellent range of foodstuffs, including Alara's well-known, own-brand muesli.

## Natural Kitchen
- 77-78 Marylebone High Street, W1
- 020 7486 8065
- www.thenaturalkitchen.com
- Baker Street, Bond Street LU
- Mon-Fri 8am-8pm, Sat 9am-7pm
  Sun 10am-6pm

Smart and spacious, this store-cum-restaurant offers organic and artisanal foods. The butchers' counter is particularly popular. *Branch: 15-17 New Street, Fetter Lane, EC4*

## Planet Organic
- 22 Torrington Place, WC1
- 020 7436 1929
- www.planetorganic.com
- Goodge Street LU
- Mon-Fri 8am-9pm,
  Sat 9am-8pm, Sun 12noon-6pm

A large branch of Planet Organic, complete with a juice-bar and café area offering organic, vegan and vegetarian food. It is particularly busy at lunchtime.

## Whole Foods Market
- The Barkers Building
  63-97 Kensington High Street,W8
- 020 7368 4500
- www.wholefoodsmarket.com
- High Street Kensington LU
- Mon-Sat 8am-10pm, Sun 12noon-6pm

Housed in what was formerly Barkers department store, this London flagship store of the American health food chain is vast. It carries a correspondingly comprehensive stock of 'natural and organic' foodstuffs as well as an eat-in foodhall.

## Whole Foods Market

- 69-75 Brewer Street, W1
- 020 7434 3179
- www.wholefoodsmarket.com
- Piccadilly Circus LU
- Mon-Fri 7.30am-9pm,
  Sat 9am-9pm, Sun 11.30am-6.30pm

In a sign of the times, what was once a veteran, independent butchers shop, is now a branch of the American health food giant.

# North

## Bumblebee

- 30, 32 & 33 Brecknock Road, N7
- 020 7607 1936
- www.bumblebeenaturalfoods.co.uk
- Kentish Town LU/Rail, then the 29 bus
- Mon-Wed, Fri & Sat 9am-6.30pm,
  Thur 9am-7pm

Spread out over this particular stretch of Brecknock Road, this trio of busy shops offers an excellent range of health foods, from fresh organic produce to vegetarian cheeses. Staff are very friendly and helpful.

## Earth Natural Foods

- 200 Kentish Town Road, NW5
- 020 7482 2211
- www.earthnaturalfoods.co.uk
- Mon-Sat 8.30am-7pm

A pleasant, spacious healthfood business, offering a range of organic and vegetarian products, with friendly, helpful staff.

## Haelan Centre

- 41 The Broadway, N8
- 020 8340 4258
- www.haelan.co.uk
- Finsbury Park LU, then W7 bus
- Mon-Sat 9am-6pm, Sun 12noon-6pm

Just by Crouch End's Clock Tower, this corner shop is very much a local institution. The groundfloor shop sells fresh organic produce and health-food groceries ranging from goat's milk to honey, while upstairs there is a health clinic.

## Just Natural

- 304 Park Road, N8
- 020 8340 1720
- Finsbury Park LU, then the W7 bus
- Mon-Sat 9am-7pm, Sun 11am-3pm

This health food store is housed in an old, tiled butcher's shop in an old-fashioned parade of shops at the foot of Muswell Hill. The stock is both vegetarian and 100% organic, from the wheat grass juices and babyfood to the spices and Rocombe Farm ice cream. Staff are friendly and Mums with buggies are particularly well catered for.

## Planet Organic

- 64 Essex Road, N1
- 020 7288 9460
- Angel LU
- Mon-Sat 8am-9pm, Sun 10am-8pm

A branch of the organic supermarket chain.

## Planet Organic

- 111-117 Muswell Hill Road, N10
- 020 8452 2910
- Highgate LU, then 134 bus
- Mon-Fri 8am-9pm
  Sat 8.30am-9pm, Sun 10am-3pm

A branch of the organic supermarket chain.

## Unpackaged

- 42 Amwell Street, EC1
- 020 7713 8368
- www.beunpackaged.com
- Angel LU
- Mon-Fri 10am-7pm, Sat 9am-6pm
  Sun 10am-3pm

Attractively housed in a vintage dairy,
Catherine Conway's friendly shop appeals
on many levels. At its core, is a desire to
cut down on packaging, so customers are
encouraged to bring their own containers and
fill them with anything from Ecover washing
up liquid to organic basmati rice, earning
a discount in the process. Good things to
eat and drink range from free-range eggs to
Neal's Yard Dairy cheeses and organic wines.

## Whole Foods Market

- 49 Parkway, NW1
- 020 7428 7575
- www.wholefoodsmarket.com
- Camden Town LU
- Mon-Sat 8am-9pm, Sun 10am-8pm

A popular branch of the Whole Foods chain.

## Whole Foods Market

- 32-40 Stoke Newington Church St, N16
- 020 7254 2332
- www.wholefoodsmarket.com
- Stoke Newington rail
- Mon-Sat 8am-9pm, Sun 9am-8.30pm

A spacious branch of the Whole Foods chain.

# West

## As Nature Intended

- 201 Chiswick High Road, W4
- 020 8742 8838
- www.asnatureintended.uk.com
- Turnham Green LU
- Mon-Fri 9am-8pm, Sat 9am-7pm,
  Sun 10.30am-6.30pm

This 'organic supermarket' offers a
comprehensive range of organic foodstuffs.

## As Nature Intended

🏠 *17-21 High Street, W5*
☎ *020 8840 1404*
🚇 *Ealing Broadway*
🕐 *Mon-Sat 9am-7pm, Sun 9am-11pm*

A large, neatly-arranged shop offering a comprehensive range of organic foodstuffs.

## Daylesford Organic

🏠 *208-212 Westbourne Grove, W11*
☎ *020 7313 8050*
🚇 *Notting Hill LU*
🕐 *Mon-Sat 8.30am-7pm, Sun 10am-4pm*

An elegant, spacious establishment housing a restaurant, café and shop selling all kinds of organic foods.

## Planet Organic

🏠 *42 Westbourne Grove, W2*
☎ *020 7221 7171*
🚇 *Bayswater LU, Queensway LU*
🕐 *Mon-Sat 8am-9pm, Sun 12noon-6pm*

This stylish superstore, Planet Organic's largest establishment, sells everything for a healthy lifestyle, from freshly-pressed juices at the juice bar to organic muesli. There is a large grocery section, a seafood and butcher's counter, and a particularly extensive fresh produce section.

# South-West

## As Nature Intended

⌗ *186-188 Balham High Road, SW12*

☎ *020 8675 2923*

🚇 *Balham LU*

🕐 *Mon-Fri 9am-8pm, Sat 9am-7pm, Sun 10.30am-6.30pm*

An established organic supermarket offering a wide selection health foods.

## Brixton Wholefoods Transatlantic

⌗ *59 Atlantic Road, SW9*

☎ *020 7737 2210*

🚇 *Brixton LU*

🕐 *Mon 9.30am-7pm, Tue-Thur & Sat 9.30am-5.30pm, Fri 9.30am-6pm*

This well-established shop, now well over 30 years old, has a loyal following and is a friendly, laid-back establishment, so-named because its former premises were on the other side of Atlantic Road. Stock is extensive, from grains, nuts and pulses to a popular self-serve selection of around 300 herbs and spices (organic and non-organic).

## Dandelion Foods

⌗ *120 Northcote Road, SW11*

☎ *020 7350 0902*

🚇 *Clapham Junction Rail*

🕐 *Mon-Sat 9am-6pm, Sun 11am-4pm*

Long established, this narrow shop is crammed with health foods, from a full range of Dove flours to organic baby foods. Lunchtime customers come by for the vegan, gluten-free soup, vegetarian lasagne and gluten-free cakes – all cooked in the kitchen at the back.

## Daylesford Organic

⌗ *44B Pimlico Road, SW1*

☎ *020 7881 8060*

🖰 *www.daylesfordorganic.com*

🕐 *Mon-Sat 8am-6pm, Sun 10am-4pm*

🚇 *Pimlico LU*

In an appropriately select neighbourhood, Daylesford's elegant white shop offers a ground floor café area, bakery, grocery and basement butchers selling organic meat.

## Whole Foods Market

⌗ *305-311 Lavender Hill, SW11*

☎ *020 7585 1488*

🚇 *Clapham Junction Rail*

🕐 *Mon-Fri 9am-9pm, Sat 8.30am-7.30pm, Sun 12noon-6pm*

This large branch of the US based organic food specialists features an impressive display of fresh produce. There's also a juice bar offering delicious juices and healthy shots of wheatgrass.

### Here

🏠 *Chelsea Farmers Market*
*125 Sydney Street, SW3*
☎ *020 7351 4321*
🚌 *Sloane Square LU*
🕐 *Mon-Sat 9.30am-8pm, Sun 10am-6.30pm*

A distinctly stylish health food shop. It has an attractively displayed, top end range of organic foods and helpful staff.

### Oliver's Wholefood Store

🏠 *5 Station Approach, TW9*
☎ *020 8948 3990*
🚌 *Kew Gardens LU*
🕐 *Mon-Sat 9am-7.30pm,*
*Sun 10am-7.30pm*

This attractive airy shop boasts an impressive overall stock. Its good selection of fresh organic produce is delivered daily. Shelves of groceries include basics such as organic grains and pulses as well as treats like organic chocolate. On offer in the chill counter are Sheepdrove's organic meat, and a range of dairy products.

# South-East

### Baldwin's Health Food Centre

🏠 *171-73 Walworth Road, SE17*
☎ *020 7703 5550*
🚌 *Elephant & Castle LU*
🕐 *Mon-Sat 9am-6pm, Thur 9am-7pm*

A South London institution, this established business carries a truly impressive range of herbals remedies. They also have a good general organic and health food stock.

### SMBS Foods

🏠 *75 Lordship Lane, SE22*
☎ *020 8693 7792*
🚌 *East Dulwich Rail*
🕐 *Mon-Fri 9am-6.30pm,*
*Sat 9am-6pm, Sun 10am-4.30pm*

Kash Rao's splendidly eclectic shop has been selling organic foods since 1985. Stock ranges from fresh fruit and vegetables to grains and pulses, spices, ice cream, dairy products, meat and poultry. The stock is impressively wide-ranging and globe-trotting.

# East

### The Grocery

🏠 *54-56 Kingsland Road, E2*
☎ *020 7729 6855*
✉ *www.thegroceryshop.co.uk*
🚌 *Liverpool Street/Old Street LU*
🕐 *Mon-Sun 8am-10pm*

The Grocery carries an extensive range of organic and fair-trade foodstuffs and household goods. Under the vaulted ceilings, stock ranges from chilled organic soups and tofu to assorted coffees. An organic café area completes the picture.

Markets

Marylebone Farmers' Market

# Markets

One of the most exciting recent developments on London's food shopping scene has been the growing number of new, specialist food markets, most famously Borough Market. Look out for the the Real Food Market at Covent Garden as well as other occasional food events. Many of London's down-to-earth, traditional street markets still survive – among them, Chapel Street Market, Portobello and Walthamstow – offering fresh produce at bargain prices.

## Berwick Street Market

- *Berwick Street, W1*
- *Oxford Circus / Piccadilly Circus LU*
- *Mon-Sat 9am-5pm*

Berwick Street is London's most central food market right in the heart of Soho. It has seen better days but still offers fruit and veg, and a fresh fish stall.

## Borough Food Market

- *Southwark Street, SE1*
- *London Bridge LU/Rail*
- *Thur 11am-5pm, Fri 12noon-6pm, Sat 8am-5pm*

Housed in Borough's wholesale market (atmospherically situated under the railway arches next to Southwark Cathedral)

Borough food market has become a major attraction. Fundamental to its success is the range and quality of the food. Shoppers can choose from great raw ingredients – scallops, grass-fed beef, wild mushrooms– to luxuries such as Joselito hams, artisanal European cheeses and great olive oils. Take-away foods are also available, from fiery chorizo sandwiches to proper pork pies. The nearby are food specialists such as Neal's Yard Dairy, Monmouth Coffee House, Konditor & Cooke and De Gustibus.

## Broadway Market

- *Broadway Market, E8*
- *London Fields Rail*
- *Sat 8.30am-4.30pm*

This appealing Hackney market has become a success in recent years with all kinds of stalls including clothing and crafts, but one of the main draws is the food. Here you can find delicious fruit and veg, fresh cakes and breads, charcuterie, fresh fish and meat and lots of food-to-go, from falafels to roast hog rolls.

## Chapel Market

- *Chapel Market, N1*
- *Angel LU*
- *Tue-Sat 9am-6pm, Thur & Sun till 4pm*

This local market still has a vibrant atmosphere and plenty of good quality fresh food – from fruit and veg to French cheeses.

## Greenwich Market

*Greenwich Church Street, SE10*
*Greenwich LU*
*Sat-Sun 9.30am-5pm*

The covered market in the centre of Greenwich still has a great deal of charm and lots of good food from traditional sausages to fresh breads

## Portobello Market

*Portobello Road, W11*
*Notting Hill Gate / Ladbroke Grove LU*
*Mon-Wed, Fri-Sat 8am-6pm,*
*Thur 8am-1pm*

Best known for its antique market on a Saturday, Portobello also has a lively food market throughout the week. The food part of the market takes place between Lonsdale Road and Lancaster Road and has some really good fruit and veg stalls.

## Partridges Food Market

*Duke of York Square, SW3*
*Sloane Square LU*
*Sat 10am-4pm*

Partridges, the well-established grocers, have enterprisingly set up a food market in the square outside their store. Saturdays see a cosmopolitan selection of around 50 food stalls, selling foods ranging from French fish soups, Scandinavian berry jams, to delicious hog roast sandwiches.

## Ridley Road Market

*Ridley Road, E8*
*Dalston Kingsland Rail*
*Mon-Sat 9am-5pm,*

This is one of the most vibrant food markets in the capital with all kinds of fruit and veg, fresh fish and meat to be found on this long pedestrianised street. There are several very good Turkish food stores along the route that are well worth a visit

## Northcote Road Market

*Northcote Road, SW11*
*Clapham Junction (Rail)*
*Mon-Sat 9am-5pm, Wed 9am-1pm*

This market compliments to the quality food shops on the Northcote Road. There are two good fruit and veg stalls, a trader selling quality pastries and breads and usually a few deli stalls. The best day to visit is Saturday, when the market is at its busiest.

Markets

# Farmers' Markets

Farmers' markets (an idea imported from America) can now be found throughout Britain. London is no exception with Islington hosting the first of the capital's farmers' markets in 1999. The capital now hosts a great number of farmers' markets, spread across the city. London Farmers' Markets (www.lfm.org.uk) were the pioneers but they have been joined by City and Country Markets (www.weareccfm.co.uk). There are also a few independents such as Growing Communities (www.growingcommunities.org) in Stoke Newington and Peckham Farmers' Market, which are locally organised and have a fantastic community atmosphere and great locally sourced food.

Shopping at farmers' markets is an excellent way to support local producers. Being able to buy seasonal produce at its best is obviously one of the attractions of the farmers' markets. There is more on offer at farmers' markets, however, than simply fresh fruit and vegetables: meat, fish and shellfish, breads, cakes, cheeses and fruit juices are just some of the other foodstuffs to be found.

LFM = London Farmers' Market
CCM = City & Country Markets
Indie = Independent Market

## Central

### Marylebone (LFM)
- *Cramer St car park, corner Moxton St, off Marylebone High St, W1U*
- *Sundays 10am-2pm*

### Pimlico Road (LFM)
- *Orange Square, corner of Pimlico Road & Ebury St, SW1*
- *Saturdays 9am-1pm*

### South Kensington Market (LFM)
- *Bute Street, SW7*
- *Saturdays 9am-1pm*

## North

### Alexandra Palace (CCM)
- *Alexandra Palace, Muswell Hill, N10*
- Sundays 10am-3pm

### Islington London (LFM)
- *Chapel Market, Between Penton Street and Baron Street.*
- *Sundays 10am-2pm*

### Parliament Hill (LFM)
- *William Ellis School, Highgate Road, NW1*
- *Saturdays 10am-2pm*

### Stoke Newington (Indie)
- *William Patten School, Stoke Newington Church Street, N16*
- *Saturdays 10am-2.30pm*

### Queen's Park (LFM)
- *Salusbury School, Salusbury Road, NW6*
- *Sundays 10am-2pm*

## West

### Ealing (LFM)
- *Leeland Rd, West Ealing, W13*
- *Saturdays 9am-1pm*

### Hammersmith (CCM)
- *Lyric Square, Hammersmith, W6*
- *Thursdays 10am-3pm*

### Notting Hill (LFM)
- *Car park behind Waterstones, access via Kensington Place, W11*
- *Saturdays 9am-1pm*

## South-West

### Brixton (LFM)
- *Outside Recreation Centre, Brixton Station Road, SW9*
- *Sundays 10am-2pm*

### Clapham (LFM)
- *Bonneville School, Bonneville Road off Abbeville Road, SW4*
- *Sundays 10am-2pm*

### Twickenham (LFM)
- *Holly Road Car Park, Holly Rd, off King St, Twickenham, TW1*
- *Saturdays 9am-1pm*

### Wimbledon Park (LFM)
- *Wimbledon Park First School, Havana Road, SW19*
- *Saturdays 9am-1pm*

## South-East

### Eltham (CCM)
- *Passey Place, Eltham, SE9*
- *3rd Sundays of every month, 10am-3pm*

### Lewisham (CCM)
- *Corner of Erlanger Road & Arbothnot Road, SE14*
- *3rd Saturday of the month, 10am-3pm*

### Oval (CCM)
- *St Mark's Church, The Oval, SE11*
- *Saturdays 10am-3pm*

### Peckham (Indie)
- *Peckham Square, Peckham High St, SE15*
- *Sunday 9am-1pm*

## East

### Liverpool Street (CCM)
- *Devonshire Square, EC2*
- *1st, 3rd Wednesday of each month, 8am-3.30pm*

### Walthamstow (LFM)
- *High Street by Town Square, E17*
- *Sundays 10am-2pm*

Spices

If you're hunting for spices, then bear in mind that many Asian shops carry a great range of spices, often at very reasonable prices. Listed here are two of London's best specialist spice traders.

## Indian Spice Shop

- 115-119 Drummond Street, NW1
- 020 7916 1831
- Euston LU/Rail
- Mon-Sat 9.30am-9pm
  Sun 10am-9pm

Catering for both the local English and Indian communities, this shop is divided into an off-licence and corner shop on one side and an Indian grocer's on the other. It offers an excellent range of spices, chutneys, papads and dals, plus huge sacks of basmati.

## The Spice Shop

- 1 Blenheim Crescent, W11
- 020 7221 4448
- Ladbroke Grove LU
- Mon-Sat 9.30am-6pm
  Sun 12noon-5pm

Birgit Erath runs this small, aromatic shop with enormous enthusiasm and energy. She stocks an impressive range of spices and herbs for both culinary and medicinal purposes. A great place to stock up on spices when visiting Portobello Market.

# Mail Order

## Seasoned Pioneers

- 1Unit 8 Stadium Court, Stadium Road, Plantation Business Park, Bromborough, Wirral CH62
- 0800 0682 348 (freephone)
- www.seasonedpioneers.co.uk

An intelligently chosen selection of over 250 spices, spice blends and herbs are on offer from this mail order company. Spices are dry-roasted in small batches in-house and carefully blended to offer authentic flavours. In addition to more familiar spices, Seasoned Pioneers offer items such as Himalayan pink salt, Indian Tellichery black pepper, grains of paradise, sumac and Mexican mulatto chillies. Spices are ingeniously packaged in funky re-sealable foil packets.

## Steenbergs

- 6 Hallikeld Close, Barker Business Park, Melmerby, Ripon HG4 5GZ
- 01765 640088
- www.steenbergs.co.uk

Axel and Sophie Steenberg's company offers a wide range of attractively packaged, good-quality Fairtrade and organic spices.

Tea & Coffee

Monmouth Coffee Company

# Central

## Algerian Coffee Store

⊞ *52 Old Compton Street, W1*
☎ *020 7437 2480*
✐ *www.algcoffee.co.uk*
🚇 *Leicester Square LU*
🕐 *Mon-Sat 9am-7pm*

This much-loved, vintage Soho institution was set up in 1887 by an Algerian businessman but has now been run by the Crocetta family for decades. The fragrant scent of coffee and spices wafts out of the door – a clue to the extensive range of coffees and teas inside – including Lebanese coffee with ground cardamom. Stock also includes an impressive range of tea and coffee equipment and delicious sweet treats to enjoy with your coffee.

## H. R. Higgins

⊞ *79 Duke Street, W1*
☎ *020 7629 3913*
🚇 *Bond Street LU*
🕐 *Mon-Fri 9.30am-6pm, Sat 10am-6pm*

Founded in 1942 by Harold Higgins (known as 'the coffee man'), this family-run business continues to sell quality teas and coffees. The huge copper caddies, beautiful old scales and knowledgeable, courteous service provide a glimpse into another retail era.

## Monmouth Coffee Company

⊞ *27 Monmouth Street, WC2*
☎ *020 7232 3010*
✐ *www.monmouthcoffee.co.uk*
🚇 *Covent Garden LU*
🕐 *Mon-Sat 8am-6.30pm*

With its high-backed, wooden booths and aromatic scent of coffee, this small coffee shop-cum-café, founded in 1978, has become a much-loved Covent Garden institution. On offer is a discerningly chosen range own-roasted coffee beans, sourced from single farms, estates and cooperatives. The coffee is sold whole or freshly ground, as requested and customers can sample the coffee in the small tasting area.

## Monmouth Coffee Company

⊞ *2 Park Street, SE1*
☎ *020 7232 3010*
✐ *www.monmouthcoffee.co.uk*
🚇 *London Bridge LU/Rail*
🕐 *Mon-Sat 7.30am-6pm*

Right by Borough Market, in a prime corner site, this is an attractively spacious café-cum-coffee shop (sibling to the Monmouth Street establishment). It offers Monmouth's range of excellent coffees, freshly roasted down the road at their roastery. Visitors can sit at a central table to enjoy their coffee along with a slice of baguette, jam and farmhouse butter or a selection of pastries.

*Postcard Teas*

## Postcard Teas

🖃 *9 Dering Street. W1*

☎ *020 7629 3654*

🖥 *www.postcardteas.com*

🚇 *Oxford Circus LU*

🕐 *Mon-Sat 10.30am-6.30pm*

Just off teeming Oxford Street, this aesthetic tea shop is run with courteous charm by Tim d'Offay. It is a serene haven, much appreciated by its loyal regulars who return for teas ranging from fine, refreshing oolongs to Muscatel-flavoured Second Flush. Timothy's genuine fascination with tea has led him to spend many years visiting tea estates in countries around the world from, Japan to Sri Lanka. The beautifully-packaged leaf teas stocked here are a select choice that Timothy himself imports from small-scale, artisanal producers. Also for sale is a selection of exquisite tea ware from hand-crafted Japanese metal tea caddies to linen tea cloths. Although a shop rather than a café, customers can sit and sample teas – a very pleasurable experience.

## Tea Palace

🖃 *12 Covent Garden Market, WC2*

☎ *020 7836 6997*

🖥 *www.teapalace.co.uk*

🚇 *Covent Garden LU*

🕐 *Mon-Sat 10am-7pm, Sun11am-6pm*

In the heart of Covent Garden Market, this smart shop offers a stylishly-packaged range of teas and tisanes (herbal infusions).

# North

## Angelucci's

🗓 *472 Long Lane, N2*
☎ *020 8444 9211*
🖱 *www.angeluccicoffee.co.uk*
🚇 *East Finchley*
🕐 *Mon-Fri 8am-2pm*

This veteran business was founded in 1929 by Mr Angelucci and for many years has been run with courteous charm by his son and daughter – Andy and Alma Angelucci. For many years, Angelucci's was a Soho institution, based in a tiny shop in Frith Street with customers including General de Gaulle and Odette Churchill. Mark Knopfler of Dire Straits fame, immortalised Angelucci in his song Wild West End. Now relocated to roomier premises in East Finchley, Angelucci continues to sells its excellent coffees, including Mokital, a special blend created by Mr Angelucci and served to this day in Soho's famous Bar Italia.

## Camden Coffee Shop

🗓 *11 Delancey Street, NW1*
☎ *020 7387 4080*
🚇 *Camden Town LU*
🕐 *Mon-Wed & Fri 9.30am-5.30pm*
   *Thur 9.30am-2.30pm, Sat 9.30am-5pm*

"Fresh roasted coffee" reads a simple sign outside this small, old-fashioned shop, established in 1950. Inside the store, George (who has run the business since 1978) roasts his coffees in batches in a small coffee-roaster, which clatters noisily as it turns, filling the air with the rich scent of roasting coffee. The choice is confined to ten coffees from Central and South America and Africa, ranging from light to dark roasts, and all very competitively priced. "I'm the only coffee shop left like this," remarks George thoughtfully. He's absolutely right.

## W. M. Martyn

🗓 *135 Muswell Hill Broadway, N10*
☎ *020 8883 5642*
🚌 *Highgate LU, then 134 bus*
🕐 *Mon-Wed & Fri 9.30am-5.30pm,*
   *Thur 9.30am-1pm, Sat 9.30am-5.30pm*

The aroma of freshly-roasted coffee beans wafting down the Broadway marks the presence of this small, old-fashioned grocer's, which was established over 100 years ago. While best-known for its teas and coffees, the shop also stocks traditional groceries, from excellent dried fruits to sugar mice and bars of German marzipan. Staff are helpful and friendly.

# East

## Teasmith

🏠 *6 Lamb Street, E1*
☎ *020 7247 1333*
🚇 *Liverpool Street LU/Rail*
🖥 *www.teasmith.co.uk*
🕐 *Mon-Sun 11am-6pm*

Housed in Spitalfields Market, this high-ceilinged 'tea bar' offers its customers a chance to savour fine teas, from green teas to aged Puers. Each tea is sampled in a number of infusions, making for a leisurely experience. Also on offer are patisserie and chocolates from chocolatier William Curley, such as matcha-flavoured financiers. Staff are friendly and helpful and happy to guide you through the intricacies of tea making and drinking. There is also a fine selection fo teaware on sale.

# MAIL ORDER

## Leaf

🖥 *www.leafshop.co.uk*

Delphine de Chabalier's business offers an attractive range of hand-packed leaf teas and herbal infusions. Flavours range from flavoured black teas to verbena and linden.

## Nardo Organic Coffee

🖥 *www.florestaorganic.co.uk*

This small Brazilian company, which represents a community of Brazilian coffee-growers, offers its own biodynamic and organic Arabica coffee.

## Rare Tea Company

🖥 www.rareteacompany.com

Run with an infectious enthusiasm for tea by founder Henrietta Lovell, this boutique company offers a small but carefully sourced range of leaf teas. Products include fragrant green, white, and jasmine silver tip teas from China and Lost Malawi and an African single-estate black tea.

## Union Coffee Roasters

🏠 *The New Roastery, Unit 2*
*7a South Crescent, London, EC16 4TL*
☎ *020 7474 8990    fax 020 7511 2786*
🖥 *www.unionroasted.com*

Coffee afficionados Jeremy Torz and Steven Macatonia of Union Coffee Roasters specialise in hand-roasted coffee. Their discriminatingly selected, carefully sourced coffees range from the popular Revelation blend to Rwanda Maraba. Union Coffee Roasters make a point of ethically sourcing their coffee working in partnership with coffee farmers and co-operatives.

Wines & Spirits

*Gerry's Wines and Spirits*

In addition to wine shop chains, London is also home to some wonderful independent wine and spirits merchants. The stores range from venerable institutions to relaxed, innovative shops, all proud of the knowledgeable service which they offer.

# Central

## Berry Bros & Rudd

🏠 *3 St James Street, SW1*
☎ *0800 280 2440*
🌐 *www.bbr.com*
🚇 *Green Park LU*
🕐 *Mon-Fri 10am-6pm Sat 10am-5pm*

Founded in 1698, Berry Brothers and Rudd has a venerable and fascinating history, starting life as a grocer's shop supplying the aristocracy, before moving into the wine trade. It is still owned and managed by members of both the Berry and Rudd families. The business began supplying wine to the British Royal Family in 1760 and currently holds two Royal Warrants. Entering the atmospheric, elegantly understated shop offers a glimpse of the past, including the huge scales on which notable customers such as William Pitt and Lord Byron were weighed, with their weight ceremoniously recorded. The cellars which were at one time home to Napoleon III are now used as a venue for wine tastings and lunches as well as for storing wine. Elegantly dressed staff offer courteous advice to delights in stock including King's Ginger, a liqueur created by Berry Bros for King Edward VII. Despite the companies history they were early pioneers of on-line wine shopping and have an award-winning website.

## Gerry's Wines and Spirits

🏠 74 Old Compton Street W1
☎ 020 7734 4215
🌐 www.gerrys.uk.com
🚇 Leicester Square LU
🕐 *Mon-Thur & Sat 9am-6.30pm,*
*Fri 9am-7.30pm, Sun 12noon-6pm*

Set up in 1984 by Michael Kyprianou, this characterful drinks emporium is a much-loved Soho institution. Noted especially for its range of spirits (200 different rums, 150 tequilas, 150 vodkas), the shelves here are lined with a colourful array of bottles, each neatly labelled with name and price. Photos of assorted happy customers testify to Gerry's popularity. Stock ranges from Pisco (much sought-after by Chilean and Peruvian ex-pats) to Lillet Vermouth (featured in the film Casino Royale) and a huge range of flavoured syrups for making cocktails. Staff are friendly and helpful and take pride in tracking down the most obscure alcoholic request from their loyal customers.

## Milroy's of Soho

- 🏠 *3 Greek Street, W1*
- ☎ *020 7437 9311*
- 🖥 *www.milroys.co.uk*
- 🚇 *Tottenham Court Road LU*
- 🕐 *Mon-Sat 10am-7pm*

This veteran whisky shop was set up in 1964 by brothers John and Wallace Milroy and soon became known to locals simply as "the whisky shop". Now part of the Jeroboams group, Milroy's stocks over 700 carefully sourced whiskies from around the world, with the emphasis on Highland single malts. Stock also includes fine wines and other spirits such as rums and Cognacs.

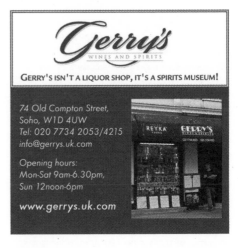
# North

## The Sampler

- 🏠 *266 Upper Street, N1*
- ☎ *020 7226 9500*
- 🖥 *www.thesampler.co.uk*
- 🚇 *Angel, Highbury & Islington (LU)*
- 🕐 *Mon-Sat 11.30am-9pm*
  *Sun 11.30am-7pm*

This relaxed and friendly wine shop offers customers a chance to sample over 1,000 assorted, carefully selected wines. Ten wine sampling machines rotated a range of 80 wines from sherries to fine wines. An additional lure is the extensive range of around 120 various grower Champagnes.

# West

## Moreno Wine Merchants

- 🏠 *11 Marylands Road, W9*
- ☎ *020 7286 0678*
- 🖥 *www.morenowinedirect.com*
- 🚇 *Warwick Avenue*
- 🕐 *Mon-Fri 4pm-8pm, Sat 12noon-8pm*

This well-established, affable wine merchants specialises in Spanish wines, but also has wines from other countries too. The service here is excellent and they have a keen eye for up-and-coming producers.

## Roberson's

348 Kensington High Street. W14

020 7371 2121

www.robersonwinemerchant.co.uk

Olympia LU

Mon-Sat 10am-8pm, Sun 12noon-6pm

Established in 1991, this smart, spacious wine shop is noted for its collection of quality Bordeaux and Burgundy wines. They also stock wines from other European countries among their 2,000 wines, with the emphasis on classic wines. Wine buffs can stock up their cellars from the 'Fine and Rare Wines' section, kept securely under lock and key, while bargain-hunters enjoy browsing the ongoing sales section. Wine tastings are an added attraction.

# South

## Bedales

5 Bedale Street, SE1

020 7403 8853

www.bedaleswines.com

London Bridge LU/rail

Tue-Sat 10am-10pm

Atmospherically housed in Borough Market, this relaxed wine shop and wine bar carries a diverse range of stock from around the world. The staff are friendly and willing to offer advice when required.

# South-West

## Jeroboams

50-52 Elizabeth Street, SW1

020 7730 8108

www.jeroboams.co.uk

Victoria LU

Mon-Fri 9.30am-7pm, Sat 10am-5pm

This showcase shop of the noted wine merchants is a smart affair, as befits its Belgravia surroundings. On offer here are around 500 fine wines, including excellent wines from Bordeaux, Burgundy and Champagnes. Jeroboams staff are knowledgeable and helpful.
*There are 9 branches in London (see website for details).*

## Lea & Sandeman

170 Fulham Road, SW10

020 7244 0522

www.leaandsandeman.co.uk

Gloucester Road LU

Mon-Sat 10am-8pm

Founded in 1988 by Charles Lea and Patrick Sandeman, this acclaimed wine shop has always prided itself on sourcing and bringing interesting wines to the public.
*Branches:*
*211 Kensington Church Street, W8*
*51 High Street, SW13*
*167 Chiswick High Road, W4*

### Philglass & Swiggot

- *21 Northcote Road, SW11*
- *020 7924 4494*
- *www.philglass-swiggot.co.uk*
- *Clapham Junction rail*
- *Mon-Fri 11am-7pm, Sat 10am-6pm, Sun 12noon-5pm*

Founded in 1991, this smart wine shop has carved out a loyal following among the local community. Always innovative it offers a great range of quality wines and is renowned for its service.

# East

## Bottle Apostle

- *95 Lauriston Road, E9*
- *020 8985 1549*
- *www.bottleapostle.com*
- *London Fields Rail*
- *Tue-Fri 12noon-9pm*
  *Sat 10am-8pm, Sun 10am-6pm*

This smart, sophisticated wine shop offers self-service wine sampling, with prices for the samples ranging from a few pence to a few pounds. The globe-trotting stock ranges from beers and ciders to wines and spirits and the friendly staff are happy to offer advice and make suggestions.

# Wine Tastings

If you'd like to learn more about wine, then there are a number of wine tasting classes and courses in the capital.

• **Berry Brothers and Rudd** offers an extensive range of wine courses, from one day events to evening classes (*www.bbr.com*).

• **Jeroboams** offer a range of informal wine tasting events, held at **Milroy's in Soho** (*www.jeroboams.co.uk*).

• Award-wining wine writer, **Ray O' Connor** offers a range of wine education events, including drop-in wine tastings and individually tailored tutoring (*www.rayoconnor.com*).

• Wine expert **Michael Schuster**, much acclaimed for his teaching, offers courses at **Bordeaux Index** in Hatton Garden (*www.schuster.f9.co.uk*).

# London Honey

*Fortnum & Mason Honey*

Although people tend to associate bees and honey with the countryside rather than cities, London supports a number of hives. London's bees enjoy easy pickings with parks, green spaces and gardens offering a fruitful source of nectar. The current interest in local food has provided an additional appeal to the idea of London-produced honey. Next time you buy a jar of honey, spare a thought for the difficulties of honey production. Beekeepers, as in other parts of the world, are currently faced with the problem of the varroa mite, which undermines the bees' health and resistance to disease to an alarming extent. Weather conditions, too, are a major factor in how much honey the bees are able to produce. Despite these adversities, interest in beekeeping is very much on the rise and there are several key London producers who are worth seeking out for their distinctive flavour.

## Fortnum and Mason Honey

⌂ *Fortnum & Mason*
*181 Piccadilly, W1*
☎ *020 7734 8040*
🖝 *www.fortnumandmason.co.uk*
🚇 *Piccadilly Circus LU*

What is surely London's poshest honey is available from established grocers Fortnum and Mason's. They house their bees in elegant, architectural-themed, Eau de Nil-coloured hives on the roof of their Piccadilly store. The bees fly within a three-mile radius of their hive in search of nectar; an area which includes the grounds of Buckingham Palace, St James Palace and numerous London parks.

## The Hive Honey Shop

⌂ *93 Northcote Road, SW11*
☎ *020 7924 6233*
🖝 *www.thehivehoneyshop.co.uk*
🚇 *Clapham Junction rail*
🕐 *Mon-Sat 10am-5pm*

James Hamill has been promoting the culinary and medicinal virtues of honey from his idiosyncratic Battersea shop for many years. The store comes complete with a glass-walled bee hive in addition to a huge, ever-changing selection of raw honeys. For those with a passion for honey, James also offers beekeeping courses.

## The London Beekeepers' Association

🖝 *www.lbka.org.uk*

An association representing beekeepers in central London offering advice and courses to those interested in urban beekeeping.

## Pure London Honey

🖝 *www.purelondonhoney.com*

Cold-filtered honey produced by beekeeper Orlando Clarke from hives in Kings Cross and South London. The honey is prepared using natural methods and sold through a handful of London delicatessens.

## Regent's Park Honey Pure Food

🖝 *www.purefood.co.uk*

Beekeeper Toby Mason produces his distinctive, perfumed, cold-filtered honey from his hives in Regents Park. As the honey is produced in very limited quantities, it is available for sale only in a few places including delicatessen Melrose & Morgan and the Regent s Park Garden Café.

## Urban Bees

🖝 *www.urbanbees.co.uk*

In addition to supplying his own London honey produced in the areas of Queen's Park and Battersea, Brian McCallum offers beekeeping courses.

Featured here are schools which offer the chance to learn all kinds of cooking skills and techniques from filleting fish to making fresh pasta.

## Billingsgate Seafood Training School

⌨ *Billingsgate Market*
   *Trafalgar Way, E14*
☎ *020 7517 3548*
✎ *www.seafoodtraining.org*
🚌 *Canary Wharf DLR/LU*

From how to identify really fresh fish to filleting and cooking fish, the Billingsgate Seafood Training School, based at bustling Billingsgate Market, is a mine of piscine information. Cookery classes here are admirably hands-on and informative. The guided tours offer a fascinating insight into this historic market.

## Books For Cooks

⌨ *4 Blenheim Crescent, W11*
☎ *020 7221 1992*
✎ *www.booksforcooks.com*
🚌 *Ladbroke Grove LU*

This much-loved, gastronomic bookshop also offers an appetising programme of cookery workshops. See p. 322 for more details.

## Le Cordon Bleu London

⌨ *114 Marylebone Lane, W1*
☎ *020 7935 3503*
✎ *www.lcblondon.com*
🚌 *Baker Street/Bond Street LU*

The London branch of this famous French cookery school offers a programme of diplomas and certificates. Pupils learn through both demonstrations and practical classes.

## Leiths School of Food and Wine

⌨ *16-20 Wendell Road, W12*
☎ *020 8749 6406*
✎ *www.leiths.com*
🚌 *Stamford Brook LU*

This well-established cookery school offers both 'Professional Courses' and 'Enthusiasts' Courses'. There is a wide-ranging syllabus offering both courses in Practical Cookery and classes in subjects such as Knife Skills and Seasonal French Cooking.

## Cookery School

- 15B Little Portland St, W1
- ☎ 020 7631 4590
- ✎ www.cookeryschool.co.uk
- 🚌 Oxford Circus LU

This friendly, informal cookery school offers a wide-ranging, seasonal selection of classes and courses. Founder Rosalind Rathouse aims to pass on her passion for and knowledge of food and cookery and offers students the chance to learn anything from thrifty cooking with meat to pastry-making techniques.

## Cucina Caldesi

- 118 Marylebone Lane, W1
- ☎ 020 7487 0750
- ✎ www.caldesi.com
- 🚌 Bond Street LU

Run by restaurateurs Giancarlo and Katie Caldesi, this cookery school specialises in Italian cookery. There are classes and courses on subjects from making fresh pasta to Venetian cuisine.

## The Kitchen

- 275 New King's Road, SW6
  Parsons Green
- ☎ 020 7736 8067
- ✎ www.visitthekitchen.com
- 🚌 Parsons Green LU

Run by Natalie Richmond and Michelin-starred chef Thierry Laborde, the idea here is simple but ingenious – choose your menu from the website, book a time-slot that suits you and turn up to cook the meal from the first-class ingredients provided, with Thierry and his team on hand to offer guidance, then take your meal home, leaving the washing up behind.

## Angela Malik Cookery School

- 6, Churchfield Road, W3
- ☎ 020 8992 5011
- ✎ www.angelamalik.co.uk

Angela Malik's hands-on cookery school offers a lively programme of cookery classes on subjects ranging from Thai Express Lunches to Indian Home Cooking.

## Recipease

- 48-50 St John's Road
  Clapham Junction, SW11
- ☎ 0845 2797272
- ✎ www.jamieoliver.com/recipease
- 🚌 Clapham Junction rail

Jamie Oliver's jaunty, spacious, Battersea-based 'food shop' offers 'Easy to Learn' cookery lessons making dishes such as risotto, 'the perfect steak' or stuffed seabass. The 'Easy to Make' sessions allow you to assemble a pre-selected dish to be taken home.

# Best Breakfasts

## Ottolenghi

287 Upper Street, N1
020 7288 1454
www.ottolenghi.co.uk
Angel, Highbury & Islington LU

Beautiful food on offer at this cool, elegant branch of Ottolenghi's includes a beguiling breakfast menu. Diners can enjoy immaculately cooked dishes such as cinnamon French toast, freshly-baked savoury muffins or scrambled egg with smoked salmon.

## E. Pellicci

332 Bethnal Green Road, E2
020 7739 4873
Bethnal Green LU/rail

Founded in 1900, this classic caff with its vintage interior is still run with warmth and charm by the Pellicci family. The caff still serves quality fry-ups to appreciative customers, ranging from builders to bankers.

## The Providores

109 Marylebone High Street, W1
020 7935 6175
www.theprovidores.co.uk
Baker Street LU

New Zealand chef Peter Gordon is noted for his creative culinary talents and uses ingredients from around the globe with cosmopolitan aplomb. The monthly-changing breakfast and brunch menu in the Tapa Room at his relaxed Marylebone eaterie features dishes such as Turkish eggs with whipped yoghurt and chilli butter, freshly-baked muffins and banana-and-pecan-stuffed French toast with bacon.

## Princi

135 Wardour Street, W1
020 7478 8888
www.princi.co.uk
Leicester Square LU

Offering a glamorous taste of Italy, this Soho bakery-cum-café does a roaring trade in espressos and cappuccinos and a mouthwatering array of freshly baked pastries.

## The Wolseley

160 Piccadilly, W1
020 7499 6996
www.thewolseley.com
Green Park LU

Splendidly housed in a former 1920s car showroom, this European-inspired café and restaurant offers a chance to sample classic breakfast dishes. Omelette Arnold Bennett, grilled kipper and kedgeree are all deliciously prepared and served with aplomb.

African & Caribbean

Brixton Market

In his monumental book, 'Staying Power', Peter Fryer points out that the first Black presence in Britain dates back to Roman times, when Black men were among the conscripts in the Roman army. The growth of a domestic Black community, however, was connected with Britain's slave trade, which was started in 1562-3 by the first 'triangular voyage' between Britain, Africa and the West Indies. The demand for sugar and the labour-intensive sugar cane plantation system in the Caribbean encouraged the slave trade's growth, making it enormously profitable to those running it.

Africans came to Britain as slaves until the slave trade was outlawed in 1807. Before this date some free Blacks, such as seamen, servants and street entertainers were established in Britain, with the London community living mainly along the Thames in Limehouse. Records such as that of freed slave Ukawsaw Gronniosaw, give a vivid picture of ill-treatment and discrimination, which forced many into destitution. After 1807 the Black community in Britain declined, although Black loyalists returned after fighting in the American War of Independence, and some seamen settled after serving in the Napoleonic Wars (1792-1815). In the late nineteenth century a small community of Somali seamen settled in the London docks.

The coming of the First World War meant a change of attitude towards the Black community. Instead of being rejected for work on racial grounds, their help was now needed in the munitions factories. Black seamen also filled the gaps in the Merchant Navy caused by conscription. By 1919 there were 20,000 Black people in Britain. But once the war was over the picture changed again, with the seamen's unions closing the door firmly against any Black labour.

A similar pattern occurred in the late 1940s and 1950s when, as Britain struggled to rebuild its war-torn economy, a call went out to the Commonwealth for workers to come to the 'Mother Country'. The 1948 Nationality Act granted British citizenship to people living in Britain's current and former colonies. For many West Indians this was an opportunity to be seized; unemployment was high in the West Indies and in 1951 a hurricane added to Jamaica's problems. Corporations such as London Transport actively recruited labour in Barbados in 1956, and by 1966 had also turned to Trinidad and Jamaica. Between 1945 and 1958, over 125,000 West Indians emigrated to Britain. The different stages of African

immigration into London in the post-war years have been triggered by the ebb and flow of African politics. The 1950s and 1960s saw an influx of West Africans made up largely of students and lawyers. During the 1970s, African and Asian Ugandans fled Idi Amin; while recent years have seen an increase in immigration from Ghana, Zaire and Ethiopia.

There is no single centre for the African community in London, with pockets of different African nationalities scattered throughout the capital. There are, however, focal points such as Brixton and Notting Hill for the West Indian community. Many of the first post-war Jamaican immigrants who sailed over on the Empire Windrush settled in Brixton, a formerly prosperous suburb which had become cheap and run-down. This community attracted further Jamaican immigrants during the 1950s and 1960s. Notting Hill, in which mainly Trinidadians settled, hosts the famous Carnival; what originated as a 1964 Bank Holiday street party for local children has since developed into Europe's largest open-air street festival. The costume parades and rhythmic steel drums all derive from Trinidad's own spectacular Carnival.

*Breadfruit at Brixton Market*

# African & Caribbean Cuisine

'African food' is a blanket term covering a huge number of countries, each with their own characteristic cuisines. Ethiopian cuisine, for example, is marked by its richly spiced dishes and its use of teff, a grain so small that there are 2,500-3,000 seeds to the gram. Teff is traditionally used to make Ethiopia's staple flatbread – injera, which has a characteristically sour tang. Certain staples, such as maize, cassava, plantain and beans, are shared across different African countries and crop up in Black cuisine in many parts of the world. Dried foods, such as smoked or salted fish and meat, are another common element in the African kitchen, reflecting the need to preserve food before the days of refrigeration or canning. Many of these ingredients are now used to add a distinctive flavour to dishes.

West African slaves brought their cuisine to the West Indies and its influence is still marked in today's Caribbean cooking. Many of the staples are the same (several brought from Africa): cassava, yams, taro, plantain and groundnuts. Dishes in common include coo-coo (cornmeal pudding) and fufu, the latter being a Fanti word used on the Cape Coast. In West Africa fufu is pounded yam, plantain and cassava dough dipped into a soup, while in Jamaica fufu now means both the pounded yam and the soup. The slaves' restricted diet also included salted meat and fish and these are still popular, although the latter is now something of a luxury.

Caribbean cooking is very much a melting pot of a cuisine, influenced by a series of colonisers and immigrants. Chillies were brought from South America by the Spanish colonisers and 'escovished fish' (fresh pickled fish) originated from the Spanish dish escabeche. The arrival in Trinidad of indentured workers from India means that dishes like roti and curry goat are popular there today.

The fertility of the Caribbean islands meant many plants could be introduced successfully. Many foods were introduced from other countries, such as breadfruit, now a staple, which was introduced by Captain Bligh. Fresh seafood is characteristic of West Indian cuisine and increasingly fish such as colourful snappers are becoming available in Britain.

Brixton Market

# Glossary

**Ackee:** a red-skinned fruit that is only safe to eat when the fruit is fully ripe. The white, fleshy base called an aril is the part that is eaten. Fresh ackee is very rarely found but it is available in tins. Saltfish with ackee is one of Jamaica's famous dishes. The Latin name of the fruit, Blighia sapida, is a tribute to Captain Bligh, who introduced it to Jamaica.

**Agbono:** sometimes spelt ogbono, this is the inner kernel of the African bush mango. The kernel is the size and shape of an almond but browner and much harder. Available both whole and ground.

**Allspice:** peppercorn-sized berries, with a flavour that combines cloves, cinnamon and nutmeg – hence the name.

**Annatto:** small, orange-red seeds, used to add colour and flavour.

**Arrowroo:** a starch extracted from the underground stem of a water-plant.

**Avocado:** this green-skinned, soft-fleshed fruit is called 'pear' in the Caribbean.

**Bananas:** green bananas, which are the unripe fruit of certain varieties, and ripe yellow bananas are treated as both a vegetable and a fruit in Caribbean and African cuisines.

**Bitter leaf:** A distinctively flavoured African leaf, related to the lettuce family. Available dried or frozen.

**Breadfruit:** a football-sized fruit with thick, green, pimply skin and creamy flesh, used both as a starchy vegetable and in pies and puddings.

**Callaloo:** green leaves of the dasheen plant, used to make a famous soup of the same name. Available tinned and fresh.

**Cassava:** large, brown, hand-shaped tubers of the cassava plant, also called manioc or yucca. Bitter cassava, despite the fact it contains toxic prussic acid which must be removed by either cooking or pressing, is a staple food. Yellow-fleshed sweet cassava is eaten as a vegetable. Dried, ground cassava is used in Africa to make gari. Ground cassava meal is used in the West Indies to make a type of bread and the flavoured juice of grated cassava is used to make cassareep, a key ingredient of pepperpot.

**Catfish, dried:** small blackened fish, with a distinctive large head, used to add flavour to soups and stews in West African cooking.

**Cho-cho (christophene, chayote):** a pear-sized member of the squash family, with a wrinkled skin ranging in colour from white to green, and watery white flesh.

**Coconut:** coconut flesh and milk are widely used in Caribbean cookery.

*Cho-cho*

**Cornmeal:** coarsely or finely ground dried corn kernels.

**Crayfish, dried:** although called 'crayfish' in Africa, these are a type of shrimp. Used whole or ground as flavouring.

**Custard apple:** apple-sized fruit with a knobbly, green skin. The white, sweet pulp has a custard-like texture, hence the name.

**Dasheen:** potato-sized fibrous tubers with white starchy flesh. Some varieties of dasheen have an acrid taste.

**Eddoe:** a small, rounded fibrous tuber with white starchy flesh.

**Egusi:** pumpkin seeds, which are available shelled, either whole or ground. Egusi is used in West African cooking, providing a nutty texture in soups and stews.

**Fish:** *flying fish*, a distinctive 'winged' fish; *king fish*, a firm-fleshed 'meaty' fish, often sold as steaks; *parrot fish*, a brightly-coloured fish with a beaky head; *snapper*, a popular, firm-fleshed fish, available in colours from grey to pinkish-red; and *trevalli*, a large, firm-fleshed oily fish. *Jacks* is the name given to the smaller fish of the same family.

**Gari:** coarsely-ground cassava, an African staple.

**Guava:** small, yellow-green, hard-skinned fruit with pinkish flesh filled with small seeds. It has a distinctive fragrance and is eaten raw or used to make jams and jellies.

**Guinep:** small, round, green fruit which grows in bunches. The pink flesh has a delicate flavour.

**Irish moss:** white, curly seaweed from which an eponymous drink is made. Available either dried or ready to drink.

**Jackfruit:** a large, green fruit with a pimply skin, similar in appearance to breadfruit.

**Kenke:** West African dumpling, made from fermented maize flour wrapped in corn husks or banana leaves and cooked.

**Landsnails:** giant snails, sold either alive, frozen, tinned or smoked. If bought alive, keep them and feed them on lettuce leaves for a few days before cooking to make sure they have excreted anything toxic.

**Mango:** this large, kidney-shaped fruit, with its succulent orange flesh and sweet, resiny flavour, comes in numerous varieties. One of the best-known West Indian varieties is the Julie mango.

**Okra (ladies fingers, ochroes):** finger-sized, ridged, tapering green pods, introduced into the Caribbean from West Africa.

*Okra*

**Ortanique:** a cross between an orange and a tangerine, this looks like an orange with a flattened end.

*Ortanique*

**Palm hearts:** tender palm tree hearts, usually found tinned.

**Palm oil:** a thick, orange-red oil, made from the fruit of the oil palm, which adds flavour and colour to African dishes.

**Pawpaw:** long, oval fruit, with soft orange flesh, varying in skin colour from green to orange.

*Scotch Bonnet Peppers*

**Peppers:** among the hottest and most flavourful of the peppers used in African and Caribbean cooking is the squat, rounded Scotch bonnet pepper, available in green, yellow and red varieties.

**Pepper sauce:** the sauce comes in a variety of textures from liquid to paste, but is always hot!

**Pigeon pea (gunga):** ridged pea pods, with every pea in its own section. Unusually, the peas within a single pod vary in colour from cream through green and brown. Available fresh, tinned or dried.

*Plantain*

**Plantain:** similar in appearance to green bananas, plantain have starchy flesh and are cooked and eaten as a vegetable. They can be chipped, boiled or cooked in stews.

**Pomelo:** often called shaddock, after the merchant ship captain who introduced the fruit to the Caribbean, this is a large, thick-skinned citrus fruit, similar in flavour to grapefruit.

**Saltfish:** preserved foods such as salted fish were brought over to the Caribbean to feed the plantation workers. It is now something of a luxury item. Stockfish is a popular salted fish.

**Sapodilla (naseberry):** a fruit very similar in appearance to kiwi fruit, with a brown, furry skin. Inside it has pinky-brown, granular flesh with a few glossy pips and a distinctive sweet flavour.

**Sorrel (rosella):** the red sepals of a flowering plant, used either fresh or dried to make a dark-red, aromatic drink, traditionally at Christmas.

**Soursop:** a large, oval-shaped fruit with a thick, green, spiny skin. The pinkish-white flesh inside is custard-textured with a delicate, tart flavour.

**Sugar cane:** similar in appearance to bamboo, this plant has played a considerable part in Caribbean history as the sugar cane plantations demanded extensive labour, provided by slaves. Short lengths of the woody stalk are either chewed and sucked for their sweet refreshing juice.

**Sweet potato:** a sweet-fleshed tuber, available in many varieties.

*Sweet Potato*

**Yam:** a family of large, brown-skinned, starchy tubers, which come in many varieties, both yellow and white-fleshed.

# Food Shops

For the best range of African and Caribbean foodstuffs, head to bustling markets such as Brixton Market in South London or Ridley Road Market in East London.

# North

## Engocha

⌨ *143 Fortess Road, NW5*
☎ *020 7485 3838*
🚌 *Tufnell Park LU*
🕒 *Daily 10am-8.30pm*

This tiny, frankincense-scented Ethiopian food shop has a meat counter and a small stock of basics, including green Ethiopian coffee beans, spices and tef (an Ethiopian grain). Home-made injeera (Ethiopian bread) is particularly popular.

## France Fresh Fish

⌨ *99 Stroud Green Road, N4*
☎ *020 7263 9767*
🚌 *Finsbury Park LU/Rail*
🕒 *Mon-Sat 9.30am-7pm, Sun 11am-5pm*

An eye-catching window display marks out this established shop, specialists in tropical fish and run by the same family who own Chez Liline, the Mauritian fish restaurant next door. Good things on offer include raw prawns, samphire (when in season) and exotic fish and seafood, including barracuda, conch and parrot fish.

## K. M. Butcher's Grocer's

⌨ *29 Stroud Green Road, N4*
☎ *020 7263 6625*
🚌 *Finsbury Park LU/Rail*
🕒 *Mon-Sat 8am-8pm, Sun 8am-6pm*

A large store, complete with a counter piled high with goat meat and chickens. Groceries range from Mauby syrup drinks to bags of cornmeal.

## Stroud Green Food Store

⌨ *65 Stroud Green Road, N4*
☎ *020 7272 0348*
🚌 *Finsbury Park LU/Rail*
🕒 *Daily 8am-8pm*

A neatly-arranged store with an attractive display of fresh fruit and vegetables outside, including breadfruit, mangoes, plantain and bunches of thyme, and grocery staples inside.

## Walthamstow Market

⌨ *Walthamstow High Street*
🚌 *Walthamstow LU*
🕒 *Tue-Sat 8am-5pm*

Among the stalls at this huge street market – reputedly Europe's longest outdoor street market – are several selling African and Caribbean ingredients.

# West

## Portobello Road Market

🏠 *Portobello Road, W12*
🚌 *Notting Hill Gate LU*
🕐 *Mon-Sat 9am-5pm*

Beyond the antique shops is a lively fruit and vegetable market. Several of the stalls here sell West Indian produce such as yams, Scotch bonnet peppers and okra.

## Shepherd's Bush Market

🏠 *Uxbridge Road, W12*
🚌 *Goldhawk Road LU,*
   *Shepherd's Bush LU*
🕐 *Mon-Wed, Fri-Sat 9am-5pm,*
   *Thur 9am-1pm*

Fifteen years ago this was a more food-orientated market. Among the fabric, lingerie and kitchenware stalls, however, one can find stalls selling Caribbean produce such as yams, mangoes and plaintain.

# South- East

## Choumert Road Market

🏠 *Choumert Road, SE15*
🚌 *Peckham Rye Rail*
🕐 *Mon-Sat 9am-3pm*

Off Rye Lane – itself lined with African and Caribbean butchers, fishmongers and grocers – this street market offers stalls selling tropical fish and staple produce, such as breadfruit plantain and yams.

# South- West

## Brixton Market

🏠 *Brixton Station Road, Pope's Road,*
   *SW9 Atlantic Road, Electric Road and*
   *Electric Avenue*
🚌 *Brixton LU/Rail*
🕐 *Mon, Tue, Thur-Sat 8am-5.30pm,*
   *Wed 8am-1pm*

This is the best market in London for West Indian and African foodstuffs. Spread out through streets and arcades alongside a mixture of household goods, wig and fabric shops are a range of fruit and vegetable stalls, piled high with yams, red Scotch bonnet peppers, green and yellow plantains, breadfruit, mangoes, limes and bunches of thyme. Fishmongers here sell an array of tropical fish while the butchers (some with signs advertising 'meat so tender you don't need teeth') offer goat, offal, cow's feet and pig's trotters. Saturday is the busiest market day and the noise is tremendous: music blaring from the record shops and people exchanging greetings, catching up on news and arguing over prices.

## Broadway Market & Tooting Market

🏠 *Upper Tooting Road, SW17*
🚇 *Tooting Broadway LU*

Both these covered markets offer a large selection of African and Caribbean foodstuffs, from fresh produce such as breadfruits and Scotch bonnet peppers, to tropical fish.

# East

## Queen's Market

🏠 *Green Street, E7*
    *(on the corner of Queen Road)*
🚇 *Upton Park LU*
🕐 *Tue, Thur-Sat 8am-5pm*

Among the clothing and household goods are a number of stalls and shops selling Caribbean foodstuffs. Tropical fish such as red snapper and halal meat are among the foods on offer.

## Ridley Road Market

🏠 *Ridley Road, E8*
🚇 *Dalston Junction Rail*
🕐 *Tue-Sat 9am-5pm*

A large, bustling market with a mixture of English and West Indian fruit and vegetable stalls, fishmongers and butchers. The quality of the food is generally good and the stalls really cater for the West Indian community with goat meat and pigs trotters among the delicacies on display.

# MAIL ORDER

## Tobia Teff

✉ *www.tobiateff.co.uk*

A chance to buy teff, the ancient Ethiopian grain, so small that its name 'teff' comes from the Arabic 'teffa' meaning 'lost'.

# Eating Places

## Central

### Jerk City  ££
- 189 Wardour Street, W1
- 020 7287 2878
- Tottenham Court Road LU

A small, relaxed café specialising in classic Caribbean dishes including saltfish and ackee and jerk chicken.

### Savannah Jerk  ££
- 187 Wardour Street, W1
- 020 7437 7770
- Tottenham Court Road LU

A popular restaurant offering a taste of Caribbean cuisine with hearty portions of dishes such as barbecue chicken and rice and peas.

## North

### Cottons  £££
- 55 Chalk Farm Road, NW1
- 020 7485 8388
- Camden Town or Chalk Farm LU

Attractively decorated in bright tropical colours this funky restaurant serves up generous portions of excellent Caribbean food such as mixed jerk grilled fish (red snapper, squid, goat fish and mullet).  Drinks include cocktails, sorrel and a serious range of rums in the Rum Shack.

### Hummingbird  ££
- 84 Stroud Green Road, N4
- 020 7263 9690
- Finsbury Park LU/Rail

This veteran Trinidadian restaurant is a relaxed place in which to try classic Trinidadian dishes such as rotis, curries and rice and peas, accompanied by delicious punches.

### Lalibela  ££
- 137 Fortess Road, NW5
- 020 7284 0600
- Tufnell Park LU

This small, friendly restaurant offers a chance to enjoy lovingly prepared classic Ethiopian dishes such as 'wot', richly-spiced stews and injeera, the flat sour bread with which one scoops up and eats the wot. Finish off with Ethiopian coffee, a leisurely experience during which one inhales the fragrance of the freshly roasted beans, heated in a heavy metal saucepan, before being presented with a pottery flask of the freshly made coffee served with aromatic burning frankincense on the side.

## Mango Room  £££

⌨ *10-12 Kentish Town Road, NW1*
☎ *020 7482 5065*
🚌 *Camden Town LU*

An attractive restaurant with a mellow atmosphere serving great, contemporary Caribbean food.

## Queen of Sheba  ££

⌨ *12 Fortess Road, NW5*
☎ *020 7284 3947*
🚌 *Kentish Town LU/rail*

A hospitable, well-established Ethiopian restaurant, offering dishes such as tibs firfir and misir we't.

# South-West

## Asmara  ££

⌨ *386 Coldharbour Lane, SW9*
☎ *020 7737 4144*
🚌 *Brixton LU/Rail*

This small, homely restaurant serves up delicious, carefully cooked Eritrean food.

*Brixton Market*

# Cookbooks

## Creole Caribbean Cookery
*Kenneth Gardiner*
A nicely written book with appetising recipes.

## Caribbean and African Cookery
*Rosamund Grant*
A well-written, informative and readable cookbook.

## A Taste of Africa
*Dorinda Hafner*
A look at African and Caribbean cookery, written with exuberance.

## Trade Wind: Caribbean Cooking
*Christine Mackie*
An evocative mix of text and recipes.

## Caribbean Cooking
*Elizabeth Lambert Ortiz*
An excellent look at Caribbean cuisine.

## Caribbean Food Made Easy
*Levi Roots*
An attractive and accessible Caribbean cookbook by the creator of Reggae Reggae Sauce.

Asian London

*Chhappan Bhog*

The term 'Asian' covers what was once the Indian subcontinent but is today Bangladesh, India, Pakistan and Sri Lanka. An Asian presence in Britain can be traced back to the seventeenth and eighteenth centuries. Some early settlers were performers but many were servants brought back from India by the newly prosperous nawabs. Through the East India Company others came as lascars, Indian seamen.

A fascinating book, Across Seven Seas (edited by Caroline Adams), describes how many of these lascars were from one small, land-locked part of Bengal called Sylhet. There was a tradition in rural India of men leaving their villages to work and support their family. Work as seamen was offered at large ports such as Calcutta. In the words of Haji Kona Miah, "The Sylhet people were in the ship because these people follow each other, and some went there and others saw them and thought they could get jobs too". The serangs, agents who chose workers for the ships, preferred to employ people from their own village or locality. Once Sylhetis became serangs, a pattern of using Sylheti sailors was established.

Those who settled in London lived in the East End, near the docks. For many

of them earning a living was difficult and in 1858 the 'Strangers Home for Asiatics, Africans and South Sea Islanders' was opened in West India Dock Road, Limehouse. The major growth in the Bengali community came this century in 1956, when passports were finally granted and thousands of people came to London. By 1962, the number of Bengali immigrants living in the East End had swelled from approximately 300 to 5,000.

Of course, it was not only Bengali seamen wae to London: doctors, politicians and lawyers were also among the immigrants. Indeed, three men pivotal to India's independence studied law in London at the turn of the century: Mohandas Karamchand (later Mahatma) Gandhi, Mohammed Ali Jinnah and Jawaharlal Nehru. In 1892 Dabadhai Naoroji, a campaigner for Indian rights, was elected as Britain's first Asian MP by a majority of three votes.

It was in the period following the Second World War that the Asian presence in Britain expanded considerably, the 1948 Nationality Act granted the right of British citizenship to Britain's colonies and former colonies. After Indian Independence the violent partition of India and Pakistan left

thousands dispossessed. Britain officially encouraged mainly unskilled workers from India and Pakistan to come to Britain and by 1958 there were around 55,000 Asians in Britain. The next wave of immigration came in the late 1960s when Asians were expelled from Uganda, and in 1972, when Idi Amin expelled nearly 30,000 Ugandan Asians who arrived in Britain within the space of three months.

The Asian community today, like the complex Indian subcontinent, is made up of people from different countries who speak different languages and practice different faiths. Certain areas in London are linked to particular groups. Brick Lane, which over the centuries has housed different waves of immigrants, is now predominantly Bengali, the Sylhet seamen who first settled there having paved the way for others. The history of Brick Lane is encapsulated in the story of one building on Fournier Street, built as a Huguenot chapel in 1774, it later became a Methodist chapel, in 1898 it was converted into a Jewish synagogue, and nowadays it functions as the London Jamme Masjid mosque.

Wembley is a Gujarati area, while Southall is predominantly Punjabi and Sikh. There are various theories about Southall's roots. One is that workers brought in to construct the new airport at Heathrow settled near their worksite. Alternatively, it is thought that work was provided for Asian labourers in local factories and the community grew up around this. Southall today is a thriving community with everything from Sikh temples to bookshops and restaurants. In South London Tooting houses a diverse Asian community, including Sri Lankans, East African Asians, Pakistanis and Gujuratis. London's Hindu community, meanwhile, is justly proud of 'Shri Swaminarayan Mandir' (020 8965 2651), the traditional Hindu temple recently built in Neasden. The gleaming white marble temple, which rises like a mirage in an urban desert just off the North Circular, is unique in Europe as an example of traditional Indian temple construction. It is made from blocks of limestone and marble which were hand-carved in India then shipped over and assembled in London. There is an adjourning Haveli (community centre) decorated with intricate wooden carvings – visitors to the temple complex are courteously welcomed.

# Asian Cuisine

The term 'Indian cuisine' is a catch-all phrase, covering the diverse cuisines of India, Pakistan, Bangladesh and Sri Lanka and a spectrum of regional, religious and cultural differences. The hallmark of all Indian cuisine is the emphasis on spices and herbs. These numerous flavourings, from aromatic crocus stamens (saffron) to pungent resin (asafoetida), are used in intricate and varying ways: dry-roasted, fried in hot oil or mixed with other spices to form a masala (spice mix). Underlying their culinary use is an ancient belief in the health-giving properties of spices. In the Holy Hindu Scriptures, the medicinal properties of herbs and spices are listed. Turmeric and cloves both have antiseptic properties. Asafoetida, a digestive which prevents flatulence, is added to lentil dishes. Spices are divided into 'warm', generating internal heat, and 'cool', lessening it.

Underneath this culinary umbrella are diverse cuisines influenced by religion (the main Indian faiths being Hinduism, Islam, Buddhism, Jainism and Sikhism), geography and culture. Religions have laid down rules and taboos as to what can or cannot be eaten. For example, the Hindus will not eat beef as the cow is sacred. Some Hindus are vegetarian, while for strict vegetarians even the flavourings associated with meat (garlic and onion) are not allowed. For Muslims, pork is a forbidden meat.

When describing Indian cuisine in regional terms, it is possible to draw a crude north-south boundary, although there are exceptions. Flat wheat breads such as paratha and chapati are a staple in the north while rice is the staple in the south. Northern cuisine was influenced by Mogul rulers who came down to India through Persia. The Persian influence is apparent in the subtle spicing, the use of nuts and in dishes such as pullao, a descendant of the pilaff. From this luxurious court cuisine came techniques used today: korma (braising in a thick, often nut-based sauce); pot-roasting (in a traditional charcoal stove); and kebab, kofte and tandoori (dishes cooked in a tandoor oven). The Indian food that is most frequently served in restaurants is based on this Mogul cuisine. In Southern Indian cookery the coconut palm has an influential role, with sweet coconut milk used in many dishes. Rice is eaten not just as a grain but is ground, mixed with dal, and used to make light pancakes called dosai. As in other hot climates, fermentation is a well-used culinary technique.

# Glossary

**Angled loofah:** a green gourd with distinctive raised ridges running down its length and a bitter flavour.

**Asafoetida (heeng:** a pungent brown resin, valued for its digestive properties, sold in either lump or powder form.

**Bitter gourd (karela):** a knobbly-skinned, cucumber-shaped green gourd with a distinctive bitter flavour and digestive properties.

Bitter Gourd

**Bottle gourd (dudi):** a large, smooth, bottle-shaped, green-skinned gourd with marrow-like flesh.

**Cardamom:** a fragrant spice pod sold whole, hulled or ready-ground. The small green or white cardamoms are used in both sweet and savoury dishes while the larger wrinkled black cardamom is used only in savoury dishes.

**Carom (ajwan):** a tiny seed spice, like miniature fennel seeds, with a medicinal scent and sharp, thyme-like flavour.

**Chayote (chow-chow):** A pear-sized, wrinkled, green-skinned squash with a single large seed and marrow-like flesh.

**Chenna:** a ricotta-like curd cheese.

**Chickpea flour (gram or besan):** ground chickpeas are the basis for many breads and fritters. Madhur Jaffrey recommends fridge storage.

**Chick–peas (channa):** fresh chickpeas are small, puffy green pods which need peeling to reveal the kernel.

**Chikoo (sapodilla):** similar looking to kiwi fruit with fine brown, furry skin, pinky-brown granular flesh, glossy pips and a distinctive sweet flavour.

**Chillies:** sold both fresh and dried. Fresh green chillies and dried red chillies are used in Indian cookery to add both pungent heat and a distinctive flavour.

**Chilli powder:** a hot red powder made from ground, dried red chillies.

119

**Cluster beans (guar):** fine, straight green beans.

**Coconut milk:** a thick white liquid made from grated coconut flesh and not, as is sometimes thought, from the cloudy liquid inside the coconut which is called 'coconut water'. Home-made coconut milk can be made by blending together dessicated coconut with hot water, then sieving it. Alternatively, tinned coconut milk is a convenient, ready-to-use product; Madhur Jaffrey recommends the Chaokoh brand. Creamed coconut or coconut milk powder needs diluting before use.

**Coriander:** both the aromatic green leaves (similar in appearance to flat-leafed parsley) and small rounded seeds are used extensively in Indian cookery.

*Curry Leaves*

*Moong Dal*

**Cumin:** small, greenish, finely-ridged oval seeds, similar to caraway seeds, with a distinctive, slightly sharp flavour, widely used in Indian cookery. Black cumin, which is rarer, has a more pronounced herbal flavour.

**Curry leaf:** a spicy-smelling leaf which resembles a small bay leaf. It's usually sold dried but sometimes branches of fresh curry leaves are available.

**Dal:** a generic term covering the three types of pulses (lentils, beans and peas) used in Indian cookery: *chana dal*, small yellow split peas; *masoor dal*, tiny pink split lentils (sometimes called red split lentils); *moong dal*, yellow split mung beans (sold both skinned and unskinned); *rajma dal*, red kidney beans; *toovar dal*, a large split yellow pea; *urad dal*, ivory-coloured hulled black gram beans (used in Southern Indian vegetarian cookery in dishes such as pancakes and fried dumplings).

**Drumsticks:** long, green, ridged pods with thick skin, fibrous pulp and a distinctive flavour. Usually available tinned but sometimes found fresh.

*Drumstick*

**Fennel:** aniseed-flavoured, greenish ridged seeds, valued as a digestive. Candied fennel seeds are eaten after a meal.

**Fenugreek (methi):** both the small, stubby, hard, yellow seeds and the spicy-smelling, bitter green leaves are used in Indian cookery. The seeds have a strong, bitter flavour and are used in pickles. The dark green trefoil leaves, which look similar to clover, are sold both fresh and dried.

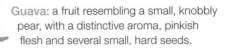
*Fenugreek*

**Fish:** *hilsa*, a prized freshwater fish from Bangladesh; *pomfret*, a flat, round-shaped and white-fleshed fish.

**Garam masala:** a fragrant spice mix, available in many versions.

**Ghee:** clarified butter with a nutty flavour. Because of the clarification, ghee can be used for deep frying and stored at room temperature.

**Ginger:** this knobbly, lightbrown root is a key flavouring prized for its aromatic flavour and digestive qualities.

*Green Mango*

**Guava:** a fruit resembling a small, knobbly pear, with a distinctive aroma, pinkish flesh and several small, hard seeds.

**Hyacinth bean (seim):** a broad-podded, thick-skinned, curved green bean; a member of the hyacinth bean family.

**Jackfruit:** a huge fruit with a thick, green studded skin. The creamy-textured flesh inside is eaten as a vegetable when unripe and as a fruit when ripe.

**Jaggery:** a pale brown sugar with a nutty flavour, made from sugar cane juice or palm sap. Used in Indian sweets.

**Kohlrabi:** a pale green or purple bulbous vegetable, resembling a sprouting turnip – but with a more delicate flavour.

**Kokum:** a variety of mangosteen, sold in dried pieces and used as a souring agent.

**Lemon crystals:** light-coloured crystals used as a souring agent.

**Mango:** a kidney-shaped fruit, with succulent orange flesh and a sweet, resiny flavour, and enormously popular in India. Tart, green unripe mangoes are used to make pickles, chutneys and relishes while orange-red ripe mangoes are eaten on their own or used in desserts. Over a thousand varieties are grown in India, but the Alphonso mango is one of the best known in Britain.

Mango powder (amchoor): sour, beige-coloured powder made from dried, unripe mangoes, used to add a tart flavour to food.

Mustard oil: a pungent yellow oil, made from mustard seeds.

Mustard seeds: tiny, black round seeds, often used in pickles.

Okra (bhindi, ladies fingers): a tapering, ridged green pod which exudes a sticky juice when cooked.

Onion seed (kalonji or nigella): tiny tear-shaped black seeds – not related to onions. Used primarily in pickles but also on tandoori naan bread.

Panch phoran: a Bengali five-spice mix, containing cumin, fennel, onion seeds, fenugreek and black mustard seeds.

Paneer: a firm white cheese, made from pressed Indian curd cheese called chenna (similar to ricotta).

Okra

Panch Phoran

Patra: large, green taro leaves which are spread with a gram flour paste, rolled and steamed to make a dish called 'patra'.

Phalooda (falooda): transparent, thread-like noodles made from wheatberry starch and flavoured with pine or rose essence, used in desserts, to garnish kulfi or in a drink of the same name.

Pistachio: green-fleshed, delicately-flavoured nuts, used in Indian sweetmeats and ice cream or as a nibble.

Pointed gourd (parwal): this is a small, green squash (sometimes striped with white)

Pomegranate seeds (anardana): dried pomegranate kernels, used to add sourness.

Poppadums (papar): small round wafers made from split-peas and flavoured with garlic or spices. When fried in hot oil they puff up and become crispy.

Poppy seed (khas khas): white poppy seeds, used ground to thicken sauces.

Rice: the most famous and expensive of rice varieties grown in India is basmati, with its nutty aroma and flavour.

**Rose essence:** a delicate rose-scented essence used in desserts. Rose water is a diluted form of rose essence.

**Saffron:** the dried stigmas of a crocus variety, sold as both thread and powdered.

**Sevian:** fine golden-brown wheat vermicelli, used in desserts.

**Snake gourd:** a long, narrow, twisted green gourd with marrow-like flesh.

**Spiny bitter gourd (kantola):** a small, spiky, egg-shaped relation of the bitter gourd.

**Sweetmeats:** many Indian sweetmeats are made from milk boiled down slowly until it thickens (rabadi) or until it takes on a fudge like consistency (khoya). Varieties include: *barfi*, a crumbly Indian fudge often flavoured with nuts; *gulub jamun*, deep-fried dumplings in syrup; *halwa*: nuts, fruits and vegetables cooked with ghee and sugar to a firm texture; *jalebi*: bright orange, crisp batter squiggles filled with syrup; *kulfi*, ice cream made from slow-cooked milk which gives a slightly grainy texture; and *rasmalai*: delicate, soft chenna dumplings served in *rabadi* (slow-cooked milk).

*Tindola*

**Tamarind:** a brown fleshy pod with a sour-sweet flavour, used as a souring agent. Both tamarind pulp and tamarind paste are available.

**Taro:** the term applies to a whole range of fibrous tubers, recognisable by their brown hairy skins and white starchy flesh.

**Tinda:** a small, rounded member of the marrow family, with pale green skin and white flesh.

**Tindola (tindori):** walnut-sized 'ivy' gourds with variegated markings and a crisp, crunchy texture.

**Turmeric (haldi):** a small-fingered, orange-fleshed root from which comes the powdered yellow spice powder of the same name.

**Vark:** fine edible foil, made from ground silver or gold, used to adorn dishes on special occasions.

**White radish (mooli):** long, thick white radish, with a mild flavour, used to stuff parathas in Pakistani cooking.

**Yard-long beans:** exceedingly long, thin green beans.

**Yoghurt:** traditionally made from buffalo milk, Julie Sahni suggests stirring a little soured cream into normal yoghurt to reproduce the necessary tangy flavour.

# Food Shops

The range of stock in Asian food shops is huge, from fresh fruits and vegetables to staples like dals and flours. Often the emphasis is on bulk-buying and stocking up with large sacks of basmati or huge packets of spices.

# Central

Tucked away behind Euston Station, the quiet backwater of Drummond Street is home to a number of excellent, good-value Indian restaurants, and a few food shops.

## Ambala

- 112 Drummond Street, NW1
- 020 7387 7886 / 3521
- www.ambalafoods.co.uk
- Euston LU/Rail
- Daily 9am-9pm

Ambala have been selling Asian sweets since 1965, when their first small shop opened on this site. Ambala is now a thriving chain and the original shop has been revamped in bright colours with marble counters. Customers return again and again for excellent fudge-like barfis, sticky jalebi and takeaway packets of ras malai. Savoury snacks include crisp vegetable samosas and packets of Bombay mix.

## Indian Spice Shop

- 115-119 Drummond Street, NW1
- 020 7916 1831
- Euston LU/Rail
- Mon-Sat 9.30am-9.30pm, Sun 10am-9pm

Catering for both the local English and Indian communities, Indian Spice is divided into an off-licence-cum-corner shop on one side and an Indian grocer's on the other. It offers a truly impressive range of spices, as well as other groceries including chutneys, papads and dals, plus huge sacks of basmati, with fresh produce outside.

# North

## Ambala

- 61 Turnpike Lane, N8
- 020 8292 1253
- www.ambalafoods.co.uk
- Turnpike Lane
- Daily 9am-9pm

A branch of the established Indian sweet company.

## Chhappan Bhog

- 143-145 Ballards Lane, N3
- 020 8371 8677
- Finchley Central LU
- Daily 10am-6pm

A branch of the confectioners selling Indian sweets plus savoury snacks.

## Goodeats

⌨ *124 Ballards Lane, N3*
☎ *020 7349 2373*
🚌 *Finchley Central LU*
🕐 *Mon-Sat 9am-7pm*

This well-established, neatly arranged foodstore has an excellent range of stock. In addition to a good selection of Indian groceries, there is a fresh fruit and vegetable section, including fresh methi and patra.

## Q Stores

⌨ *19 Lodge Lane, N12*
☎ *020 8446 2495*
🚌 *Woodside Park LU*
🕐 *Mon-Sat 9.30am-5.45pm, Sun 10am-1pm*

Tucked away just off North Finchley's busy high street, this small, neat shop has a good selection of fresh Indian produce, from mangoes to mustard seed, plus store cupboard staples.

# North-West

Wembley's Ealing Road has long been noted for its range of Asian food shops including enormous greengrocers. Be warned, however, that it becomes very busy over the weekend and finding a parking space can be a challenge. Kingsbury also has a useful cluster of Asian food shops, including grocers, confectioners and halal butchers.

## Chhappan Bhog

⌨ *560 Kingsbury Road, NW9*
☎ *020 8204 7009*
🚌 *Kingsbury LU*
🕐 *Daily 10am-6pm*

A branch of the confectionary chain, selling assorted sweets plus savoury snacks.

## Fudco

⌨ *184 Ealing Road, HA0*
☎ *020 8902 4820*
🚌 *Alperton LU*
🕐 *Daily 10.30am-6.30pm*

As importers and packagers, Fudco are a major supplier of foodstuffs from spices to dried fruits. Their own grocer's shop stocks an impressive range all neatly displayed.

## Gayatri

⌨ *467 Kingsbury Road, NW9*
☎ *020 8206 1677*
✎ *www.gayatri.co.uk*
🚌 *Kingsbury LU*
🕐 *Mon-Fri 10.30am-6.30pm,*
    *Sat 10.30am-6pm, Sun 9am-4pm*

Warmly recommended by Gujurati friends, this sweet shop produces a range of traditional vegetarian sweets (such as tutti frutti burfi and shrikhand) plus savoury nibbles. It is especially noted for its Diwali specialities, doing huge business in the run-up to Diwali.

## Kingsbury Fruit and Veg Ltd

- 🏠 *477-481 Kingsbury Road, NW9*
- ☎ *020 8905 0295*
- 🕐 *Daily 10am-7pm*

This large store carries a comprehensive range of stock, from fresh fruit and vegetables to store cupboard groceries.

## Royal Sweets

- 🏠 *280 Ealing Road, HA0*
- ☎ *020 8903 9359*
- 🚌 *Alperton LU*
- 🕐 *Tue-Sun 10am-7pm*

A friendly branch of the established Asian sweetmeat shop, selling brightly coloured halvas and savoury nibbles.

## Sira Fruit–Veg

- 🏠 *288 Ealing Road, HA0*
- ☎ *020 8903 5769*
- 🚌 *Alperton LU*
- 🕐 *Daily 8am-8pm*

A roomy shop with a large fresh fruit and vegetable section, including okra, fresh curry leaves and bunches of methi. In addition, there is a selection of basic Asian groceries.

## V. B. & Sons Cash and Carry

- 🏠 *738 Kenton road, HA3*
- ☎ *020 8206 1770*
- 🚌 *Kingsbury LU*
- 🕐 *Mon-Sat 9am-6.45pm, Sun 10am-4pm*

A large, well-established shop offering an impressive range of stock. They have their own-label, from pulses and flours to frozen vegetables and savouries such as kachoris.

## V. B. & Sons Cash and Carry

- 🏠 *218 Ealing Road, HA0*
- ☎ *020 8902 8579*
- 🚌 *Alperton LU*
- 🕐 *Mon-Fri 9.30am-6.45pm,*
  *Sat 9am-6.45pm, Sun 11am-5pm*

A huge, neatly-arranged store, aromatic with spices and bustling with customers tracking down the numerous special offers. V.B. specialises in groceries, with a wide range of spices, nuts, dried fruits, dals and flours. The freezer section contains yucca and mogo chips, samosas and samosa pastry.

## Wembley Exotics

- 🏠 *133-135 Ealing Road, HA0*
- ☎ *020 8900 2607*
- 🚌 *Alperton LU*
- 🕐 *Daily 24 hours*

Mounds of chillies, root ginger and peanuts under an awning mark this cavernous self-service store, which specialises in fresh produce. Inside is a staggering array of Asian fruits and vegetables, from guvar beans and pigeon peas to guavas and mangoes.

# South-West

The main highway through Tooting is lined with a real variety of Asian food shops (halal butchers, greengrocers, foodstores and sweetshops). There is also a tempting choice of eateries, ranging from veteran South Indian vegetarian to Pakistani restaurants offering halal meat dishes.

## Ambala

- ▣ 48 Upper Tooting Road, SW17
- ☎ 020 8767 1747
- 🖉 www.ambalafoods.co.uk
- 🚌 Tooting Bec LU. Tooting Broadway LU
- 🕐 Daily 9am-9pm

A branch of the established Asian sweet manufacturers.

## Dadu's

- ▣ 190-198 Upper Tooting Road, SW17
- ☎ 020 8672 4984
- 🚌 Tooting Bec LU, Tooting Broadway LU
- 🕐 Mon-Sat 9am-7pm, Sun 10am-6pm

This huge store has an extensive stock of Asian foodstuffs, from papads, pulses and chutneys to a freezer section crammed with everything from samosas to parathas.

## Daily Fresh Foods

- ▣ 152 Upper Tooting Road, SW17
- ☎ 020 8767 7861
- 🚌 Tooting Bec LU, Tooting Broadway LU
- 🕐 Daily 8am-8pm

As the name suggests, there's an eye-catching outdoor display of fresh fruit, vegetables and herbs. Inside is a halal counter and a grocery section offering a limited choice of basics.

## Deepak Food and Wine

- ▣ 953 Garratt Lane, SW17
- ☎ 020 8767 7819
- 🚌 Tooting Broadway LU
- 🕐 Mon-Sat 9am-7.30pm, Sun 10am-4pm

An enormous supermarket with an extensive range of Asian foodstuffs, particularly strong on store-cupboard staples such as spices, pulses and chutneys.

## Patel Brothers

- ▣ 187-91 Upper Tooting Road, SW17
- ☎ 020 8672 2792
- 🚌 Tooting Bec LU, Tooting Broadway LU
- 🕐 Daily 9am-6.30pm

This well-established business was the first Asian food store on Upper Tooting Road. Stock ranges from fresh produce to pickles, curry pastes and spices, ghee and tinned foods. A side room is devoted mainly to rice, pulses and flours.

## Pooja Sweets

⌑ *168-170 Upper Tooting Road, SW17*
☎ *020 8672 4523/8682 5148*
⌕ *www.poojasweets.com*
🚃 *Tooting Bec LU/Toorting Broadway LU*
🕐 *Mon-Sun 9am-9pm*

This smart establishment offers an extensive array of over 100 sweets and savouries, from assorted ladoo to chat.

# West

Southall, in London's western suburbs, is a busy Indian shopping area full of sari shops, jewellers, halal butchers, greengrocers. There are also stalls selling everything from mobile phones to sweet corn snacks or freshly-fried jalebi. Southall also has several large-scale cash-and-carry stores, where the emphasis is on bulk-buying.

## Ambala

⌑ *107 The Broadway, UB1*
☎ *020 8843 9049*
⌕ *www.ambalafoods.co.uk*
🚃 *Southall Rail*
🕐 *Daily 10am-8pm*

A branch of the established Asian sweet manufacturers.

## Chhappan Bhog

⌑ *1 The Broadway, UB1*
☎ *020 8574 7607*
🚃 *Southall Rail*
🕐 *Daily 10am-8pm*

This small sweet shop comes complete with an outside stall selling freshly-fried jalebis and samosas. Inside, a colourful selection of assorted sweets is on display.

## Dokal & Sons

⌑ *133-135 The Broadway, UB1*
☎ *020 8574 1647*
🚃 *Southall Rail*
🕐 *Daily 9am-8pm*

What appears at first to be a small corner shop widens out into a huge store. It is filled with a comprehensive stock of groceries such as chutneys, flours, tinned vegetables, nuts and spices and is run with friendly enthusiasm by Mr Dokal and his family.

## Moti Mahal

⌑ *94 The Broadway, UB1*
☎ *020 8574 7682*
⌕ *www.motimahal.co.uk*
🚃 *Southall Rail*
🕐 *Daily 10am-11pm*

Food writer Roopa Gulati highly recommends the jalebis (freshly fried in a stall outside) and the kulfi ice creams from this established Southall eaterie.

Sira Cash & Carry

## Quality Foods

- 47-61 South Road, UB1
- 020 8917 9188
- www.quality-foods.co.uk
- Southall Rail
- Mon-Sat 7am-7.30pm,
  Sun 12noon-6pm

This store is recommended by food writer Roopa Gulati. It is a huge, spacious store with an impressive stock ranging from fresh produce such as round dudhi, white turmeric and bunches of saag to store cupboard items such as huge 2.5kg tins of chick peas and beans. Gulab, the in-house brand, is extensively stocked.

## Sira Cash and Carry

- 128 The Broadway, UB1
- 020 8574 2280
- Southall Rail
- Daily 8am-8pm

Established in 1969, this friendly shop carries a range of stock including flours, pulses, spices and chutneys. In addition there is an excellent, extensive greengrocery with an aisle of fruit including chikoo, limes, guavas and tiny green mangoes for pickling. The store also has unusual Asian vegetables such as karela, tindola and fresh chickpeas.

## Sira Cash and Carry

- 43 South Road, UB1
- 020 8571 4529
- Southall Rail
- Daily 8am-9pm

Usefully comprehensive, this spacious shop stocks fresh fruit and vegetables, grocery items, confectionary and kitchenware.

## Sira Supermarket

- Amrit House, Springfield Road, Hayes UB4
- 020 8569 1112
- www.siras.co.uk
- Mon-Sat 8am-9pm, Sun 12noon-6pm

Billed as 'the biggest Asian supermarket in London', this huge, brightly-lit, spic-and-span wholesale store comes complete with colourful murals, statues, piped music and an Ayurvedic clinic upstairs. The range of goods is extensive, including fresh produce, a confectionary counter from Royal Sweets, a butchers counter selling halal lamb, mutton and chicken, freezers full of Bangla fish and an extensive range of Sri Lankan foodstuffs. The fresh jalebi stall is also a popular feature. Weekends see the store filled with shoppers stocking up, some from as far away as Bournemouth and Oxford.

# East

Focal points for Asian shopping in the East End are the area around Brick Lane (home to the Bengali community). Further out, Green Street in the Upton Park are is also a great place to find Asian groceries.

## Ambala

🖃 *55 Brick Lane, E1*
☎ *020 7247 8569*
🚌 *Aldgate East LU*
🕐 *Mon-Sat 10am-8pm,*
    *Sun 9.30am-7.30pm*

A branch of the Asian sweet manufacturers (see under Central for more details).

## Taj Stores

🖃 *112-14a Brick Lane, E1*
☎ *020 7377 0061*
🚌 *Aldgate East LU*
🕐 *Daily 9am-9pm*

A comprehensive food store, serving the local Bengali community. It combines a halal meat counter, a greengrocery section and a mini-supermarket selling grocery items such as pulses and spices.

## Green Street, E7

This long East End road has a mash shop and an assortment of Asian stores, selling everything from wedding saris a to bargain boxes of mangoes and sweetmeats.

## Bharat

🖃 *4-6 Carlton Terrace, Green Street, E7*
☎ *020 8472 6393*
🚌 *Upton Park LU*
🕐 *Daily 9am-8pm*

This large store is aimed at those who buy in bulk, stocking things like huge 15 litre tins of ghee and 10 kilogram sacks of basmati. The freezers are jammed with Indian fast food. Fresh fruit and veg can be found at Bharat's small sister shop, over the road at No. 263.

## Queen's Market

🖃 *Green Street, E7*
    *(on the corner of Queen's Road)*
🚌 *Upton Park LU*
🕐 *Tue, Thur-Sat 9am-6pm*

Handily positioned right by Upton Park tube, this large, keenly-priced, down-to-earth market bustles with shoppers stocking up and looking out for bargains. Stalls and shops here sell an assortment of goods, from kitchenware to ribbons. The presence of a local Asian community is reflected in a number of halal butchers and stalls offering a huge range of Asian fruit and vegetables.

# Eating Places

The long standing British love affair with Indian food continues unabated. Asian eateries in London range from the cheap and cheerful to the luxuriously expensive. There are several simple cafés listed below, offering remarkably good value, flavourful food from spicy kebabs to dosai (pancakes). The glamorous, expensive restaurants are also worth a try for a more sophisticated, contemporary Indian cuisine..

# Central

## Imli   ££-£££
🍴 *167-69 Wardour Street, W1*
☎ *020 7287 4243*
🖥 *www.imli.co.uk*
🚌 *Leicester Square LU*

Smart and spacious, this new-wave restaurant offers Indian 'tapas', ie fashionable small plates of both classic and creative Indian food. Set menus offer excellent value for money.

## Indian YMCA   £
🍴 *41 Fitzroy Square, W1*
☎ *020 7387 0411*
🚌 *Warren Street LU*

The appetising smell of Indian cooking wafts out from this large building, adding character to its institutional air. On offer is good home-style food at student prices in a canteen atmosphere.

## Malabar Junction   ££
🍴 *107 Great Russell Street, WC1*
🖥 *www.malabarjunction.com*
☎ *020 7580 5230*
🚌 *Tottenham Court Road LU*

A rather drab frontage hides a large, airy restaurant complete with a glass-roofed dining room. South-Indian cuisine is the speciality here, from tangy idlee (steamed rice and black gram cakes) to spicy Keralan fish curry. Service is courteous and prices very reasonable given the standard of the cooking.

## Raavi Kebab   £-££
🍴 *125 Drummond Street, NW1*
☎ *020 7388 1780*
🚌 *Euston LU/rail*

This small, unpretentious halal restaurant (an alcohol-free zone) serves up very reasonably priced dishes including very tasty, chilli spiced kebabs.

## Ragam  ££

⌨ *57 Cleveland Street, W1*
☎ *020 7636 9098*
🚌 *Goodge Street LU, Warren Street LU*

A small, modest and friendly restaurant serving excellent, good value food including South-Indian dishes such as avial or uthappam, and delicious breads.

## Rasa Samudra  ££££

⌨ *5 Charlotte Street, W1*
☎ *020 7637 0222*
🚌 *Goodge Street LU*

An attractive Indian restaurant, specialising in Keralan seafood dishes. Dishes such as kingfish and green mango curry and crab in coconut milk are both recommended.

## Rasa W1  £££

⌨ *6 Dering Street, W1*
☎ *020 7629 1346*
🚌 *Oxford Circus LU, Bond Street LU*

Keralan vegetarian cuisine is on offer here, giving diners the chance to try distinctive spiced dishes such as green banana and mango curry and cashew nut patties. Round off your meal with Keralan desserts such as banana dosa (pancakes) or pal payasum (cashew rice pudding).

## Veeraswamy  £££

⌨ *99 Regent Street, W1*
☎ *020 7734 1401*
🚌 *Piccadilly Circus LU*

London's oldest Indian restaurant has shed its Raj image. Now owned by the Chutney Mary team it has become a sleek example of the new-wave of Indian restaurants. New features include vividly painted walls, smartly dressed staff and a menu featuring well prepared regional dishes.

# North

## Diwana Bhel Poori House  £

⌨ *121 Drummond Street, NW1*
☎ *020 7387 5566*
🚌 *Euston LU/Rail*

Tucked away behind Euston station this well-established, unpretentious South-Indian vegetarian restaurant serves up dosai, idlee and good value thali at remarkably reasonable prices.

## Great Nepalese  ££

⌨ *48 Eversholt Street, NW1*
☎ *020 7388 6737)*
🚌 *Euston LU/Rail*

A Euston institution, much-frequented by hungry commuters. In addition to standard curry house fare it serves a selection of Nepalese specialities.

## Majjo's £

⌨ *1 Fortis Green Road, N2*
☎ *020 8883 4357*
🚇 *East Finchley LU*

This small, smart, friendly take-away serves up superior Pakistani home-cooking. The meat is halal and there is a range of more unusual vegetarian dishes such as patra. Sample tastes are offered to those trying to choose from the array of dishes available.

## Raavi Kebab Halal Tandoori £

⌨ *125 Drummond Street, NW1*
🚇 *Euston Square LU*
☎ *020 7388 1780*

A small, unpretentious restaurant which specialises in delicious, chilli-hot kebabs, freshly grilled over charcoal.

## Rani ££

⌨ *7 Long Lane, N3*
☎ *020 8349 4386/2646*
🚇 *Finchley Central LU*

Authentic Gujarati vegetarian cuisine. All dishes, from the home-made chutneys to the breads, are carefully prepared. The exciting menu includes delights such as banana methi and tindora curry.

## Ravi Shankar £-££

⌨ *133-135 Drummond Street, NW1*
☎ *020 7388 6458*
🚇 *Euston LU/Rail*

A popular Indian vegetarian restaurant offering reasonably priced dishes such as masala or de luxe dosai.

# West

## New Asian Tandoori Centre (Roxy) ££

⌨ *114-118 The Green, Southall, UB2*
☎ *020 8574 2597*
🚇 *Southall Rail*

This large, spic-and-span Punjabi eaterie offers both take-away food and an eat-in restaurant. Prices are cheap and this is a great place for group eating allowing you to sample lots of dishes.

## Ram's £

⌨ *203 Kenton Road, HA3*
☎ *020 8907 2022*
🚇 *Kenton LU/rail*

Known for its Gujurati vegetarian cuisine, this down-to-earth café is warmly recommended by food writer Roopa Gulati.

## Sagar ££

- 157 King Street, W6
- ☎ 020 8741 8563
- 🚇 Hammersmith LU

Food writer Roopa Gulati also recommends this South Indian vegetarian café which has made a name for itself for its delicious dosais and idlis.

## Zaika ££££

- 1 Kensington High Street, W1
- ☎ 020 7795 6533
- 🚇 High Street Kensington

This sumptuous restaurant offers creative and innovative Indian cuisine to match its glamorous décor.

# North-West

## Sakonis £

- 119-121 Ealing Road, HA0
- ☎ 020 8903 9601
- 🚇 Alperton LU

This bright, cheery vegetarian diner attracts queues of would-be diners (many of them in family groups), waiting patiently by the paan stall and take-away counter to sit down in the back room. The menu promises a wide range of snacks, mains, drinks and desserts: seriously chilli-hot dosai, chilli paneer, falooda, chikoo ice cream and delicious, salty-sweet freshly-squeezed lime juice.

# South-West

## Apollo Banana Leaf £

- 190 Tooting High Street, SW17
- ☎ 020 8696 1423
- 🚇 Tooting Broadway LU

This popular restaurant offers a chance to sample Sri Lankan food at remarkably reasonable prices.

## Chutney Mary ££££

- 535 King's Road, SW10
- ✉ www.chutneymary.com
- ☎ 020 7351 3113
- 🚇 Fulham Broadway LU

This large, glamorous restaurant, complete with an attractive conservatory dining area, serves top-notch Indian cooking in an enjoyably buzzy atmosphere. The menu features carefully chosen regional specialities, with the chilli-marinated lamb chops and Alphonso mango ice cream being particular highlights.

## Sree Krishna £-££

- 192-194 Tooting High Street, SW17
- ☎ 020 8672 4250
- 🚇 Tooting Broadway LU

Established in 1973, this restaurant is full of enthusiasts who appreciate both the good South Indian vegetarian food and the reasonable prices.

# South-East

## The Painted Heron  ££££
🔲 *205-209 Kennington Lane, SE11*
🚌 *Kennington LU*
☎ *020 7351 5232*

This is a light, spacious modern Indian restaurant, complete with a large courtyard dining area. It specialises in refined contemporary dishes, using fresh and unusual ingredients to elegant effect.

# East

## Café Spice Namaste  ££££
🔲 *16 Prescott Street, E1*
☎ *020 7488 9242*
🚌 *Aldgate East LU, Tower Hill LU*

Chef Cyrus Todiwala is committed to bringing true Indian cookery, in all its variety, to the London restaurant scene. From within a brightly-decorated old courthouse he serves up an extensive menu, including many unusual Goan and Parsee dishes.

## Lahore Kebab House  £
🔲 *2 Umberston Street, E1*
☎ *020 7488 2551*
🚌 *Aldgate East, Whitechapel LU*

This modest-looking restaurant has acquired a cult following, serving up gutsy Punjabi food to an appreciative audience

# Cookbooks

## Curry Lovers
*Roopa Gulati*

A slender but appetizing Indian cookbook, offering delicious recipes for dishes from tamarind chutney to an elaborate lamb biriyani.

## Madhur Jaffrey's Ultimate Curry Bible
*Madhur Jaffrey*

This wonderful cookbook lives up to its grandiose title, with Madhur Jaffrey exploring all kinds of curry, from fish curry in Singpore to Pakistani-style kofta curry. The recipies are both appetising and achievable.

## Madhur Jaffrey's Indian Cookery
*Madhur Jaffrey*

A clearly-written, accessible introduction to this great cuisine.

## Fifty Great Curries of India
*Camellia Panjabi*

A beautifully-presented, illustrated guide which takes readers through the art of making curries clearly and in detail. Recipes range from classic dishes, such as Goanese pork Vindaloo, to less familiar ones such as Gujurati mango and yoghurt curry.

## The Calcutta Kitchen
*Simon Parkes and Udit Sarkhel*

An attractive collection of recipes and writing, offering an appetizing insight into Bengali cuisine.

## Classic Indian Cooking
*Julie Sahni*

A well-written Indian cookery book which is readable, practical and authoritative.

## Classic Indian Vegetarian Cooking
*Julie Sahni*

An inspirational book filled with appetising recipes conveying the less well-known world of Indian vegetarian cuisine in all its subtlety.

## Curry
*Edited by Jeni Wright*

A wide-ranging collection of curry recipes from around the globe by an impressive collection of contributors..

Chinese London

New Loon Moon

The original points of entry for the Chinese community in Britain were Liverpool and London: the ports into which Chinese seamen with the East India Company arrived and settled. The Limehouse area, near the docks in the East End, was London's first 'Chinatown', with the first immigrants arriving during the eighteenth century when Britain's tea trade with China was booming. Sailors jumped ship and set up businesses running laundries, shops or becoming ship's chandlers. In the 1950s, the development of the laundromat and the domestic washing machine badly affected the laundry business, so catering became an alternative source of work.

Limehouse was practically destroyed in the Blitz, and post-war restrictive regulations imposed on non-British workers by the Seamen's Union hit affected Chinese seamen hard. So, both alternative livelihoods and accommodation had to be found. Soho, a run-down, derelict area with a bad reputation and low property prices, saw an influx of Chinese around the Gerrard Street area in the 1950s. The first Chinese restaurants in Soho were chop-suey outlets, opened in the 1940s to cater for American GIs and British servicemen who had acquired a taste for Chinese food overseas. Restaurants catering specifically for the growing Chinese community also opened in the area. The Communist revolution in China in 1949 meant a further wave of immigration from China into Britain in the 1950s and 1960s, mostly from the British colony of Hong Kong. As a result, the Chinese community in Soho expanded further.

The area bounded by Shaftesbury Avenue, Leicester Square, Charing Cross Road and Wardour Street is a rectangle of predominantly Chinese shops, businesses, gambling clubs and restaurants. Gerrard Street, now pedestrianised, comes complete with Chinese-style arches and pagoda-style phone boxes.

Two annual festivals have become major events in London, attracting people from outside the Chinese community. Chinese New Year, according to the Chinese lunar calendar, takes place either in late January or early February, and is celebrated with gifts to children of 'ang pow', money in lucky red envelopes, and a lion dance procession. Special dishes appear on menus in the restaurants. Each year is attributed to one of the twelve animals in the Chinese zodiac – with the Year of the Dragon being especially auspicious – and the New Year celebrations feature the animal to which the year belongs. The autumnal Moon Festival, around September, is marked by special moon cakes and a lion dance. During both these festivals, Chinatown is filled with Chinese of all generations, colourful lanterns and decorations and street-stalls selling snacks and gifts.

# Chinese Cuisine

This ancient cuisine is both complex and various. Underlying it are the 'yin and yang' principles, translated in culinary terms into hot, cold and neutral, with ingredients allocated different properties. A huge range of ingredients is used, with nothing wasted. There is an old saying that 'A Cantonese will eat anything with four legs except for a piece of furniture and anything that flies apart from a kite'. Textures play an important role in Chinese cooking and include some that are foreign to Western sensibilities, with slippery, jelly-like textures being prized.

Each of China's regions has its own characteristic cuisine, influenced by climate and the availability of ingredients. It's customary, however, to group China culinarily into four broad geographical groups: Peking/Northern, Shanghai/Eastern, Sichuan/Western and Cantonese/Southern. The cuisine of the North is distinguished by its use of grains other than rice, such as wheat, corn and millet, in the form of breads, noodles, dumplings and pancakes. Because the ancient Imperial Court was situated in Peking, elaborate dishes such as Peking Duck are characteristic of this cuisine. The Mongols introduced lamb, which is eaten more widely here than in other parts of China.

Eastern cuisine is famous for its fresh fish and seafood. Rich, sweet seasonings are a hallmark and popular techniques include stir-frying, steaming, red-cooking (slow simmering in soy sauce) and blanching. Sichuan cooking, from the provinces of Hunan, Yunnan and Sichuan in Western China, is marked by its use of fiery chillies, garlic, ginger and Sichuan peppercorns producing a vigorous, strongly flavoured cuisine. Two regional foodstuffs are aromatic peppercorns and chilli-pickled mustard plant.

Cantonese cuisine is the best-known Chinese cooking outside China, because of the large numbers of Chinese from southern Canton who emigrated in the nineteenth century. Strong, overwhelming flavourings are avoided and, instead, a harmonious blend of colours, textures and flavours is sought. Stir-frying epitomises Cantonese cooking, with the freshness and colours of ingredients retained and a minimum of seasonings added. Dim sum, the small steamed and fried dumplings eaten at lunchtime, are another Cantonese speciality.

# Glossary

**Agar agar:** a vegetarian setting agent obtained from seaweed which does not require refrigeration to set. Available either in powdered form or translucent strands.

**Azuki beans:** small red beans, used primarily in cakes and desserts and available both whole and in sweetened paste form.

**Bamboo shoots:** fresh bamboo shoots are occasionally available. Tinned bamboo shoots, either whole or sliced, are easily found.

**Bean curd (doufu):** a soya bean product which has always been a valuable source of protein in Chinese cooking. Fresh ivory-coloured bean curd has a firm custard texture and bland flavour. It is sold in the chilled section, packed in water. Deep-fried bean curd has a golden colour and spongy texture and is found in packets in the chilled section. Bean curd 'cheese', either red or white, is fermented bean curd with a strong, salty taste and is sold in jars. Dried bean-curd sheets are sold in packets.

*Black Beans*

**Bean sprouts:** white crispy sprouts of the mung bean; also available are the larger, nuttier soya bean sprouts, which should be cooked before eating.

**Beche-de-mer:** sea cucumber or sea slug, it is sold dried and prized as a delicacy.

**Bird's nest:** the key ingredient of the famous delicacy, bird's nest soup. The nests of a cave-dwelling species of swallow are coated with a gelatinous saliva and it is this which gives the soup its prized consistency. The nests are sold either whole or in fragments for high prices.

**Black beans:** small black soya beans, fermented with salt and spices, with a pungent flavour.

**Chilli oil:** a transparent oil, tinted red from chillies, sold in small bottles and with a powerful chilli kick.

**Chinese broccoli (gaai laan):** a thick-stalked vegetable with large rounded leaves and white flowers.

**Chinese cabbage (bok choy):** similar in appearance to Swiss chard, with dark green leaves and thick white stems.  Green bok choy, with green leaves and stems, is also available.

*Bok Choy*

**Chinese chives:** long, dark green, flat leaves, with a stronger and more pungent odour and flavour than English chives; also sold blanched and complete with buds.

**Chinese cinnamon:** cassia bark, sold in sticks similar to cinnamon but larger and rougher with a stronger flavour.

**Chinese flowering cabbage (choi sum):** a leafy vegetable with rounded leaves, small yellow flowers and long stems.

**Chinese leaves:** a large tight head of white-green crinkly leaves with a crunchy texture; widely available.

*Chinese Chives*

**Chinese mushrooms:** black, dried shitake mushrooms with distinctive meaty flavour. Prices vary according to the size and thickness of the caps.

**Chinese sausages:** these resemble small, fatty salamis, but they must be cooked before eating. There are two sorts: pork and pork and liver, the latter being darker in colour.  They are found in packets or hanging up in bunches with other dried meats.

**Coriander:** this green herb, similar in appearance to flat-leaved continental parsley but with a distinctive sharp flavour, is one of the few herbs used in Chinese cooking.

**Five-spice powder:** fragrant, golden-brown powder made from five or sometimes six ground spices, with the four base spices being star-anise, Chinese cinnamon, cloves and fennel seeds. Sichuan peppercorns, ginger and cardamom are the additions.

**Ginger:** an aromatic root available fresh.

**Glutinous rice:** rounded rice grains with a sticky texture when cooked, used in both sweet and savoury dishes.

**Golden needles:** long dried buds of the tiger-lily flower.

**Longan:** a small brown-skinned fruit, related to the lychee, with translucent flesh and glossy black seed (also known as 'dragon's eye' fruit). Available either tinned or fresh.

**Lotus leaves:** the large leaves of the water-lily plant, available dried and used to wrap food for cooking.

**Lotus root:** a crunchy root with a decorative tracery of holes, available fresh, in sausage-like links, or tinned.

**Mooli:** a large, long white radish, with crispy white flesh.

**Mustard Greens (gaai choi):** a green large-leafed plant. The bitter varieties are pickled rather than cooked.

**Noodles:** *cellophane noodles* (also known as beanthread, glass or transparent noodles): fine thread-like noodles made from mung beans which need soaking before they can be easily cut; *egg noodles*: made from wheat flour, egg and water, distinguished by their yellow colour; *rice noodles* and *vermicelli* are dried, white noodles of varying widths made

*Egg Noodles*

from rice flour which need soaking before use; *river rice noodles* (sarhor noodles) are made from ground rice and water, steamed in thin sheets and cut into strips. Fresh-river rice noodles are sold in clear packets, and usually stored near the chilled section.

**Potato flour:** fine white flour, made from cooked potatoes, used as a thickener.

**Rice vinegar:** mild vinegars, ranging from delicate white rice vinegar to sweet red rice vinegar and rich black rice vinegar.

**Rice wine:** made from glutinous rice, yeast and water, this is used for both drinking and cooking.

**Sauces:** *chilli bean sauce*, a hot, spicy, dark sauce made from soya beans and chillies; *chilli sauce*, a bright red sweet chilli sauce; *hoisin sauce*, a thick, brown fruity sauce; *oyster sauce*, a thick, brown sauce made from oysters; *soy sauce*, a dark brown salty liquid made from fermented

*Oyster Sauce*

soya beans (available as thin, salty Light Soy Sauce or as thicker, sweeter Dark Soy Sauce); and *yellow bean sauce*, a thick, brown sauce made from fermented yellow beans.

Sesame oil: a nutty, golden-coloured oil made from sesame seeds.

Shrimps, dried: small, shelled, dried pink shrimps, with a strong salty flavour.

Spring roll wrappers: white paper-thin wrappers, available in different sizes. Found in either the chilled or freezer sections.

Star-anise: dark brown, star-shaped pod with a distinctive liquorice flavour and scent.

*Water Spinach*

Straw mushrooms: cone-shaped mushrooms, usually available canned.

Sichuan peppercorns: fragrant, reddish-brown 'peppercorns', which are the dried berries of a shrub.

Sichuan pickled vegetables: mustard green tubers, pickled in salt and hot chillies, which are a speciality of Sichuan province.

Tangerine peel: in its dried form, in dark-brown pieces, this is used as a flavouring in Chinese cooking.

Thousand-year-old eggs: preserved duck eggs, with a pungent flavour, which are in fact only about a hundred days old.

Water chestnuts: the crunchy bulbs of a waterplant. Fresh, brown-skinned bulbs are sometimes found, but tinned water chestnuts are easily available.

Water spinach (ong chai): a triangular-leafed plant with a mild, spinach-like flavour.

Winter melon: a large green gourd with white flesh, available whole or in pieces, and often used to make soup.

Wonton skins: small squares of yellow egg-noodle dough, used to wrap up dumplings. Found in either chilled or freezer sections.

Wood ears: black, crinkled, dried fungus with a beige underside.

# Food Shops

For decades, Gerrard Street and its side-streets have housed Chinese food shops, an important and thriving part of London's Chinese community. Recent years have seen several Chinese food shops opening round the corner on Shaftesbury Avenue. Dotted around London there are also a number of huge Chinese cash-and-carry stores, stocking an impressive range of ingredients.

# Central

## Golden Gate Grocers

🏠 *100-102 Shaftesbury Avenue, W1*
☎ *020 7437 0014*
🚌 *Leicester Square LU*
🕐 *Daily 10am-7pm*

This veteran Chinatown food shop relocated here from its former premises in Newport Place. Although it appears initially to be a small shop, in fact the shop extends downstairs to a basement area and to stalls outside. Golden Gate stocks everything from noodles (fresh and dried), sauces, condiments and fresh fruit and vegetables.

## Good Harvest Fish and Meat Market

🏠 *65 Shaftesbury Avenue, W1*
☎ *020 7734 4900*
🚌 *Leicester Square LU*
🕐 *Daily 11am-7pm*

In the heart of theatreland, this veteran Chinese fishmonger offers fresh scallops in their shells, live lobsters, raw king prawns and fish such as catfish and pomfret. Food writer Fuchsia Dunlop, author of Sichuan Cookery, recommends their 'very fresh' sea bass.

## Loon Fung Supermarket

🏠 *42-44 Gerrard Street, W1*
☎ *020 7437 7332*
🚌 *Leicester Square LU*
🕐 *Daily 10am-8pm*

Loon Fung is the oldest and largest Chinese supermarket in Soho, occupying a key position on Gerrard Street and always bustling with customers. Boxes of fresh fruit from kumquats to longans, are displayed outside on the pavement with a large fresh vegetable section inside. A butcher's counter sells a range of Chinese pork cuts, plus more unusual items such as duck and chicken feet and duck tongues. The shop's size means that it offers a comprehensive range of store-cupboard staples.

## New China Gate

⌖ *19 Newport Place, WC2*
☎ *020 7287 8969*
🚌 *Leicester Square LU*
🕑 *Daily 11am-9.30pm*

A small food shop offering a limited range of both fresh fruit and vegetables outside and store cupboard ingredients inside.

## New Loon Moon Supermarket

⌖ *9a Gerrard Street, W1*
☎ *020 7734 9940*
🚌 *Leicester Square LU*
🕑 *Daily 10.30am-8pm*

In the heart of Gerrard Street, this veteran food shop catches the eye with an attractive display of consistently good quality fresh fruit and vegetables, such as gai lan and longans. Inside, the busy shop is crammed with Chinese foodstuffs: noodles, sauces, tinned ingredients and teas. A large backroom contains chilled and freezer sections, cookware and an impressive range of spices.

## Newport Supermarket

⌖ *28-29 Newport Court, WC2*
☎ *020 7494 9222*
🚌 *Leicester Square LU*
🕑 *Daily 10am-9.45pm*

A corner shop with a small assortment of fresh produce and an eclectic range of stock, from condiments to beancurd.

## Oriental Delight

⌖ *14 Gerrard Street, W1*
☎ *020 7439 1183*
🚌 *Leicester Square LU*
🕑 *Mon-Sun 11am-8pm*

The ground-floor of this corner shop is crammed with Chinese biscuits, sweets and snacks. The roomy downstairs basement stocks an array of tinned, bottled and jarred Chinese foodstuffs, from sauces to canned fruits.

## See Woo

⌖ *19 Lisle Street, WC2*
☎ *020 7439 8325*
🚌 *Leicester Square LU*
🕑 *Daily 10am-8pm*

This large, sprawling shop has an excellent, comprehensive stock of chilled, frozen, dried, tinned and bottled ingredients. There is a large fresh fruit and vegetable section, which regularly features more unusual items. A basement room contains Chinese bowls of all sizes, woks, steamers and other Chinese cookware.

Chinese Food Shops

# North

## Loon Fung

⌕ *111 Brantwood Road, N17*
☏ *020 8365 1132*
🚌 *Bus 123, W3*
🕓 *Mon-Sat 9.30am-6.30p*
*Sun 11am-5pm*

An extensive range of Chinese ingredients, from fresh vegetables and frozen seafood to store-cupboard ingredients such as sauces and dried noodles.

## Wing Yip (London) Ltd

⌕ *395 Edgware Road, NW2*
☏ *020 8450 0422*
🚌 *Colindale LU*
🕓 *Mon-Sat 9.30am-7pm*
*Sun 11.30am-5.30pm*

This enormous superstore at Staples Corner is the place for bulk-buying Chinese food. It has an impressive selection, ranging from freezers of dim sum to delicacies such as bird's nest and shark's fin. There is a small selection of fresh vegetables and foodstuffs such as bean curd and noodles.

# West

## Impress Food Oriental Supermarket

⌕ *69 Queensway, W2*
☏ *020 7792 8620*
🕓 *Mon-Thur & Sun 10am-10pm,*
*Fri-Sat 10am-11pm*

A roomy shop with a range of chilled, frozen, canned and bottled Chinese foodstuffs.

## Loon Fung

⌕ *1 Glacier Way, Alperton, Middlesex HA0*
☏ *020 8810 8188*
🚌 *Alperton LU*
🕓 *Mon-Sat 9.30am-7pm, Sun 11am-5pm*

A large Chinese cash-and-carry stocking an impressive range of Chinese foodstuffs.

## Oriental City Supermarket

⌕ *26 Queensway, W2*
☏ *020 7313 9217*
🚌 *Queensway LU*
🕓 *Daily 10.30am-11pm*

Canned, tinned and bottled 'Oriental' foodstuffs are on offer here, though not in the depth that one would find in shops such as Loon Fung, See Woo or Wing Yip.

# South-West

## Wing Tai Supermarket
⊞ *13 Electric Avenue, SW9*
☎ *020 7738 5898*
🚌 *Brixton LU/Rail*
🕐 *Mon-Sat 10am-7pm*

Tucked away behind the bustling fruit and veg stalls outside, this roomy store has a small fresh produce section and fish counter at the front but is particularly strong on bottled, tinned and frozen goods.

# South-East

## See Woo Cash and Carry
⊞ *Furlong House Horn Lane, SE10*
☎ *020 8293 9393*
🚌 *Westcombe Park Rail*
🕐 *Mon-Sun 9.30am-7pm*

A cavernous Chinese cash-and-carry store stocking an extensive range of Chinese foodstuffs.

## Wing Tai Supermarket
⊞ *Unit 11A The Aylsham Centre, Rye Lane, SE15*
☎ *020 7635 0714*
🚌 *Peckham Rye Rail*
🕐 *Mon-Fri 9am-9pm, Sat-Sun 10am-8pm*

A friendly down-to-earth shop with stock ranging from fresh fish to noodles and Thai fragrant rice.

## Wing Tai Supermarket
⊞ *52-54 Denmark Hill, SE5*
☎ *020 7737 6788*
🚌 *Denmark Hill Rail*
🕐 *Mon-Fri 9am-9pm, Sat-Sun 10am-8pm*

Despite its slightly ramshackle appearance, a good range of Chinese foodstuffs can be found here.

# East

## Loon Fung
⊞ *Factory Road, Silvertown E16*
☎ *020 7055 1888*
🚌 *North Woolwich Rail*
🕐 *Mon-Sat 9.30am-6.30pm*
   *Sun 11am-5pm*

A spacious Chinese superstore carrying an ample range of Chinese foodstuffs, complete with a reasonably-priced noodle bar in which to have a meal.

# Chinese Bakeries

Freshly baked sweet and savoury buns and pastries, such as custard tarts, can be bought at a number of bakeries around London's Chinatown. Many of them also offer a café area.

## Far East

🔲 *13 Gerrard Street, W1*
☎ *020 7437 6148*
🚌 *Leicester Square LU*
🕐 *Daily 10am-7pm*

During the day Far East functions as a friendly bakery-cum-tea-shop offering Chinese breakfast dishes and an appetising array of Chinese cakes and pastries. At night the place becomes a great value restaurant.

## Golden Gate Cake Shop

🔲 *13 Macclesfield Street, W1*
☎ *020 7287 9862*
🚌 *Leicester Square LU*
🕐 *Daily 10am-6pm*

A well-established Chinese bakery, which despite its small size offers a good range of custard tarts buns and mango puddings.

## Golden Gate Dessert House

🔲 *110 Shaftesbury Avenue, W1*
☎ *020 7494 3886*
🚌 *Leicester Square LU*
🕐 *Daily 10am-7pm*

A bright red façade marks this cake house as does its eye-catching window display of gaudily-iced cakes. Here one can buy an array of Chinese cakes and desserts.

## Kowloon Chinese Café Cake Shop

🔲 *29 Gerrard Street, W1*
☎ *020 7437 1694*
🚌 *Leicester Square LU*
🕐 *Daily 10am-7pm*

This bakery-cum-café does brisk business in Chinese buns and cakes which can be eaten in or taken away

## Sun Luen

🔲 *4 Little Newport Street W1*
☎ *020 7437 0251*
🚌 *Leicester Square LU*
🕐 *Daily 10am-6.30pm*

A down-to-earth, well-established bakery and café offering a selection of freshly baked, sweet and savoury goods.

## Wonderful Patisserie

🔲 45 Gerrard Street, W1
☎ 020 7734 7629
🚌 Leicester Square LU
🕐 Daily 11am-7pm

This bright and cheerful cake shop does a roaring trade in Chinese biscuits and cakes.

Far East Bakery

# Eating Places

For many years, London's Chinese restaurants offered predominantly Cantonese food. As a result several places offer excellent dim sum – an assortment of steamed and fried dumplings traditionally served at lunchtime – which are a speciality of Canton. Today, however, Chinese restaurant cuisine is beginning to reflect China's regional diversity with restaurants and cafés offering Fujianese or Sichuan dishes beginning to appear.

With Chinatown overrun by tourists, standards have slipped in many of its restaurants, though there are some offering excellent food. If you enjoy good Chinese cuisine, then you should also head for Bayswater, where a cluster of excellent Chinese restaurants attracts enthusiastic and discerning diners.

# Central

## Baozi Inn   £-££
*25 Newport Court, W1*
☎ *020 7287 6877*
🚌 *Leicester Square LU*

Hidden down a small alleyway, this homely café serves up gutsy streetfood-inspired snacks such as chilli oil-slathered Chengdu dumplings and their own delicious plump buns. A great place for cheap and delicious Chinese food.

## Bar Shu   £££
*28 Frith Street, W1*
☎ *020 7287 6688*
🚌 *Leicester Square LU*

Upmarket and atmospheric, Bar Shu offers a chance to sample Sichuan's famously chilli-hot cuisine. There are dishes with names such as Ants Climbing Tree (spiced minced pork with glassthread noodles) and Pock-Marked Old Woman's Beancurd.

## Café de HK   £-££
*47-49 Charing Cross Road, WC2*
☎ *020 7534 9898*
🚌 *Leicester Square LU*

One of a new-wave of more contemporary, casual eateries opening up in Chinatown – good for a quick one-dish meal.

## Four Seasons   ££
*12 Gerrard Street, W1*
☎ *020 7494 0870*

A Chinatown veteran, run with businesslike efficiency and famous for its roast duck.

## Golden Dragon   ££
*28-29 Gerrard Street, W1*
☎ *020 7734 2763*
🚌 *Leicester Square LU*

This is a quintessential Chinatown restaurant. It's noted for its dim sum and is busy at lunchtime on Sundays.

## Hakkasan  ££-£££

- 8 Hanway Place, W1
- ☎ 020 7927 7000
- 🚌 Tottenham Court Road LU

Intriguingly situated down a back-alley, this is a glamorous restaurant (set up by Wagamama founder Alan Yau). It has a night-club décor and popular cocktail bar and is noted for its dainty dim sum.

## Imperial China  ££

- White Bear Yard, 25A Lisle Street, WC2
- ☎ 020 7734 3388
- 🚌 Leicester Square LU

Picturesquely tucked away in a courtyard, this upmarket restaurant offers reasonable dim sum during the day.

## Joy King Lau  ££

- 3 Leicester Street, WC2
- ☎ 020 7437 1132
- 🚌 Leicester Square LU

A Chinatown veteran, housed in a long narrow town house on a Soho side-street. It offers a classic Cantonese menu, with dim-sum especially popular.

## New World  ££

- 1 Gerrard Place, W1
- ☎ 020 7434 0396
- 🚌 Leicester Square LU

Vast and invariably busy, New World is very much an old-style Chinatown restaurant. It is one of the few serving dim sum from trolleys, rather than à la carte.

## Phoenix Palace  ££

- 3-5 Glentworth Street, NW1
- ☎ 020 7486 3515
- 🚌 Baker Street LU

This spacious restaurant is perpetually filled to the brim with diners. It is an impressively smooth-running operation, noted for its high-quality dim sum and a la carte menu.

## Royal China  ££

- 24-26 Baker Street, W1
- ☎ 020 7487 4688
- 🚌 Baker Street LU

This Baker Street branch of Royal China offers a chance to enjoy excellent dim sum in spacious, attractive surroundings.

## Shanghai Blues £££-££££

*193-197 High Holborn, WC1*

*020 7404 1668*

*Holborn LU*

For sheer glamour, this strikingly-decorated restaurant is hard to beat. The menu offers an upmarket selection of dim-sum and mains, with the emphasis on luxurious ingredients such as fresh scallops, sea bass, lobster and fillet steak.

## Yauatcha ££-£££

*15 Broadwick Street, W1*

*020 7494 8888*

*Oxford Circus LU*

Set up by restaurateur Alan Yau, this basement restaurant is a stylish establishment, complete with a long tank of eye-catching tropical fish, a light-studded ceiling and embroidered turquoise-coloured seating. Jewel-like dim sum, such as vegetarian shark's fin with gold leaf, look as good as they taste, with fresh seafood figuring prominently. The ground floor serves exquisitely presented East-West fusion patisserie and a fine selection of teas.

# North

## Yum Cha ££

*27-28 Chalk Farm Road, NW1*

*020 7482 2228*

*Chalk Farm LU*

This restaurant specialises in dim sum, offering respectable versions of classic dishes such as steamed barbecued pork buns or pan-fried turnip paste.

# West

## Golden Palace ££

*146-150 Station Parade, Harrow HA1*

*020 8863 2333*

*Harrow-on-the-Hill LU, Rail*

A well-established Cantonese restaurant, particularly popular for its dim sum.

## Mandarin Kitchen £££

*14-16 Queensway, W2*

*020 7727 9468*

*Bayswater LU, Queensway LU*

Peering in through the large windows to the dimly-lit interior, one is reminded of an aquarium. Appropriately so, as this large, busy restaurant specialises in Cantonese seafood. Among the delicious dishes on offer are succulent steamed scallops in the shell and fresh crab with ginger.

## Royal China ££

13 Queensway, W2

☎ 020 7221 2535

🚌 Bayswater LU, Queensway LU

Such is the fame of the dim sum here that, at the weekend, queues start forming before the restaurant opens at noon. Inside, the large, roomy dining area is decorated with 70s opulence; shiny black tiled walls festooned with golden lacquerwork and masses of mirrors. Service is efficient, which is just as well considering how busy it gets. The dim sum dishes are spot on, from delicate mangetout dumplings (filled with pea-shoots) to soft, spongy char siu bau.
*Branch: 24-26 Baker Street, W1*

# East

## Shanghai ££

41 Kingsland High Street, E8

☎ 020 7254 2878

🚌 Dalston Kingsland Rail

What was formerly a pie and mash shop, complete with traditional tiles, has now been transformed into a busy Chinese restaurant. Good dim sum and a bargain lunchtime buffet pull in the punters.

# Cookbooks

## Sichuan Cookery
*Fuchsia Dunlop*
This elegantly written, attractively packaged cookbook offers a fascinating and appetising insight into Sichuan cuisine.

## The Chinese Kitchen
*Deh-Ta Hsiung*
Offering a considerable insight into Chinese cuisine, this is an attractive, well-illustrated book. There is extensive information on Chinese ingredients and an appealing range of recipes.

## Heart and Soul
*Kylie Kwong*
Kylie Kwong's appetising book combines personal recollections with tasty, clearly written recipes

## Classic Chinese Cookbook
*Yan-Kit So*
A classic Chinese cookbook by a wonderful food writer who knew how to share her knowledge in the most accessible way. This is both lucidly written and well-illustrated with mouthwatering, workable recipes.

French London

*Le Pascalou*

ondon's first serious experience of the French was when it fell under Norman rule following the 1066 Conquest. French became the language both of the Court and local government. London saw an influx of merchant traders from northern France and a number of religious orders, including the influential Knights Templar, established themselves in the city.

The next major increase in London's French community was due to the arrival of French-speaking Protestants, known in France as 'Huguenots', who came to England to escape Catholic persecution. In France, the limited privileges granted to Huguenots by the 1598 Edict of Nantes were gradually eroded, with restrictions placed on Protestant worship. In 1680 many Huguenots fled, and Charles II offered them asylum in 1681. Four years later in France, the Edict of Nantes was revoked and Protestant churches were ordered to be destroyed. Following this, between 40,000 and 50,000 Huguenots moved to England, with half of them thought to have settled in London. By the year 1700, Huguenots formed around five per cent of London's population.

Spitalfields and Soho were the two main areas in London in which the Huguenots settled. Spitalfields

(also home to a community of Flemish weavers) attracted the Huguenot weavers, who eventually contributed to a prosperous period in the British silk industry. In Soho, where the Huguenots took over a chapel built for Greek Christians and used it until 1822, the new immigrants were craftspeople, such as watch and clockmakers, bookbinders and gold and silversmiths.

Our popular perception of the French as stylish and fashionable was apparent even then, with a 1700 report declaring, 'The English have now so great an esteem for the workmanship of the French refugees that hardly any thing vends without a gallic name'. Huguenot merchants, alongside other immigrants, played an important part in London's financial life. When the Bank of England was setup in 1694, several of the founder directors were Huguenots. In addition to influencing crafts and business, Huguenot academics played a notable role in the worlds of science and technology, with many joining the Royal Society.

London's French community were joined by subsequent groups of refugees, with an influx of royalists fleeing the 1789 French Revolution, and political refugees escaping the 1870

Commune. Gradually, further institutions catering to French expats were set up, from a chapel in the French Embassy to French schools in Lisle Street in 1865. In 1867, the French Hospital and Dispensary in Shaftesbury Avenue was established, while 1893 saw the completion of the French Protestant Church in Soho Square. Paul Villars wrote in 1905 in 'Living London' of the French community that 'In London, as in France, they use the café as a club' – the Café Royal was a favourite haunt. During the eighteenth and nineteenth centuries, however, the French community slowly became assimilated into English society. Huguenot families such as the Courtaulds and Oliviers became established members of British society. Today, Spitalfields' Georgian houses and Huguenot names like Fournier Street are reminders of the area's former prosperity under the silk merchants.

During the Second World War, Soho, once home to the Huguenots, became a focal point for the French Resistance, with the York Minster pub acting as the headquarters of the Free French Forces. Generally known 'the French pub' it has now been renamed the French House; General de Gaulle used to shop for his coffee at Angelucci's around the corner on Frith Street.

Today, London is home to a large French community. The heartland of this Gallic presence is found in elegant, affluent South Kensington, with the French Lycée on Cromwell Road and the French Institute at Queensberry Place providing two focal points. Serving this community are a cluster of upmarket food shops and chic patisseries.

sélection raoul

Spécialité
Aromatisée façon
Limonade Artisanale

VIOLETTE

75cl

LE RENDEZ-VOUS DES GO...

sélection raoul

Spécialité
Aromatisée façon
Limonade Artisanale

MANDARINE

75cl

LE RENDEZ-VOUS DES GO...

sélection raoul

Spécialité
Aromatisée façon
Limonade Artisanale

MENTHE
GLACIALE

75cl

sélection raoul

Spécialité
Aromatisée façon
Limonade Artisanale

MENTHE
GLACIALE

75cl

LE RENDEZ-VOUS DES GO...

*Le Pascalou*

# French Cuisine

French cuisine has been highly influential throughout Europe, with Britain especially living in its shadow. As the current edition of the Larousse Gastronomique baldly states, 'At the beginning of the twentieth century, French cookery gained supremacy throughout the world.' Today the language of the kitchen continues to be French, from 'chef' to culinary terms such as 'sauté'.

Still a predominantly agricultural country, France has retained many of the regional ingredients such as cheeses, hams and herbs which give its cuisine character and flavour; local markets still abound selling locally-grown seasonal produce. Standards of produce have remained high and the simple pleasures of life, such as a decent loaf of bread and some good cheese, are easily found.

An enduring regionalism means that even in the twenty-first century local dishes are cherished, rather than discarded in a mass move towards uniformity. As a result, French cuisine contains wonderfully contrasting strands: from the Mediterranean flavours of Provençal cooking, laden with tomatoes, basil and olive oil, to the cream, cider and calvados based dishes of Normandy.

French cooking can be divided broadly into 'haute cuisine', the cookery of grand restaurants and hotels; 'cuisine du terroir', regional cooking found in provincial restaurants; and 'cuisine grand-mère', the everyday food found in people's homes and in cheap, down-to-earth bistros. Haute cuisine has influenced chefs and cookery schools around the world. Naturally, it has followed trends and fashions. In the 1970s and 1980s 'nouvelle cuisine' – a move away from the over-rich dishes of the classic cuisine – was highly influential, although reviled in some quarters for its affectation. In contrast, regional and home cooking continues to stick to a traditional repertoire of classic French dishes, such as cassoulet or tarte tatin.

# Glossary

**Anchovy (anchois):** a small sea fish, generally available salted in cans or jars, filleted or whole. The distinctive salty, fishy flavour of anchovies plays a key part in dishes like tapenade and pissaladière.

**Bayonne ham:** a famous salt-cured, smoked ham, originally from Bayonne but now manufactured all over France.

*Banon*

**Butter:** beurre d'Isigny from Normand, sold both unsalted and salted, is highly prized in French pastry-cooking.

**Calvados:** a spirit distilled from cider traditionally from Normandy. Pays d'Auge Calvados is a particularly high-quality brand.

**Capers:** the unopened buds of a Mediterranean shrub, used pickled either in brine or vinegar as a distinctive sour flavouring.

**Celeriac (céleri-rave):** the white, firm-textured, bulbous root of a variety of celery with a distinctive nutty flavour.

**Cep (cèpe):** a brown-capped, thick-stemmed edible wild boletus mushroom, valued for its rich flavour and meaty texture.

**Cheeses:** French cheeses are one of the glories of French cuisine. There are hundreds of different French cheeses, with the following only a tiny selection. *Banon*, a soft, small, round cheese, traditionally wrapped in chestnut leaves; *Beaufort*, a Gruyère-like hard cow's milk cheese from the mountain pastures of the Savoie; *Brie*, a circular, soft, unpressed cow's milk cheese, with its origins in the thirteenth century; *Brie de Meaux* is a classic brie, farm-made from unpasturised milk; *Camembert*, a round, flat, soft cheese, traditionally from Normandy; *chèvre*, goat's milk cheese (mi-chèvre refers to cheeses made with a mixture of goat's and cow's milks); *Comte*, a Gruyère-type cow's milk cheese from the Jura mountains; *crottin de chavignol*, a soft goat's milk, cheese made in Sancerre, shaped like a small flattened ball; *explorateur*, a mild, cylindrical, triple-cream cow's milk cheese; *Fourme d'Ambert*, a semi-soft, cow's milk veined cheese; *fromage frais*, fresh curd cheese made from cow's milk, used in cooking;

*Livarot*, a soft Normandy cow's milk cheese; *lucullus*, a soft, cylindrical cow's milk cheese; *Munster*, a soft cheese from the Alsace with an orange-red rind; *Pont l'Eveque*, a square-shaped, soft cow's milk cheese from Normandy; and *Roquefort*, a famous veined, semi-soft sheep's milk cheese, ripened for three months in the limestone caves of Les Causses.

**Chervil:** a subtle-flavoured green herb, with fine fronds, resembling a delicate continental parsley.

**Crème fraîche:** soured cream containing a minimum of 30% butterfat.

**Dandelion (dent-de-lion, pissenlit):** a jagged-leafed, wild meadow plant, dismissed as a weed in England but eaten when young as a salad leaf in France.

**Lard de poitrine:** a fatty version of streaky bacon used for flavouring dishes such as stews; also available smoked.

**Marrons glacés**: sweet, glazed, syrup-poached chestnuts, eaten as a costly sweetmeat and used in desserts. Available whole, in pieces or in purée form.

*Marrons glacés*

**Mustard (moutarde):** pale yellow Dijon mustard made from black or brown mustard seeds, verjuice and white wine; mild, aromatic dark-brown Bordeaux mustard; and grainy-textured Meaux mustard made from mixed mustard seeds.

**Olive oil:** Although a small producer, France's olive oil is well-regarded, with the best thought to come from Provençe.

**Pâtés:** *pâté de campagne*, coarse-textured pâté; pâté de foie, containing 15% pork liver and 45% fat.

**Purslane (pourpier):** a green salad vegetable with rounded, clover-shaped leaves.

**Puy lentil:** a prized small, green-brown lentil which retains its shape and has a good flavour when cooked.

**Rocket (roquette):** a peppery, jagged green salad leaf; a traditional element of Provençal mesclun (a wild leaf salad).

**Salt cod (morue):** dried, salted cod which needs pre-soaking before cooking and which is used in classic dishes such as brandade.

**Saucisson sec:** Dried sausages including: *Jésus*, a large, pork sausage; *saucisson d'Arles*, made from pork and beef; *saucisson de campagne*, made with pork, fat, garlic and spice; *rosette*, a slowly-matured pure pork sausage.

**Sausages:** *andouillette*, a thick, bumpy sausage, sometimes smoked; *boudin blanc*, a creamy white sausage containing meat such as veal, chicken or pork; *boudin noir*, a dark-skinned blood sausage made from pig's blood; *cervelas*: a short, stocky pork sausage; *merguez*, a spicy red-coloured Algerian lamb and beef sausage; *Toulouse*: a popular pork cooking sausage, used in cassoulet.

**Shallot:** a small, russet-skinned, mild member of the onion family.

**Snails (escargot):** an edible gastropod mollusc, enjoyed by the Gauls, available canned or frozen and sometimes found fresh.

**Sorrel:** a green, leafy herb with a distinctive sour flavour, used to flavour soups, omelettes and salads.

**Tarragon:** a fine-leafed green herb with a distinctively aromatic, faintly aniseed flavour.

**Truffle (truffe):** rare and costly black and white tubers, with a distinctive aroma and flavour. Black Périgord truffles are particularly prized.

**Vanilla sugar:** vanilla-flavoured caster sugar, available commercially but easily made at home by placing two or three vanilla pods in a jar of caster sugar and leaving it to infuse.

**Wine vinegar:** red and white wine vinegars are key flavourings in French cookery, essential in salad dressings. Orleans wine vinegars are particularly valued.

# Food Shops

As one would expect from a country famous for its baking, several of London's best French food shops are elegant patisseries. These stores offer Londoners the welcome chance to enjoy decent croissants, delectable cakes and proper bread.

# Central

## Comptoir Gascon Food Hall

🏠 *61-63 Charterhouse Street, EC1*
☎ *020 7608 0851*
✍ *www.clubgascon.com*
🚌 *Farringdon LU/Rail*
🕐 *Tue-Sat 9am-10pm*

This handsome shop boasts an excellent pedigree, linked as it is to the Michelin-starred restaurant Club Gascon. Pride of place here goes to an array of home made foie gras – the sweet wines stocked here are specifically chosen as good accompaniments to foie gras. Own-made traiteur dishes range from pig's cheek in Armagnac to Gascony pies. On-site bakers produce top-notch viennoserie, a range of breads, cakes and pastries – including canele, a speciality from South Western France.

## La Fromagerie

🏠 *2-4 Moxon Street, W1*
☎ *020 7935 0341*
✍ *www.lafromagerie.co.uk*
🚌 *Baker Street LU*
🕐 *Mon-Fri 8am-7.30pm, Sat 9am-7pm, Sun 10am-6pm*

Discreetly positioned just off Marylebone High Street, Patricia Michelson's attractive food shop is filled with good things to eat. As the name suggests, cheeses are the shop's forte, stocked in a separate, temperature-controlled cheeseroom. Here can be found between 100 and 150 seasonal farmhouse cheeses, many of which are French with Alpine cheeses, such as Beaufort, being a speciality. Patricia, whose passionate enthusiasm for cheese is genuine and infectious, makes a point of sourcing cheeses herself, direct from small farms and suppliers. Other Gallic edibles include exquisite walnut oil, delectable jams and superb Normany cider and wines, chosen to complement the cheeses on offer. A tasting room area offers a chance to sample charcuterie and cheeses as well as dishes made in the kitchen downstairs.

French Foodshops

French Foodshops

## Laduree
🔲 *71-72 Burlington Arcade, W1*
☎ *020 7491 9155*
🖥 *www.laduree.fr*
🚌 *Green Park, Piccadilly LU*
🕐 *Mon-Sat 9am-6pm*

This petite, golden-coloured shop offers a chance to sample Laduree's famous macaroons. These are exquisitely colourful, dainty creations with flavours ranging from striking liquorice or coffee to delicate orange blossom or pistachio. The branch at Harrods in Knightsbridge also offers a splendidly opulent café.

## Maison Bertaux
🔲 *28 Greek Street, W1*
☎ *020 7437 6007*
🚌 *Leicester Square LU*
🕐 *Mon-Sat 8.30am-11pm,*
*Sun 8.30am-9pm*

Founded in 1871, this characterful patisserie is the area's last surviving food shop link to Soho's nineteenth-century French community. Tucked away down a side-street, it has a loyal clientele who enjoy the excellent pastries, good coffee and Bohemian atmosphere, lovingly sustained by Michelle, the manager. As one sits sipping coffee, trays of freshly made croissants or fruit tarts are brought out from the kitchen and regulars pause at the till for a few moment's gossip.

## Paul
🔲 *29 Bedford Street, WC2*
☎ *020 7836 3304*
🖥 *www.paul-uk.com*
🚌 *Covent Garden LU*
🕐 *Mon-Fri 7.30am-9pm*
*Sat-Sun 9am-9pm*

The first London branch of an established French bakery chain. It combines a bakery with a salon de thé in which to indulge in a coffee éclair or sample a slice of authentic quiche Lorraine. All the goods are baked on the premises.
*Branches throughout London (see website).*

## Poilâne
🔲 *46 Elizabeth Street, SW1*
☎ *020 7808 4910*
🖥 *www.poilane.fr*
🚌 *Sloane Square LU, Victoria LU/Rail*
🕐 *Mon-Fri 7am-7.30pm, Sat 7.30am-6pm*

This small, dainty shop is the first London branch of a much-loved Gallic institution. A replica of Lionel Poilâne's famous bakery in Paris. The shop's basement contains a huge, wood-fired brick oven where the master baker works through the night. Here one can buy the distinctive tangy sourdough loaves for which Poilâne is famous as well as delicious patisserie.
*Branches throughout London (see website).*

# North

## La Fromagerie

- 30 Highbury Park, N5
- 020 7359 7440
- www.lafromagerie.co.uk
- Highbury & Islington LU/Rail
- Mon 11am-7.30pm,
  Tue-Sat 9.30am-7.30pm,
  Sun 10am-4.30pm

Under a dark blue awning, a window filled with appetising tarts and pastries marks the presence of this attractive shop. Inside, the shelves are packed with carefully chosen delicacies. Pride of place goes to the cheese room at the back with its range of artisanal cheeses, a large proportion of which are French.

# West

## Maison Blanc

- 102 Holland Park, W11
- 020 7221 2494
- www.maisonblanc.co.uk
- Holland Park LU
- Mon-Wed 8am-7pm
  Thur-Fri 8am-7.30pm,
  Sat 7.30am-7pm, Sun 8.30am-6pm

This is the first London branch of a well-established chain. A striking display of elegant cakes draws customers into this attractive French patisserie shop and café. The baked goods on offer include rustic-style French breads and exquisitely stylish cakes and pastries. Among the traditional French treats on offer are classic tarte au citron, Bûches de Noel (at Christmas) and Tarte Bonne Femme.

# South-West

## Bagatelle Boutique

- 44 Harrington Road, SW7
- 020 7581 1551
- www.bagatelle.co.uk
- South Kensington LU
- Mon-Sat 8am-8pm, Sun 8am-6pm

This established shop sells its own high-quality viennoiserie, patisserie, breads and cakes. In addition, there is a traiteur counter offering dishes such as salmon quenelles and home made foie gras.

## La Grande Bouchee

🏠 *31 Bute Street, SW7*
☎ *020 7589 8346*
🚌 *South Kensington LU*
🕐 *Mon-Fri 8am-7pm, Sat 8am-6pm*
   *Sun 12noon-4pm*

This small, well-established shop-cum-café has served generations of Lycee students with coffees, pastries and sandwiches. Foodstuffs range from French cereals, compotes and dairy products to champagne and caviar.

## Le Pascalou

🏠 *359 Fulham Road, SW10*
☎ *020 7352 1717*
🚌 *Fulham Broadway LU*
🕐 *Mon-Sat 8am-7.30pm, Sun 10am-6pm*

This upmarket, handsome Gallic shop is aimed at an affluent clientele. It sells an impressive range of foodstuffs, from savoury saucisson, pâtés and condiments to French cereals, chocolates, biscuits and confectionary. In front of the shop there's an eye-catching display of fresh fruit and vegetables as well as fish and seafood.

## Le Tour de France

🏠 *135 Sunnyhill Road, SW16*
☎ *020 8769 3554*
🖥 *www.letourdefrance.co.uk*
🚌 *Streatham Rail*
🕐 *Mon-Sat 8am-7pm, Sun 8am-2pm*

This small, neat shop is knowledgeably run by its amicable owners Regine and Jean-Pierre Bruyas. Luxury items include fresh Brittany oysters, home-made fois gras, Comte cheese, sel gris de Guerande and vintage Armagnacs. The store is also strong on basics such as vinegars, fruit juices and fresh sausages.

# South-East

## Boulangerie Jade

🏠 *44 Tranquil Vale, SE3*
☎ *020 8318 1916*
🚌 *Blackheath Rail*
🖥 *www.boulangeriejade.com*
🕐 *Mon-Sat 8am-6pm, Sun 9am-5pm*

A tempting array of French breads are all freshly baked on the premises. Cakes and pastries are also very popular with the Blackheath regulars who often stay to enjoy a coffee. Seasonal specialities include Christmas treats such buche de Noel, available in different flavours.

# Eating Places

French eateries in London range from cafés serving delicious pastries to some seriously chic and elegant establishments.

## Central

### Club Gascon   ££££-£££££

- 57 West Smithfield, EC1
- ☎ 020 7796 0600
- ✐ www.clubgascon.com
- 🚇 Farringdon LU/Rail

A luxurious establishment specialising in the cuisine of south-west France.

### Elena's L'Etoile   ££££-£££££

- 30 Charlotte Street, W1
- ☎ 020 7636 7189
- ✐ www.elenasletoile.co.uk
- 🚇 Goodge Street LU

In the heart of Fitzrovia this unashamedly cosy restaurant, with its red plush seating and signed celebrity portraits, is the sort of place which inspires loyalty in its regulars. The classic French food – such as scallops with celeriac purée – and charming service, presided over by famous maître d' Elena Salvoni, match the surroundings to perfection.

### Galvin Bistrot de Luxe   ££££-£££££

- 66 Baker Street, W1
- ☎ 020 7935 4007
- ✐ www.galvinrestaurants.com
- 🚇 Baker Street LU

This handsome restaurant, evoking a Parisian brasserie, has a well-deserved reputation for its excellent French food and wines. The courteous, knowledgeable service adds to the appeal.

### Maison Bertaux   £

- 28 Greek Street, W1
- ☎ 020 7437 6007
- 🚇 Leicester Square LU

A vintage Soho café in which to enjoy a café au lait or freshly squeezed orange juice and a freshly baked pastry. Their almond croissants are renowned.

### Mon Plaisir   £££-££££

- 21 Monmouth Street, WC2
- ☎ 020 7836 7243
- ✐ www.monplaisir.co.uk
- 🚇 Covent Garden, Leicester Square LU

London's oldest French restaurant is still going strong. Here one can enjoy well-prepared, classic dishes such as steak tartare or coq au vin in pleasantly old-fashioned, atmospheric surroundings.

## Paul  £

- 🖃 *29 Bedford Street, WC2*
- ☏ *020 7836 3304*
- 🖉 *www.paul-uk.com*
- 🚌 *Covent Garden LU*

Paul's backroom salon de thé is something of a haven with proper quiche Lorraine.

## Terroirs  ££-£££

- 🖃 *5 William 1V Street, WC2*
- ☏ *020 7036 0660*
- 🖉 *www.terroirswinebar.com*
- 🚌 *Charing Cross LU/rail*

This pleasantly informal wine bar and restaurant has rapidly gained a following for its simple, immaculately executed food and extensive wine list.

# North

## L'Absinthe  ££-£££

- 🖃 *40 Chalcot Road, NW1*
- ☏ *020 7483 4848*
- 🖉 *www.labsinthe.co.uk*
- 🚌 *Chalk Farm LU*

Run with panache by owner Jean-Christophe Slowik, this intimate French bistro hums with diners enjoying their meals. The reasonably-priced menu offers classic French fare, from chicken liver parfait to tasty steak frites. The set lunch is a bargain and the corkage added to the wines for sale is very reasonable.

## Almeida  ££££

- 🖃 *30 Almeida Street, N1*
- ☏ *020 7354 4777*
- 🚌 *Highbury & Islington LU/Rail*

This stylish Islington restaurant focuses on classic French food. Dishes to be found on the menu include hand-carved jambon du Bayonne with celeriac remoulade, superior steak au poivre and a range of tarts, presented (tongue-in-cheek) on a trolley.

## Le Crêperie de Hampstead  £

- 🖃 *Corner of Hampstead High Street and Perrins Lane, NW3*
- 🚌 *Hampstead LU*

This corner stall is something of a Hampstead institution, serving excellent take-away sweet and savoury crêpes, such as classic crêpes Suzette. Customers stand mesmerised watching thin pools of batter metamorphose into crêpes.

# South-West

## Racine  ££££-£££££

- 🖃 *239 Brompton Road, SW3*
- ☏ *020 7584 4472*
- 🚌 *Knightsbridge LU, South Kensington LU*

An elegant, smooth-running restaurant serving classic French dishes with panache. The experience is rounded off with an impressive cheese board and fine wine list.

# Cookbooks

## Mastering the Art of French Cookery (Vols 1 & 2)
*Simone Beck, Louisette Bertholle & Julia Child*
A well-respected, practical classic.

## French Country Cookery
*Elizabeth David*
An elegantly written, discriminating guide to traditional French cooking.

## French Provincial Cookery
*Elizabeth David*
A classic cookbook by a master food writer.

## Floyd on France
*Keith Floyd*
A jaunty, accessible collection of French recipes from the flamboyant Floyd.

## Charcuterie and French Pork Cooking
*Jane Grigson*
A mixture of scholarly knowledge and practical food writing.

## Larousse Gastronomique
A fascinating gastronomic encyclopaedia.

## Cooking in Provence
*Alex Mackay*
An attractively illustrated cookbook offering an appealing taste of Provence.

## I know How to Cook
*Ginette Mathiot*
An impressive tome.  This is an authentic French cookbook, offering over 1.400 recipes for classic French dishes.

## Simple French Food
*Richard Olney*
A wonderful, authoritative insight into French bourgeois cuisine, written with love and knowledge.

French Cookbooks

Greek London

Greenhill Grocers

The Greek community in London today is about 160,000 strong and largely made up of Greek Cypriots; its growth has been a purely twentieth-century phenomenon. Historically, however, there was a small mainland Greek presence in London dating back to the eighteenth century. Bishop Timotheus Catsiyannis, of the Cathedral of Aghia Sophia on Moscow Road, has traced back the histories of such prominent Greek families as the Rallis. Pandias Ralli (1793-1865), a prosperous merchant from Chios, came to Britain to expand the family business. He was a leading figure in the early Greek community in Britain, becoming Consul of Greece in 1835.

The Greek community used the Russian Chapel for their religious services and ceremonies until 1837 when a Greek Chapel of Our Saviour was established at 9 Finsbury Circus, where the Ralli brothers had their business. By 1843 Pandias felt this chapel to be inadequate and proposed building a new church. Seven years later the Greek Church of Our Saviour was opened at London Wall, followed by the completion of the Cathedral of Aghia Sophia in Moscow Road in 1878.

The real growth in London's Greek community came much later, as a result of Britain's relations with Cyprus. This Mediterranean island was leased to the British government in 1878 by the Ottomans, and annexed as a colony by Britain in 1914. During the period of British rule, the lack of opportunities in Cyprus drove many Cypriots to Britain. In the 1930s, the Christian Cypriot Brotherhood was founded in London to offer support to this ex-pat community. The number of Cypriots coming to Britain increased appreciably after the Second World World. Many found work as kitchen hands and waiters, and in the garment industry. Soho was an early focal point but there was a shift to Camden Town and in 1948 Greek Cypriots took over the Church of All Saints on Pratt Street. In 1960, Britain withdrew from Cyprus and as a result 25,000 Cypriots came to this country in 1961 seeking work. The Turkish invasion of Cyprus in 1974 caused the next major influx, with hundreds of refugees fleeing to Britain to seek refuge.

During the 1960s the Greek community moved out from Camden, many of them heading north to Turnpike Lane, Wood Green and Palmers Green. Green Lanes, a long road in Haringey, was a focal point for Greek Cypriots but today only a few veteran Greek Cypriot shops remain in the area. Green Lanes now houses a Turkish and Kurdish community while the Greek community has dispersed through London's north-eastern suburbs.

The cuisine of ancient Greece, chronicled by the second-century writer Athenaeus, has now been overlaid by other influences. A history of occupation by the Romans, Venetians and Turks has left distinct traces: pasta dishes, kebabs, coffee and honey pastries. There is a clear overlap between Greek and Turkish cooking, especially apparent in Cypriot cooking, and the debate over who originated which dish still continues today. There are also differences: alcohol and pork, prohibited to the Turks under Islam, are used in Greek cooking in dishes like stifatho and afelia. Easter, the most important religious festival in the Greek calendar, is marked by a host of traditional Greek dishes such as mayeritsa: a soup made from lamb head, heart, liver, lungs and intestines; and tsourekia: a braided loaf decorated with a red-dyed, hard-boiled egg, evoking the colour of Christ's blood.

The physical geography of Greece has influenced its cuisine. The long coastline of the mainland and the islands, shared between three seas, means an abundance of fish and seafood dishes. Mediterranean fish soups, such as bouillabaisse, may be Greek in origin. The lack of grazing ground meant that traditionally, meat was scarce and had to be ingeniously spun out: minced and layered with aubergine in moussaka or with macaroni in pastitio, or cubed and skewered in kebabs. Goats and sheep, able to thrive on the rocky hills, were more popular than cattle, with their need for pasture.

From Arcadia onwards this pastoral tradition has continued, and dairy products such as yoghurt and cheese still play an important, nutritious part in Greek cookery. The pungent flavour of sheep's, and goat's, milk provides a characteristic sharp note. In agriculture the olive and vine, able to flourish on the rocky hill tops, continue to dominate as they have done for centuries. Their products are essential to Greek cooking: olives on the table, mellow-flavoured olive oil, wine for drinking and cooking and vine leaves for dolmathes. The host of nut trees that thrive in Greece, such as almond, pistachio, walnut and stone pine, play their part, adding flavour and texture to both sweet and savoury dishes.

The lemon, also grown plentifully, sounds one of the keynotes of Greek cooking. Its fresh, sharp flavour characterises dishes such as avgolemono sauce and soup. The fragrant herbs that grow wild on the hill tops are another source of flavour. Athenaeus wrote of herbs being scattered on fish and grilled meat; rigani, or oregano, 'joy of the mountain' is especially popular. The hills are also the source of horta: wild green leaves such as dandelion, wild mustard and chicory, popularly eaten boiled with a dressing.

One Greek influence that has been embraced in kitchens all over the West stems from the Middle Ages. Cooks who entered the monasteries but continued their culinary vocation adopted tall white hats to distinguish themselves from the black-robed and hatted monks – hence the origin of the chef's white hat. The lavish feasts described by Athenaeus or Hesiod the Epicurean in one of the world's first cookbooks are no longer perceived as characteristic Greek cooking. Instead, Greek food is today valued for its flavourful simplicity.

# Glossary

**Bulgar (pourgori):** parboiled, cracked wheat grains, available either coarse or finely ground.

*Bulgar*

**Cheeses:** *anari*, a soft cheese, similar to Italian ricotta; *feta*, a salty, crumbly white cheese made from cow's, sheep's or goat's milk, often stored in brine; *halloumi*, a firm white cheese with a rubbery texture, often flavoured with mint.

**Colocassi:** a large, brown, fibrous tuber with a distinctive white stump, which is a staple of Cypriot cookery.

*Colocassi*

**Filo:** paper-thin pastry, sometimes spelled 'phyllo', used in both sweet and savoury dishes. It's usually available frozen, but occasionally fresh filo can be found. When using filo, be careful not to let it dry out.

**Glyko:** preserved fresh fruit, such as quinces and cherries, in a sweet syrup.

**Kataifi:** a vermicelli-like pastry, formed by pouring batter through a fine sieve onto a hot surface; usually found frozen.

**Loundza:** smoked pork loin, a traditional Cypriot Christmas food.

**Louvana:** a type of vetch, recognisable by its curly tendrils, eaten as a salad leaf.

**Mahlepi:** the fragrant kernel of the blackcherry stone, sold in husked form and added to sweet yeast breads.

**Mastic:** the fragrant resin of an evergreen tree, sold in powdered form for use in sweet yeast breads.

**Olive oil:** in Greek mythology the olive tree was a gift from Athena (the goddess of wisdom and warfare). The rich, fruity oil adds a distinctive flavour.

**Olives:** *Kalamata,* named after the city, are the famous, large, purple-black olives. Tiasis, or cracked olives, are partially-crushed olives which have been marinaded, often with olive oil, lemon slices, garlic and cumin seeds.

**Ouzo:** clear, anise-flavoured liquor, distilled from grapes. When diluted, this potent aperitif becomes white and cloudy and is nicknamed 'lion's milk'.

*Loukanika*

**Parsley**: the flat-leafed, flavourful variety known as 'continental parsley' is a basic herb in Greek cookery.

**Pasta**: dried pasta is a legacy of the Italian influence on Greek cookery. Shapes include macarona (long thick tubes of pasta), *manestra* (pasta kernels), and *vermicelli*, often cooked with bulgar.

**Purslane (glysterida):** a green salad vegetable with rounded clover-shaped leaves, sometimes called 'Cypriot watercress'.

**Retsina:** wine with a distinctive resin flavour, traceable back to the days when wine was kept in goat skins sealed with pitch.

**Rocket (rocca):** a green salad leaf with a distinctive peppery flavour, which is now very fashionable.

**Sausages:** bastourma, dark, short, spiced sausages; loukanika, thin sausages popularly flavoured with allspice, savory and orange peel or coriander seeds.

**Savory:** a peppery-flavoured herb, which looks similar to thyme.

**Tahini:** a smooth paste made from pounded sesame seeds.

**Tarama:** smoked grey mullet roe or, more commonly, cod roe, used to make taramasalata.

**Trahani:** brown, stubby, crumbly tubes made from fermented cracked wheat and yogurt. They have a tangy flavour and should be soaked before using.

**Vine leaves:** large, distinctively-shaped leaves, used principally to make dolmathes. Occasionally found fresh but usually preserved in brine, when they need soaking to rinse off the excess salt.

**Yoghurt:** thick, creamy Greek yoghurt, made from sheep's or cow's milk.

# Food Shops

A typical Greek and Greek Cypriot food shop is a greengrocer, proudly carrying a selection of Cypriot fruit and vegetables. In addition, stock usually includes loaves of freshly-baked village bread, bottles of olive oil, feta cheese, sheep's yoghurt, pulses and grains – the essentials of a Mediterranean diet.

# North

## Clocktower Store

- 🏠 *52 The Broadway, N8*
- ☎ *020 8348 7845*
- 🚌 *Finsbury Park LU/Rail, then the W7 bus*
- 🕐 *Mon-Fri 8.30am-7pm,*
  *Sat 8.30am-6pm, Sun 10am-5pm*

This friendly, bustling Cypriot greengrocer, just by Crouch End's landmark Clock Tower, offers an excellent range of fruit and veg including fresh herbs to huge watermelons. Inside are staples such as village bread, feta and olive oil.

## Greenhill Grocers

- 🏠 *24 Greenhill Parade, EN5*
- ☎ *020 8449 3879*
- 🚌 *High Barnet LU*
- 🕐 *Mon-Sat 9am-8pm, Sun 10am-3pm*

Christalla and George Vosku set up this greengrocers in 1989 and are still running it to this day with friendly courtesy. The front part of the shop offers an eye-catching display of fresh fruit and vegetables, from figs, pomegranates and quinces to colocassi, okra and bunches of fresh herbs. Other good things on offer range from frozen artichoke hearts and black-eye beans to olives, Greek pasta, feta and Christalla's own-made olive bread. They have a loyal local following, with one contented customer observing "This is my little bit of heaven,".

## Andreas Michli & Sons

- 🏠 *405-411 St Ann's Road, N15*
- ☎ *020 8802 0188*
- 🚌 *Harringay Green Lanes Rail*
- 🕐 *Mon-Thur 9.30am-7.30pm,*
  *Fri 9.30am-8.30pm,*
  *Sat 9.30am-7.30pm, Sun 11am-3.30pm*

Tucked away just off Green Lanes, this characterful row of shops sells everything from food to barbecue equipment and Greek statuary. Andreas takes particular pride in the fresh produce, which includes delights such as bergamot lemons, myrtle berries, juicy un-waxed oranges and spanking fresh bunches of chard and spinach.

## Tony's Continental Stores

🏠 *140 High Road, N2*
☎ *020 8444 5545*
🚌 *East Finchley LU*
🕐 *Mon-Fri 8am-7pm*
   *Sat 8am-6.30pm, Sun 10am-1pm*

From watermelons and figs in the summer to quinces and huge field mushrooms in the autumn, there is always a good range of produce at this self-service greengrocer. The place is run with friendly courtesy and efficiency by the Athanasiou family.

# West

## Adamou

🏠 *126 Chiswick High Road, W4*
☎ *020 8994 0752*
🚌 *Turnham Green LU*
🕐 *Daily 8.30am-6.45pm*

This Chiswick institution has an attractive display of fruit and vegetables outside, including pumpkins, colocassi, figs and wet walnuts. Inside, this large, old-fashioned shop offers an excellent range of general groceries.

Athenian Grocery

## Athenian Grocery

- *16a Moscow Road, W2*
- *020 7229 6280*
- *Bayswater LU*
- *Mon-Sat 8.30am-7pm*
  *Sun 9.30am-1pm*

Down the road from St Sophia is this charming corner shop. Its blue-painted exterior and boxes of vegetables strike an attractive Mediterranean note. Established for well over 40 years, its stock includes seasonal items such as green almonds and fresh vine leaves, as well as basic staples.

Banter is the name of the game here and insults are genially exchanged with regular customers, but service is friendly and heavy bags are carried out to waiting cars.

# Eating Places

## Central

### Vasis  ££

🏠 *56 Maple Street, W1*
☎ *020 7580 4819*
🖱 *www.vasisrestaurant.co.uk*
🚌 *Warren Street*

Andy Stylianou has been running this veteran Greek taverna since 1979 and continues to do so with genial hospitality and an eye for detail.  Customers can enjoy generous portions of freshly-made, home-cooked Greek food.  Meze dishes include exemplary deep-fried kalamari and more robust mains such as charcoal-grilled meats and slow-cooked dishes including rabbit stifado or kleftico.

### Konaki  ££

🏠 *5 Coptic Street, WC1*
☎ *020 7580 9730*
🖱 *www.konaki.co.uk*
🚌 *Tottenham Court Road LU*

Hidden down a Bloomsbury side-street, this well-established, friendly Greek restaurant has  a small courtyard for al-fresco dining. The food is traditional and delicious with classic dishes such as moussaka very well cooked and served with charm.

## North London

### Café Corfu  ££

🏠 *7 Pratt Street, NW1*
☎ *020 7267 8088*
🚌 *Camden Town LU*

A contemporary bar-cum-restaurant offering above average Greek cooking and an excellent Greek wine list.

### Daphne  ££

🏠 *83 Bayham Street, NW1*
☎ *020 7267 7322*
🚌 *Camden Town LU*

A convivial Greek restaurant offering decent Greek food in a traditional environment that has remained unchanged for years.  It is popular for both romantic tête-à-têtes and parties of friends.

### Lemonia  ££

🏠 *89 Regent's Park Road, NW1*
☎ *020 7586 7454*
🚌 *Chalk Farm LU*

With its lively atmosphere, friendly staff and fresh-tasting food this is a great Greek restaurant which is deservedly popular with revellers and young couples.

## Vrisiaki  ££

🖃 *73 Myddleton Road, N22*
☎ *020 8889 8760*
🚌 *Bounds Green LU*

Warmly recommended by Cypriot friends, at first sight this looks solely like a take-away kebab house. Venture in, however, past the busy charcoal grills and it opens into a large, popular restaurant. Those with gargantuan appetites should opt for mezedes, a seemingly never-ending array of dishes, starting with nibbles such as cracked olives and working up via seafood to a platter of grilled meats.

# Cookbooks

## Flavours of Greece
*Rosemary Barron*
An evocative collection of over 250 recipes, ranging from olive bread to houmous.

## A Book of Mediterranean Food
*Elizabeth David*
An informative book which, although not solely about Greek cookery, captures the flavours of the Mediterranean.

## Mediterranean Seafood
*Alan Davidson*
A fascinating and authoritative guide to Mediterranean seafood.

## The Taste of Cyprus
*Gilli Davies*
A charmingly written cookbook, combining personal memories with straightforward recipes.

## Mediterranean Cookery
*Claudia Roden*
A well-written and attractive book, dealing with Mediterranean cuisine as a whole but with plenty of Greek recipies.

## The Greek Cook
*Rena Salaman*
Attractively and clearly illustrated with mouth-watering photographs, this appetising cookbook offers a seasonal look at Greek cuisine.

## Meze
*Rena Salaman*
A pretty cookbook offering recipes for meze dishes from Greece and Lebanon.

## Vefa's Cookbook
*Vefa Alexiadou*
A magnificent, magisterial tome of traditional, regional Greek recipes. It offers a genuine and delicious insight into this ancient cuisine.

Italian London

PRUNES
SULTANAS
ALMONDS
PISTACCHIO NUTS
£ 1.00 per packet

I Camisa & Son

Italian links with London date back to the Roman invasion in AD 43 and the creation of a settlement named 'Londinium'. Over subsequent centuries Italians came to live in London, but particularly so in the first half of the nineteenth century when waves of political refugees arrived. The community continued to grow through the turbulent times of Italian Unification and war with Austria – by 1900 there were around 10,000 Italians in London.

The historical Italian quarter, founded in the mid-nineteenth century, was in Clerkenwell and Holborn, known to outsiders as 'Little Italy' and to its residents as 'The Hill'. The nickname 'The Hill' came from two important streets in the community: Back Hill and Eyre Street Hill. St Peter's Church was the community's focal point, erected in 1864 with money donated by Italian immigrants. Its importance to the Italian community continues to this day. Although the Italian population has now dispersed from Clerkenwell, the legacy of this period is still visible in the area around King's Cross and Holborn where red, white and green signs over barbers, cafés and shops patriotically signal Italy.

Every July the Feast Day of Our Lady of Mount Carmel is celebrated with a procession through Clerkenwell from St Peter's, followed by a 'sagra' or fête. One of the few religious processions to take place in London, it has been enacted since the 1880s and older Italians have fond memories of attending it as children. Even today, the procession draws Italians back to Clerkenwell from all over Britain. There is a great sense of community, with the different generations all present and participating. Stalls are set up on the streets selling delicious Italian snacks such as polenta e salsiccie (cornmeal and sausages), freshly-roasted porchetta (pork) and slices of savoury tarts – all washed down with wine.

The other traditional Italian area in London was Soho, which also saw an influx of Italians in the 1860s. Despite the internment of Italian residents as 'enemy aliens' during the Second World War and the tragic death in 1940 of 470 Italian internees being deported to Canada when the Arandora Star was sunk by the Germans, the Italian community continued to maintain its links with Britain. In the 1950s and 1960s, during the espresso bar boom, a wave of immigrants, mostly from the south of Italy, came to London seeking work and settled in Soho as waiters and restaurateurs.

# Italian Cuisine

Italian cuisine is very much a regional affair; the different parts of Italy, united only in the last century, have their own dishes and even their own ingredients. The historical divide between the prosperous, industrial north and the poor, rural south also extended to foodstuffs. Rice, cornmeal polenta, and fresh egg pasta were the staples of the north while in the south factory-made, dried durum wheat pasta was eaten. Cooking fats varied: the north used butter, middle-Italy pig fat, and the south, olive oil. With the post-war migration of labour from south to north and the growth of mass-production, regional eating patterns became less rigid. Today the Mediterranean diet, stemming from the south, is valued for its health-giving qualities. Dried pasta and olive oil, low in saturated fats, are now eaten throughout Italy.

Despite this blurring of the north-south divide, regional characteristics are still apparent. Tuscan cuisine comprises rustic, peasant food such as bean soup (the Tuscans are nick-named 'mangiafagioli', bean-eaters), bruschetta and charcoal-grilled meat such as bistecca fiorentina, as well as T-bone steak traditionally from the Val di Chiana. Rice dishes are still popular in the north, where rice was traditionally grown, and in Lombardy you find risotto alla Milanese, flavoured with saffron, wine and stock. Roman cuisine is that of the 'quinto quarto', the fifth quarter, with the poor eating what was left after the rich had eaten, hence strongly-flavoured offal dishes. Sicily has a rich, varied culinary inheritance due to a history of invasions by the Greeks, Romans, Arabs and Normans. The Arab legacy is particularly noticeable, with sultanas, aubergines, pistachio nuts and spices being popular ingredients in Sicily.

Italian cooking is noted for its emphasis on clear, simple flavours. Good ingredients are the key to Italian cooking and seasonality is valued. Foods continue to be associated with the regions, towns or villages that have traditionally produced that ingredient: the best radicchio from Treviso, with its annual radicchio festival; balsamic vinegar from Modena; prosciutto from Parma or San Daniele; fontina cheese from Val d'Aosta; and costly white truffles from Alba.

# Glossary

**Baccala** pungent salted, dried cod – needs soaking before cooking.

**Balsamic vinegar** an aromatic brown vinegar made from wine must and historically from Modena. Traditionally-matured balsamic vinegar is very expensive while cheaper, commercially produced balsamic vinegar compresses the maturing process into a few years.

**Ciabatta** a flavourful, distinctively-textured bread, named after a slipper because of its flattened, oval shape.

*Balsamic Vinegar*

**Colomba** a dove-shaped cake similar to panettone, but traditionally eaten at Easter.

**Farro** a staple of the early Romans, this ancient grain – a form of wheat – is enjoying a revival. Available either whole or cracked, it has a chewy texture and was traditionally used in hearty soups.

**Foccacia** a flat, salty bread flavoured with olive oil and sometimes additionally with rosemary, onions or sage; known as schiacciata in Tuscany.

**Fontina** semi-soft cow's milk cheese, traditionally from Val d'Aosta, and famously used to make fonduta, a fondue flavoured with white truffles.

**Gorgonzola** Italy's most famous blue cheese, made in Piedmont and Lombardy, traditionally matured in caves. Production today ranges from industrial to artisanal.

**Lardo di Colonnata** a traditional delicacy, consisting of cured pork fat, flavoured with salt, herbs and spices, and eaten sliced extremely finely as an antipasto.

**Marscapone** an extremely rich cream cheese, an essential ingredient of the popular dessert tiramisu.

**Mortadella** a large pink sausage, traditionally from Bologna, flavoured with peppercorns, garlic and pistachios. It can be eaten like a salami or used in cooking.

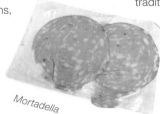

*Mortadella*

**Mozzarella** a mild white cheese, famously used on pizzas. Buffalo's milk mozzarella, with its melting texture and rich flavour, is rarer and more expensive than the wide-available cow's milk version. Baby mozzarellas are called 'bocconcini'.

*Olive Oil*

**Olive oil** a key ingredient in Italian cooking, olive oil is labelled according to its acidity levels. Extra Virgin must have no more than 1% acidity. As with wine, different regions produce different-flavoured olive oils, with Tuscan olive oil being famously piquant.

**Pancetta** the Italian equivalent of bacon, this is made from the same cut of meat – pig belly.

**Panettone** a light, brioche-style cake, containing sultanas, traditionally given at Christmas time, the season when London's Italian delis stock several versions.

*Parmesan*

**Parmesan** the best-known Italian cheese and also the largest and longest-matured cheese produced in Italy, this hard-grating cheese traditionally comes from around Parma. Grana padano is a similar cheese produced in Lombardy. Buy chunks of Parmesan and keep them refrigerated, wrapped in foil, to be used as required.

**Pasta** this famous Italian staple comes both fresh and dried and in a multiplicity of forms. Fresh pasta, made with eggs, can be bought ready-made from delicatessens. Dried pasta is made from durum wheat, with reliable Italian brands including Barilla and Da Cecco.

**Pecorino** a hard sheep's milk cheese, available in regional variations: Pecorino Romano, Pecorino Sardo, (from Sardinia) and Toscana, from Tuscany.

**Pine nuts** small ivory-coloured kernels from the stone pine tree, with a distinctive flavour.

*Panettone*

**Polenta** a Northern Italian staple made from maize, polenta flour is available in fine or coarse versions. Pre-cooked polenta flour, scorned by purists, is also available.

*Polenta*

**Porcini** wild Boletus mushrooms, prized for their flavour and priced accordingly. Dried porcini mushrooms, often in pieces, are easily found, while fresh porcini are much rarer.

*Porcini*

**Prosciutto Crudo** the most famous of these salt-cured hams is Parma ham, cured for 14 months. San Daniele, cured for 12 months, is considered another fine prosciutto.

**Ricotta** a light, bland sheep's whey cheese, drained in baskets which give it its distinctive woven markings. It is used in both sweet and savoury dishes.

**Rocket** known as 'rucola', this peppery, jagged leaf is increasingly available as a chic salad leaf. Italians are fond of pointing out that in Italy it grows wild as a weed.

*Rocket*

**Salami** ready-to-eat, salt-cured sausages, available in a range of sizes and flavours, such as fine-textured Milano or finocchiona, flavoured with fennel.

**Salsiccie** Italian sausages, usually made from pork. Luganega is a mild sausage from Lombardy, sold in long narrow coils, while in the South chilli is often added as a flavouring.

**Sun-dried tomatoes** as their name suggests, these are dried tomatoes, available either in their dry state or preserved in olive oil.

**Truffles** these rare tubers with their overwhelming and distinctive flavour are astronomically expensive, especially when sold fresh. White truffles from Alba are particularly prized. Tinned and bottled truffles are available as is truffle-flavoured olive oil.

# Food Shops

The older Italian delicatessens in London grew out of the community's needs, starting as everyday corner-shops supplying foods that had to be specially imported. In some cases the shop acted as an informal community centre, lending money, explaining English laws and providing advice. In recent years, many of these traditional Italian groceries have now gone, notably Terroni's, founded in 1890 in the heart of the Italian community in Clerkenwell. As the Italian community has become assimilated into British life this role has disappeared. With Italian food now enjoying a huge wave of fashionable popularity, newer, more upmarket delicatessens have entered the market aimed primarily at the English.

## Central

### I Camisa & Son
🏠 *61 Old Compton Street, W1*
☎ *020 7437 7610/4686*
🚌 *Leicester Square LU,*
     *Tottenham Court Road LU*
🕐 *Mon-Sat 9am-6pm*
On this bustling Soho thoroughfare, Gaby presides genially over this classic Italian deli. Established over thirty years ago, this small shop has a seemingly perpetual queue of loyal regulars, attracted by the quality of the cheeses (including excellent Parmesan), meats and delicious home-marinaded olives. Bags of fresh rocket and stunningly sweet Sicilian cherry tomatoes are another draw. Fresh, own-made pasta includes pappardelle, parma ham tortellini and gnocchi and there are excellent home-made sauces such as pesto, pomodoro and porcini.

### Gastronomeria Italia
🏠 *8 Upper Tachbrook Street, SW1*
☎ *020 7834 2767*
🚌 *Pimlico LU, Victoria LU/Rail*
🕐 *Mon-Fri 9am-6pm, Sat 9am-5pm*
This homely delicatessen is well-used by Italians and Spaniards from the local community. As well as a good basic stock of Italian ingredients, they sell tasty Italian snacks to cater to the lunchtime market.

### Gastronomica
🏠 *45 Tachbrook Street, SW1*
☎ *020 7233 6656*
🚌 *Pimlico LU,Victoria LU/Rail*
🕐 *Mon-Sat 8am-11pm, Sun 9am-10pm*
Run by an experienced team of Italian food importers, this deli-cum-café offers a range of good quality Italian foodstuffs, notably cheeses, charcuterie and fine wines.

## Lina Stores

- 18 Brewer Street, W1
- ☎ 020 7437 6482
- 🚌 Leicester Square LU,
  Oxford Circus LU,, Piccadilly Circus LU
- 🕐 Mon-Fri 7am-5.45pm, Sat 7am-5pm

The pistachio-coloured façade and the
1930s lettering on the shop sign signal this
is a vintage institution. Customers return as
much for the friendly, leisurely atmosphere
as for the delicious food. It is famous for its
excellent fresh pasta, made on the premises
every morning. The speciality is pumpkin
tortelloni, a dish from Piacanza, where the
Filippi family come from. Groceries are
wide-ranging – you feel you could ask for any
Italian ingredient and it would be conjured up.

## Princi £-££

- 135 Wardour Street, W1
- ☎ 020 7478 8889
- 🚌 Leicester Square LU ,
  Oxford Circus LU
  Piccadilly Circus LU,
- 🕐 Mon-Sat 7am-12midnight,
  Sun 9am-11pm

At last – a great Italian pasticceria in London.
On offer from the in-house bakery are freshly
baked focaccia and sweet treats such as
cannoncini, crostata, cannoli Siciliani. Seasonal
treats include colombe and panettone.

# North

## Angel Delicatessen

- 48 Cross Street, N1
- ☎ 020 7226 1951
- 🚌 Angel LU
- 🕐 Mon-Sat 8am-6pm, Sun 9am-4pm

This café and delicatessen makes a great
cappuccino along side offering quality italian
foods. The store has a good selection of cold
meats, cheeses, anti-pasta and packaged
goods from pasta to Italian biscuits and
cakes. There also sell Italian wines and beers
and have a store in Finchley:
*Amici Delicatessen*
*78 High Road, N2; Tel: 020 8444 2932*

## Gazzano's

- 167-9 Farringdon Road, EC1
- ☎ 020 7837 1586
- 🚌 Farringdon LU
- 🕐 Tue-Fri 8am-5.30pm,
  Sat 8am-5pm, Sun 10am-2pm

Founded in 1901, this veteran Italian
delicatessen, run by the Gazzano family, is
still going strong – a legacy of the days when
Clerkenwell was known as 'Little Italy'. Deli
stock is comprehensive and there's also a
café area in which customers can sit and
enjoy a cappuccino. Sundays sees the shop
filled with Italians popping in to stock up with
ingredients or grab a coffee following Mass.

*Italian Food Shops*

## Giacobazzi's Delicatessen

⊞ *150 Fleet Road, NW3*
☎ *020 7267 7222*
🚌 *Hampstead Heath Rail*
✎ *www.giacobazzis.co.uk*
🕐 *Mon-Fri 9.30am-7pm, Sat 9am-6pm*

The speciality here is ready-made fresh foods which are appetisingly display. The dishes are made on the premises by Raffaele Giacobazzi, who has a particular penchant for char-grilled vegetables ranging from radicchio to onions in balsamic vinegar. Home-made pasta, freshly made every day, includes upmarket flavours such as gorgonzola, walnut and porcini and white truffle tortellini.

## Monte's

⊞ *23 Canonbury Lane, N1*
☎ *020 7354 4335*
🚌 *Highbury & Islington LU/Rail*
🕐 *Mon-Fri 10am-7pm,*
   *Sat 10am-6pm, Sun 10am-4pm*

A smart, contemporary Italian deli, with mauve walls, glossy black floor tiles, gleaming metal shelving and jazz playing in the background. The stock is distinctly upmarket, from large bowlfuls of marinaded olives and insalata di mare to fresh funghi ravioli. Groceries include several kinds of olive oils, balsamic vinegars and polentas.

## Olga Stores

⊞ *30 Penton Street, N1*
☎ *020 7837 5467*
🚌 *Angel LU*
🕐 *Mon-Fri 9am-8pm, Sat 9am-7pm,*
   *Sun 10am-2pm*

This attractive deli is run by the charming and knowledgeable Aida. It was founded in 1988 and caters to its Islington clientele with a wide selection of foodstuffs, from marinaded olives to breads. Best-selling items include Aida's home-made lasagne, Portuguese-style salt cod fritters and her huge range of sauces – from tomato-based arrabiata and vongole to pesto.

## Saponara

⊞ *23 Prebend Street, N1*
☎ *020 7226 2771*
🚌 *Angel LU*
🕐 *Mon-Thur 8am-6pm, Fri 8am-10pm,*
   *Sat 9am-10pm*

Run with friendly courtesy by brothers Marco and Vincenzo Saponara, this roomy deli and bar offers a classic Italian mixture of delicious things to eat and drink. The store has a very good selection of authentic anti-pasta, cold meats and organic Italian wines and now offers freshly made stone-baked pizza which is served into the evening on Fridays and Saturdays.

## Salvino Ltd

⌂  *47 Brecknock Road, N7*
☎  *020 7267 5305*
🚌  *Buses 29, 253 or 10*
🕐  *Mon-Sat 9am-7pm*

An agreeably down-to-earth shop run by the Salvino brothers. As importers of Italian food their stock is above average, with a good selection of cured meats and wines.

# North-West

## L'Angolo

⌂  *120 College Road, NW10*
☎  *020 8969 5757*
🚌  *Kensal Green LU, Kensal Rise rail*
🕐  *Mon-Fri 9am-6.30pm, Sat 9am-6pm, Sun 9.30am-1pm*

Very much a local institution, Carmelo's attractive cornershop ('angolo' means corner in Italian, by the way) offers an appetising range of foodstuffs, from staples such as dried pasta, risotto rice and sauces to charcuterie, fresh pasta and fresh produce from chestnuts to porcini mushrooms. Lunchtimes see a patient queue waiting for made-to-order panini and coffees to go.

# West

## Exeter Street Bakery

⌂  *18 Argyll Road, W8*
☎  *020 7937 8484*
🚌  *High Street Kensington LU*
🕐  *Mon-Sat 8am-7pm, Sun 9am-6pm*

This small shop does a roaring trade in authentically tasty slices of pizza, Illy espressos and classic Italian breads such as pane Pugliese and ciabatta.

## Luigi's Delicatessen

⌂  *349 Fulham Road, SW10*
☎  *020 7352 7739*
🚌  *Fulham Broadway LU*
🕐  *Mon-Fri 9am-9.30pm, Sat 9am-7pm*

This roomy, cheerful delicatessen attracts a steady stream of loyal customers. The stock is extensive and high-quality; 40 olive oils, an ample stock of quality Italian dried pastas and over 300 Italian wines, spirits and aperitivos. There is an appetising display of homemade sauces and dishes.

Italian Food Shops

## Manicomio

⌖ *85 Duke of York Square, SW3*

🚇 *Sloane Square LU*

🕐 *Mon-Fri 8am-7pm, Sat 10am-7pm,*
   *Sun 10am-6pm*

Just off the King's Road, alongside smart boutiques, this spacious, elegant café and deli offers an upmarket taste of Italy. It showcases Italian food importers Machiavelli's fine products. Popular items include the fresh Italian produce like prime red peppers, cured meats and Italian cheeses, including truffle-flavoured pecorino.

## Negozio Classica

⌖ *283 Westbourne Grove, W11*

☎ *020 7034 0005*

🚇 *Notting Hill LU*

🕐 *Tue-Fri 9.30am-8pm, Sat 9.30am-7pm,*
   *Sun 11am-4.30pm*

This sleek operation is a contemporary take on the Italian 'enoteca' or wine shop. Here one can sit at the chrome bar sampling wines, eating antipasti platters or sipping on an expertly-made cappuccino made from Saint Eustachio coffee. A large range of fine Italian wines, including top notch vin santo, are available by the glass, plus select artisanal foodstuffs including chestnut honey, trout cheeks in oil and Italian saffron.

## La Picena

⌖ *5 Walton Street, SW3*

☎ *020 7584 6573*

🚇 *Knightsbridge LU*

🕐 *Mon-Fri 9am-7.30pm, Sat 9am-5.30pm*

Tucked away behind Harrods is this refreshingly down-to-earth delicatessen. It is crammed full of good-quality Italian provisions including fresh pasta and excellent homemade pasta sauces.

## Speck

⌖ *2 Holland Park Terrace, W11*

☎ *020 7229 7005*

🚇 *Holland Park LU*

🕐 *Mon-Fri 9am-8.30pm, Sat 8.30am-7pm*

This small, sleek shop carries upmarket stock. There is an attractive display of home-made dishes such as marinaded grilled vegetables and a good assortment of balsamic vinegars, Cipriani dried pasta and fine olive oils.

## Tavola

⌖ *155 Westbourne Grove, W11*

☎ *020 7229 0571*

🚇 *Notting Hill Gate LU*

🕐 *Mon-Fri 10am-7.30pm, Sat 10am-6m*

Alistair and Sharon Little's attractive food shop reflects their love of Italian cuisine with discerning products carefully sourced. Unusual Italian wines, fine balsamic vinegars and olive oils, truffle salami and artisanal dried Pugliese pasta are some of the Italian foodstuffs on offer. Alistair's own-cooked dishes, ready to take away, are often Italian-inspired, including an exemplary pasta e fagioli soup.

# South-West

## Salumeria Napoli
- 69 Northcote Road, SW11
- 020 7228 2445
- Clapham Junction Rail
- Mon-Sat 9am-6pm

A friendly corner shop with an appetising deli-counter containing olives, home-made red and green pesto sauces and a good selection of salamis and cured meats. A great shop to visit when combined with a trip to Northcote Road Market.

## Valentina
- 210 Upper Richmond Road West, SW14
- 020 8392 9127
- Mortlake Rail
- Mon-Sun 8.30am-10pm

This attractive, friendly delicatessen has a loyal local following. Particularly popular are the home-prepared dishes, from grilled vegetables to baked pasta dishes. There's a good range of grocery items and luxuries such as fresh truffles when in season.

# South-East

## La Gastronomeria
- 135 Half Moon Lane, SE24
- 020 7274 1034
- Herne Hill Rail, North Dulwich Rail
- Mon-Fri 9am-5.30pm, Sat 9am-5pm

A friendly, well-stocked Italian deli offering customers a solid range of basic groceries, from Italian dried pastas to packets of biscotti. Popular items on the deli counter include the home-made pastas and antipasti.

# East

## Gastronomica
- New Crane Wharf
  75 Garnet Street, E1
- 020 7481 8669
- Wapping LU
- Mon-Wed 8am-8pm,
  Thur-Sat 8am-10pm,
  Sun 9.30am-6.30pm

An Italian deli and café offering Italian foods, including cheeses and charcuterie.

# Eating Places

The enormous popularity of Italian food in the UK has seen a huge range of Italian restaurants opening up. In London you can find anything from chains offering pizza and pasta to elegant, expensive restaurants offering authentic, delicious and regional Italian cuisine.

## Central

### Bar Italia   £

🖃   *22 Frith Street, W1*

☎   *020 7437 4520*

🚌   *Leicester Square LU*
       *Tottenham Court Road LU*

Despite its cult status as the place for a late night espresso, Bar Italia remains thankfully down-to-earth. The place remains unchanged, complete with fruit machines, a giant video screen for Italian football and the photo of the heavyweight boxing legend Rocky Marciano glowering down from behind the bar.

### Bocca di Lupo   £££-££££

🖃   *12 Archer Street, W1*

☎   *020 7734 2223*

🚌   *Leicester Square LU, Piccadilly Circus LU*

Discreetly positioned down a tiny Soho backstreet in the heart of theatreland, this attractive restaurant is perpetually buzzing with contented diners enjoying a delicious taste of Italy. Chef Jacob Kennedy's kitchen serves up a mouthwatering range of impeccably-executed regional Italian dishes, ranging from tagiolini with sea urchin and breadcrumbs from Campania to Tuscan-style grilled quail. Delectable desserts, such as burnt almond granita with bitter chocolate sorbet, are not to be missed.

### Caffé Caldesi   £££

🖃   *118 Marylebone Lane, W1*

☎   *020 7935 1144*

🚌   *Baker Street LU, Rail*

A relaxed, well-established Italian eaterie, offering an informal café area downstairs and a more formal restaurant upstairs.

### Caffé Vergnano   1882 £

🖃   *62 Charing Cross Road, WC2*

☎   *020 7240 3512*

🚌   *Leicester Square LU*

A small, intimate café, offering excellent coffee, from espresso to cappuccino.

## Carluccio's Caffé  ££

- 8 Market Place, W1
- 020 7636 2228
- www.carluccios.com
- Oxford Circus LU

The first in what is now a chain of successful café-cum-delis. This pleasantly stylish, family-friendly eatery offers excellent value Italian food such as spaghetti alla vongole.
*Branches all over London (see website).*

## Cecconi's  ££££

- 5a Burlington Gardens, W1
- 020 7434 1500
- Green Park

This legendary, glamorous restaurant focuses on Venetian food, with a bar serving chichetta (traditional Venetian bar-snacks) and prosecco as well as a luxurious dining area.

## Manicomio  £££

- 85 Duke of York Square, SW3
- 020 7730 3366
- Sloane Square LU

Quality ingredients are at the heart of good Italian cooking and Manicomio's, set up by Italian fine food importers, has impeccable credentials on that front. The restaurant is smart in a pleasantly understated way and serves up excellent Italian food, with pasta a forte, complemented by a shrewdly chosen wine list.

## Locanda Locatelli  ££££
⌕ *8 Seymour Street, W1*
☎ *020 7935 9088*
🚌 *Marble Arch LU*

This sophisticated and elegant restaurant is a showcase for the considerable culinary talents of acclaimed Italian chef Giorgio Locatelli. Deftly executed dishes such as prawn and courgette flower risotto or calves liver with balsamic vinegar exhibit the flavourful simplicity of classic Italian cooking. Equally Italian is the welcome extended to children, with Saturday lunchtime particularly popular with families.

## Pizzeria Malletti  £
⌕ *26 Noel Street, W1*
☎ *020 7439 4096*
🚌 *Oxford Circus LU*

This diminutive pizzeria has a cult following, offering slices of freshly-made pizza, available to take-away or eat in, perching on a stool.

## Princi  £-££
⌕ *135 Wardour Street, W1*
☎ *020 7478 8889*
🚌 *Leicester Square or Piccadilly Circus LU*

This stylish eaterie offers all-day Italian eating, from brioche and cappuccino for breakfast, to freshly baked pizza slices, filled focaccia bread, salads and hearty pasta bakes at lunchtime and through the night.

## Sardo  £££
⌕ *45 Grafton Way, W1*
☎ *020 7387 2521*
🚌 *Warren Street LU*

Sardinian specialities, including traditional pasta dishes such as spaghetti bottariga or malloreddus, are a feature in this intimate, friendly restaurant.

## Theo Randall at the Intercontinental  ££££
⌕ *1 Hamilton Place, Park Lane, W1*
☎ *020 7409 3131*
🚌 *Hyde Park Corner LU*

The Intercontinental is the prefect setting for this comfortable and stylish restaurant. Theo Randall, formerly Head Chef at the River Café, already has a keen following for his accomplished, seasonal Italian cooking .

## Zafferano  ££££
⌕ *15 Lowndes Street, SW1*
☎ *020 7235 5800*
🚌 *Knightsbridge LU*

A pioneer of fine Italian food in London, this rustic but elegant restaurant continues to produce excellent Italian cooking.

# North

## Marine Ices   ££

⬜ *8 Haverstock Hill, NW3*
☎ *020 7482 9003*
🚌 *Chalk Farm LU*

In addition to Marine Ices' famous ice cream parlour, there is also a relaxed family-friendly restaurant offering tasty pizzas and pasta.

## Pane Vino   £££

⬜ *323 Kentish Town Road, NW5*
☎ *020 7267 3879*
🚌 *Kentish Town LU Rail*

This intimate restaurant enjoys a cult local following for its flavourful Sardinian food. Specialities include delicious cured meats.

# West

## Assaggi   ££££

⬜ *The Chepstow, 39 Chepstow Place, W2*
☎ *020 7792 5501*
🚌 *Notting Hill Gate LU*

Located above a pub this small restaurant is noted for its flavourful, authentic Italian food.

## Franco Manca   ££

⬜ *144, Chiswick High Road, W4*
☎ *020 8747 4822*
✍ *www.francomanca.co.uk*
🚌 *Turnham Green*

A spacious West London branch of the acclaimed Brixton Market pizzeria. There authentic pizzas are worth making a special journey to enjoy.

## The River Café   £££££

⬜ *Thames Wharf, Rainville Road, W6*
☎ *020 7381 8824*
🚌 *Hammersmith LU*

A pioneer of quality Italian cookery, in a stylish location by the Thames. The restaurant continues to use the finest seasonal produce to produce simple but delicious Italian food despite the sad death of Rose Gray. A number of best-selling 'River Café' cookbooks have helped establish this restaurant's fine reputation .

# South

## Viva Verdi   ££-£££

⬜ *6 Canvey Street, SE1*
☎ *020 7928 6867*
✍ *www.vivaverdiwinebar.com*

Just behind the Tate Modern, this bright and breezy wine-bar offers an authentic taste of Emilia-Romagna. The menu offers piadine (Italian flat breads), pasta and main courses in addition to a good range of wines. The focus is on prime Italian foodstuffs, including melting burrata cheese, Lardo di Colonnata and mature Prosciutto di Parma.

# South- West

## La Bottega   £

🖵  *25, Lower Sloane Street, SW1*
☏  *020 7730 8844*
✑  *www.labottega65.com*
🚌  *Sloane Square LU*

A small, smart Italian café, which does a roaring trade in coffees, paninis and Italian pastries. *Branch:*
*25, Eccleston Street, SW1 (020 7730 2730)*

## Donna Margherita   ££-£££

🖵  *183 Lavender Hill, SW11*
☏  *020 7228 2660*
🚌  *Clapham Junction Rail*

Pizzas freshly baked in a wood-fired oven are the particular attraction at this lively Neapolitan restaurant.

## Franco Manca   ££

🖵  *4 Market Row SW9*
☏  *020 7738 3021*
🚌  *Brixton LU/Rail*

In the heart of Brixton Market, this pleasantly casual pizzeria buzzes with a perpetual crowd of appreciative diners. A short, to-the-point, seasonal menu offers a choice of six pizzas, with the emphasis on top-notch ingredients. All pizzas have a deliciously thin sourdough base. Prices are remarkably reasonable given the quality.

## Riva   £££

🖵  *169 Church Road, SW13*
☏  *020 8748 0434*
🚌  *Barnes Bridge Rail*

A restaurant pioneer of regional Italian cooking, Riva continues to offer imaginative and tasty dishes in an elegant setting. The food and atmosphere has brought the place a loyal clientele.

# East

## Jamie's Italian   £££

🖵  *Unit 17, 2 Churchll Place, E14*
☏  *020 3002 5252*
🚌  *Canary Wharf DLR/LU*

Set up by enterprising chef Jamie Oliver, this light, airy restaurant in the heart of Canary Wharf serves up an Italian-inspired menu. The menu included truffle tagliatelle and pannacotta.

# Cookbooks

## The Italian Cookery Course
*Katie Caldesi*
Katie Caldesi draws on her years of teaching to offer an in-depth guide to Italian cuisine.

## Complete Italian Food
*Antonio and Priscilla Carluccio*
Attractively illustrated guide to Italian ingredients complete with recipes by Italian chef Antonio Carluccio and his wife Priscilla.

## The Classic Food of Northern Italy-Gastronomy of Italy
## Secrets of an Italian Kitchen
*Anna del Conte*
Offering a genuine insight into Italian cuisine, Anna del Conte's books are at once wonderfully appetising and informative.

## Italian Food
*Elizabeth David*
First published in 1954, this book is still as valid and useful as when it was first written – a classic.

## The River Café Classic Italian Cook Book
*Rose Gray and Ruth Rogers*
An elegant cookbook, bringing together a delicious collection of classic Italian recipes.

## The Classic Italian Cookbook

## The Second Classic Italian Cookbook

## Marcella's Kitchen

*Marcella Hazan*
Three wonderful cookbooks by a highly respected authority on Italian cuisine.

## Made In Italy: Food & Stories
*Giorgio Locatelli*
Acclaimed Italian chef Giorgio Locatelli offers an inspiring collection of delicious recipes and evocative anecdotes.

## The Food of Italy
*Claudia Roden*
A beautifully written guide to the regions of Italy and their local dishes – evocative and deliciously useable.

## The Silver Spoon
An English version of the classic Italian cookbook with over 2000 recipes.

# Ice Cream

The Italian community have contributed enormously to London's ice cream scene. During the nineteenth century, Italian immigrants in London worked selling ice cream on the street. Today, London hosts an increasing number of Italian gelaterias, selling their own excellent artisanal ice cream, freshly made on the premises.

## Amorino London

⌨ *41 Old Compton Street, W1*
🚌 *Piccadilly Circus LU*
🕐 *Mon-Sat 11am-11pm, Sun 12noon-9pm*

This elegant gelateria and café offers high-quality Italian-style ice cream. There are sophisticated flavours which can be enjoyed in cups, cones or sandwiched in focaccine (brioche buns).

## Cocorino

⌨ *18 Thayer Street, W1*
☎ *020 7935 0810*
🖎 *www.cocorino.co.uk*
🚌 *Bond Street, Marble Arch LU*
🕐 *Mon-Fri 7am-8pm, Sat 8am-8pm*
    *Sun 9am-9pm*

This chic gelateria, a joint venture between restaurateurs Francesco Mazzei and Caroline Yau. It offers an extensive range of seasonally-changing, own-made ice creams, available in tubs, cones or brioche.

## Cremeria Vienna

⌨ *Kiosk 2,*
    *The Spires Shopping Centre, Barnet*
☎ *020 8440 2734*
🚌 *High Barnet LU*
🕐 *Mon-Sat 10.30am-6pm,*
    *Sun 11am-4pm*

A small take-away gelateria offering its own in-house classic gelati, freshly made on the premises. Flavours range from fiordilatte (flower of the milk) to melone (melon).

## Marine Ices

⌨ *8 Haverstock Hill, NW3*
☎ *020 7482 9003*
🚌 *Chalk Farm LU*
🕐 *Tue-Sat 10.30am-11pm,*
    *Sun 11am-10pm*

A gelateria set up by Gaetano Mansi in 1930. He had been a fruiterer and the family myth goes that he began making water-ices from left over fruit. The business prides itself on its range of flavourful Italian ice creams, using ingredients such as dark-roasted Mocha. Grander desserts such as tartufo and cassata Siciliana have traditionally been purchased here for family occasions by London's Italian community.

## Oddono's Gelati

📖 *4 Bute Street, SW7*
☎ *020 7-52 0732*
🚌 *South Kensington LU*
🕐 *Mon-Thur/Sun 11am-11am,*

This smart Italian gelateria offers its own
ice cream, freshly made on the premises.
Flavours range from refreshing sorbets, such
as strawberry, to richer milk-based gelati
including chocolate, nocciola (hazelnut) and
pistachio.
*Branches: Selfridges, 400 Oxford Street, W1*
*(020 7318 3344)*
*Whiteley's, 151 Queensway, W2*
*(020 7792 6023)*

## Scoop

📖 *40 Shorts Gardens, WC2*
☎ *00044 7944779693*
🚌 *Covent Garden LU*
🕐 *Mon-Sun 11am-9pm*

Specialising in its own Italian-style ice cream,
this small gelateria offers sophisticated
flavours such as pinolo (pine nut), crema
Buontalenti (a classic recipe dating back to
Medici Florence) and zabaione, made from
quality ingredients.

*Marine Ices*

Japanese London

Japan Centre

The Japanese presence in London is a comparatively recent phenomenon. Japan's deliberate cultural isolation for hundreds of years was broken down in the seventeenth century by Portuguese traders and missionaries, but contact with the West remained limited. It was during Japan's post-Second World War business boom, as the country restored and developed its economy, that a community developed in London. It is primarily a business community, consisting of families on postings for large companies and banks. The temporary nature of most of these postings has kept the community transitory and relatively rootless. Social life, as in Japan, is conducted largely round the golf course and at business lunches.

It used to be said that the Japanese lived on the Northern Line, which provided access to all their needs, from the City for work to the leafy suburbs of Finchley and Golders Green for housing, with much-valued golf courses nearby. The presence of the Oriental City shopping plaza at Colindale was prompted by the growth of this North London community. The shifting of the Japanese School to Acton, however, has opened up a new area of surburban London for the Japanese community and the Northern Line is no longer the sole axis. Acton's Japanese community are now catered for by two kindergartens and primary schools, as well as Japanese food shops, book shops, property letting agencies and restaurants. The past decade has also seen a growing Japanese presence in the West End, with shops opening specifically to cater for the influx of prosperous Japanese tourists.

# Japanese Cuisine

This highly refined cuisine, which developed in isolation for hundreds of years, is both aesthetic and ascetic. In Japan's codified society, a meticulously disciplined approach governs food preparation as well as other aspects of life. Presentation is all-important: small portions of foods are carefully arranged, delighting both the eye and the palate. Nouvelle cuisine borrowed greatly from Japanese culinary aesthetics.

'Kisetsukan' is the Japanese term for a sympathy with nature, important in Japanese culture. Dishes are designed to echo nature, perhaps creating a miniature landscape or simply a natural gracefulness. A great value is placed on freshness and seasonality. Fish and vegetables, two key foodstuffs, are at their best fresh. Sashimi, raw fish served with a dipping sauce, epitomises this emphasis. Even though modern preserving techniques have robbed seasonality of its practical imperative, it continues to be valued. There is a whole range of dishes, such as cherry blossom rice or oden, eaten in appropriate months and seasons, with even preserved ingredients such as pickles and miso pastes changing according to the time of year. The flavour of individual ingredients is emphasised in the cooking rather than disguised. Even a Japanese stew retains the separate flavours of ingredients rather than blending them into a whole.

The range of seasonings in Japanese food is limited, falling into three broad categories: salty (provided by shoyu and dashi), sweet (from sugar, mirin and sake) and citrus (from yuzu and dai dai fruits). Shiso leaves and sansho provide an extra aromatic touch. These flavourings are used over and over again in different combinations. Pickles are carefully chosen to go with particular dishes. Fish and seafood, as befits a nation of islands, play a large part in the cuisine, from the basic soup stock to fishcakes and sausages. An extenstion of this love of seafood has been the use of seaweeds or sea-vegetables, a hallmark of Japanese cooking.

Many of the unique aspects of Japanese cuisine come from the fact that it developed to a great extent in isolation. However, over centuries, a number of foreign influences filtered through. China, between the sixth and eighth centuries, had an effect on many aspects of Japanese life including food – hence chopsticks, tea, the nutritious soya bean, rice and noodles. Zen Buddhism provided both the aesthetic criteria of Japanese cuisine and the emphasis on vegetables. It was only in the nineteenth century that the Japanese began eating red meat more widely. Certain dishes can be traced directly to outside sources, although most have been refined into something quintessentially Japanese. Portugese missionaries in the sixteenth century are said to have requested gambas fritta, fried prawns. From this developed the dish tempura: whole prawns and slices of vegetables cooked briefly in an exquisitely light batter so that the flavour and freshness of the ingredients are highlighted rather than disguised.

# Glossary

**Agar agar (kanten)** a vegetarian setting agent obtained from seaweed, available either in powdered form or in translucent strands.

**Azuki Beans** small dark red beans. In a sweetened paste form (*an*), they form a principal ingredient in Japanese cakes.

*Dashi-no-moto*

**Bean curd (tofu)** an ivory-coloured soya bean product with a firm custard texture, available either fresh or vacuum-packed. *Kinu* or silk tofu has a more delicate texture than *momen* or cotton tofu. *Koyadofu* is freeze-dried tofu, dull brown with a spongy texture. *Aburage* are thin deep-fried sheets of bean curd.

**Bonito** dried bonito fish flakes, together with kombu seaweed, are used to make dashi soup stock and also as a garnish. *Dashi-no-moto* is an instant granule form of dashi stock, available in packets.

**Burdock (gobo)** a long slender root vegetable, available fresh and canned.

**Chrysanthemum leaves (shungiku):** the leaves of the edible garland chrysanthemum (not to be confused with our ornamental inedible one), used as a garnish and a vegetable.

**Daikon:** a large, long, mild, white radish, also called mooli in greengrocers. Dried daikon strips, called *kiriboshi daikon*, need soaking before use.

**Fish and Seafood:** raw fish, either in sashimi or sushi, is one of the most famous elements of Japanese cuisine. Popular fish include mackerel (*saba*), salmon (*sake*) and tuna (*maguro*), with the latter graded according to its fattiness. Grilled eel (*unagi*) is a prized delicacy. Popular seafood includes abalone (*awabi*), horse clams (*mirugai*), scallops (*hotategai*), salmon roe (*ikura*), octopus (*tako*) and squid (*ika*).

**Fishcakes and fish sausages:** boiled, baked and deep-fried fishcakes and sausages come in various forms, and are often found in the deep freeze section. Popular varieties include: *naruto maki*, a fish sausage with a spiral pink or yellow pattern running through it; *satsuma-age*, oval-shaped fried fishcake; and *chukuwu*, a fish sausage.

**Flours:** rice flour (*joshinko*) is used for savoury doughs. Glutinous rice flour (*mochiko*) and soya bean flour (*kinako*) are used mainly for desserts.

**Gingko nuts (ginnan):** maidenhair tree kernels. Fresh gingko nuts (which need shelling) are ivory-cloured, while tinned, shelled gingko nuts are pale green.

**Kabocha:** Japanese pumpkin, often sold deep-frozen.

*Kabocha*

**Kampyo:** dried gourd or winter melon strips, used for tying food.

**Kinome:** prickly ash tree leaf, used as a garnish.

**Konnyaku:** a bland, glutinous substance made from the root of the devil's tongue plant, often labelled 'alimentary paste' and found in the chilled section or freezer. Konnyaku noodles, called *shirataki* (meaning white waterfall), are sold packaged in water.

**Kuzu:** a white starch made from the kuzu vine root, sometimes labelled 'kuzu arrowroot'.

**Lotus root (renkon):** a crunchy root with a decorative tracery of holes, available fresh, in sausage-like links, or tinned.

**Mirin:** a sweet Japanese rice wine, used as a glazing ingredient.

**Miso:** fermented soya bean paste, available in a variety of colours and flavours. In general, the light miso pastes have a more delicate flavour than the darker ones. It is usually found in the chilled or freezer section and should be stored in the fridge.

**Mochi:** cooked glutinous rice, pounded to a paste.

**Mountain yam (yama no imo):** a large, pale-skinned, sweet-flavoured tuber, which comes in different shapes.

**Mushrooms:** these include large, brown-capped *shitake* (available both fresh and dried), tiny white-capped clusters of *enokidake*, light brown *shimeji* and large, brown *matsutake*.

**Natto:** fermented soya beans with a pungent smell and sticky texture.

**Noodles:** *harusame*, fine cellophane noodles made from mung beans whose Japanese name means 'spring rain'; *soba*, brown buckwheat noodles; *somen*, fine wheatflour noodles, sometimes flavoured with green tea; *udon*, thick, white wheatflour noodles.

*Sabo Noodles*

**Pickles:** *sudori shoga*, pickled ginger, traditionally eaten with sushi; *takuan*, pickled daikon, often bright yellow in colour.

**Ponzu:** a citric vinegar.

**Potato starch (kataturika):** strongly binding sweet potato starch.

**Rice:** short grain, slightly glutinous rice is the staple. A very sticky glutinous 'sweet rice' is used to make desserts and cakes.

**Rice vinegar (su):** delicate rice vinegar, used in making sushi.

**Sake:** rice wine, both drunk and used as a flavouring in cooking.

**Sansho:** known as 'Japanese pepper' this is the seed of the prickly ash tree.

*Seaweed*

**Seaweeds:** *kombu*, a dark large-leafed seaweed used in making dashi stock; *nori*, thin green sheets of dried seaweed used for sushi, available untoasted or toasted; *wakame*, dried lobeleaf seaweed.

**Shichimi togarashi:** a piquant seven-spice mix containing chilli.

**Shiso:** the aromatic red or green leaves of the perilla or beefsteak plant, used to add both flavour and colour.

**Soya beans:** raw soya beans (*edamame*), available frozen, are a poplar snack food. Dried soya beans (*daizu*) need long cooking.

*Shiso*

**Soy sauce (shoyu):** Naturally brewed Japanese soy sauce, available both dark and light, has a different, more subtle flavour than Chinese soy sauce. Kikkoman is a reputable shoyu manufacturer.

**Trefoil (mitsuba):** a leaf herb, often found freeze-dried.

**Umeboshi:** small, deep red, pickled plums, with a tart flavour.

**Warabi:** young edible sprouts of bracken, picked before they have uncurled, available dried or vacuum-packed.

**Wasabi:** a pungent green root, compared to horseradish, sold in paste or powder form.

**Wheat Gluten (fu):** wheat gluten forms, often coloured, used rather like croutons in soups and simmered dishes.

**Yuzu:** an aromatic citrus fruit with a distinctive aroma and taste, used to flavour oil.

*Wasabi*

# Food Shops

Japanese food shops often demand high prices for their stock – something about which the Japanese ex-pat community grumble. Many of the foodstuffs are imported from Japan and all of these are beautifully packaged, from rice-paper packets of ribbon-wrapped noodles to gaudy, wacky packets of sweets, shaped like robots or calculators. Fish and meat counters are a beautiful sight, with finely-sliced meat and aesthetic displays of seafood from gracefully-coiled octopus tendril to a mosaic of mackerel fillets.

In general Japanese food shops are well-ordered, with ingredients grouped together: flavourings, pickles, noodles. Often, the goods have small labels giving the English names.

# Central

## Arigato
- 48-50 Brewer Street, W1
- 020 7287 1722
- Leicester Square, Piccadilly Circus LU
- Mon-Sat 10am-9pm, Sun 11am-8pm

This friendly supermarket and take-away caters for office workers. The stock covers basics from miso paste to soba noodles. The take-away sushi counter is very popular.

## Centre Point Food Store
- 20-21 St Giles High Street, WC2
- .020 7836 9860
- Tottenham Court Road LU
- Mon-Sat 10am-10.30pm, Sun 12noon-8pm

In the shadow of Centre Point's looming tower, the Centre Point Food Store is a large, well-stocked food shop, offering both Japanese and Korean foodstuffs. Stock is comprehensive, including freezers containing Japanese cuts of meat and fish, fresh vegetables and fruit, noodles, miso pastes and flavourings as well as a large choice of snacks and sweets. If the sight of all these Japanese ingredients gives you an appetite, simply head upstairs to the Sushi Café.

## Japan Centre Food Shop
- 14-16 Regent Street, SW1
- 020 3405 1246
- Piccadilly Circus LU
- Mon-Sat 10am-9pm Sun 11am-7pm

Formerly on Piccadilly, the Japan Centre Food Shop has relocated to Regent Street. This smart new food hall offers an extensive range of Japanese foodstuffs, from sashimi at the fresh fish counter to eye-catching Hello Kitty and Totoro buns (filled with red bean paste, chocolate or custard) which are freshly baked in-store. They also stock a wide selection of everyday store cupboard staples as well as sake. Ready-to-eat meals include bento boxes, sushi and desserts and there's a small dining area for those who can't wait. Customers range from those grabbing take-away sushi to those doing their weekly grocery shopping.

## Minamoto Kitchoan

🏠 *44 Piccadilly, W1*
☎ *020 7437 3135*
🚌 *Piccadilly Circus LU*
🕐 *Mon-Fri & Sun 10am-7pm, Sat 10am-8pm*

This dainty shop specialises in Japanese confectionery. These are exquisite-looking concoctions made from red bean paste, rice flour and fruit and bean jelly all of which are tastefully wrapped and packaged. Creations range from white peach jellies to Muscat sorbets, eaten either chilled or frozen. Prices are high – reflecting the fact that these items are traditionally given as gifts. There is a small seating area where you can sit and enjoy green tea and a cake. Particularly recommended is their Tsuya (a soft round pancake filled with red bean paste).

# North

## Atari-Ya Foods

🏠 *15-16 Monkville Parade,*
   *Finchley Road, NW11*
☎ *020 8458 7626*
🚌 *Golders Green LU, then bus 82, 102, 260*
🕐 *Mon-Fri 10am-6.30pm,*
   *Sat-Sun 10am-7pm*

This large, neatly arranged shop is particularly strong on store-cupboard staples such as rice, noodles, seaweeds and condiments but they also have a small fresh fish counter. Sunday's sushi counter is extremely popular with the local Japanese community.

## Atari-Ya Foods

🏠 *595 High Road, N12*
☎ *020 8446 6669*
🚌 *West Finchley LU; Bus 263*
🕐 *Tue-Fri 10am-6.30pm,*
   *Sat-Sun 10am-7pm*

A neat shop dominated by a long fish counter, with the staff behind it expertly preparing the fish. In addition, there is a limited selection of groceries and a small chilled cabinet containing essentials such as fresh tofu.

Japanese Food Shops

## Fuji Foods

- 167 Priory Road, N8
- 020 8347 91770
- Finsbury Park LU, then W7 bus
- Tue-Fri 9.30am-5.30pm
  Sat-Sun 9.30am-5.30pm

This small, immaculate shop offers an excellent range of Japanese foodstuffs, from frozen fish cakes to fresh tofu. Pride of place goes to the fresh fish and sushi counter. It is here that Mr Fuji lovingly and expertly prepares his own sushi rolls including prawn and avocado coated in flying fish roe. He also marinates fish with flavours such as black cod with miso.

## Hello Kitchen

- 10 North End Road, NW11
- 020 8209 3487
- Golders Green LU
- Mon-Sat 10am-8pm, Sun 11am-7pm

Opposite Golders Green tube station, a few doors down from the Japanese Homes letting agency, this friendly shop stocks a good and competitively-priced range of Japanese foodstuffs. In addition to basic foodstuffs the shop does a brisk business with its take-away sushi which is freshly prepared at the back of the shop.

## Wing Yip (London) Ltd

- 395 Edgware Road, NW2
- 020 8450 0422
- Colindale LU
- Mon-Sat 9.30am-7pm,
  Sun 11.30am-5.30pm

This massive Chinese supermarket, located just off Staples Corner, contains all the basics for the Japanese kitchen from noodles to dried seaweed. It also stocks a wide selection of Japanese teas and Sake.

# North-West

## Tetote Factory

- Pacific Plaza, Unit 16, The Junction
  Wembley Retail Park, Engineers Way
  Wembley, HA9
- 020 8903 2559
- Wembley Park
- Mon, Wed-Sun, 10am-6pm

Part of the Pacific Plaze complex, this Japanese bakery offers a chance to sample freshly baked Japanese breads and buns.

# West

## Atari-Ya Foods

🏠 *7 Station Parade, Noel Road, W3*
☎ *020 8896 1552*
🚌 *West Acton LU*
🕐 *Tue 11am-6.30pm,*
*Wed-Fri 10am-6.30pm,*
*Sat 9am-7pm, Sun 10am-7pm*

In West Acton's leafy suburbs, this small corner food shop, is particularly strong on fresh seafood, with stock ranging from dressed crab to black cod and razor clams. Other foods in stock include storecupboard basics and a selection of fresh fruit and vegetables, such as gobo or daikon, displayed outside.

## Natural Natural

🏠 *20 Station Parade, Uxbridge Road, W5*
☎ *020 8992 0770*
🕐 *Mon-Sat 9am-8pm, Sun 9am-7pm*

This friendly, down-to-earth shop caters comprehensively for West London's Japanese community, with stock ranging from fresh fruit and vegetables in boxes outside to shelves of sake, freezers filled with frozen vegetables such as burdock and huge sacks of sushi rice stacked on the floor inside. Take-away foods such as tonkatsu and Japanese cakes are a popular draw with Japanese commuters returning home.

# Eating Places

Once Japanese restaurants in London were exclusive, expensive affairs. With sushi now stocked alongside sandwiches in British supermarkets, Japanese food has now become far more widely available, but the best sushi is still to be found in Japanese foodshops and restaurants. While London boasts a number of extremely elegant and luxurious Japanese restaurants, diners can also choose from casual noodle bars and the popular conveyor-belt sushi restaurants.

# Central

## Abeno  ££

🏠 *47 Museum Street, WC1*
✎ *www.abeno.co.uk*
☎ *020 7405 3211*
🚌 *Holborn LU, Tottenham Court Road LU*

This small, tranquil restaurant offers a chance to sample 'okonomi-yaki' – tasty Japanese pancakes made from a thick batter containing shredded cabbage, and topped with ingredients ranging from meat to seafood. Each okonomi-yaki is freshly cooked to order on a table griddle in front of the diner by polite, friendly staff.
*Branch: Abeno Too, 17-18 Great Newport Street, WC2  (020 7579 1160)*

## Chisou   £££

📖 *4 Princes Street, W1*
☎ *020 7629 3931*
✎ *www.chisou.co.uk*
🚌 *Oxford Circus LU*

A short stroll from Oxford Circus, this established restaurant is a discreet, smart and perpetually buzzing with diners. Quality ingredients, an interesting and extensive menu and friendly attentive service make a winning combination. Popular dishes here include the seared steak with ponzu dressing, deep-fried oysters and sashimi and avocado salad.

## Dinings   £££-££££

📖 *22 Harcourt Street, W1*
☎ *020 7723 0666*
🚌 *Marylebone LU, Rail*

A serene, sophisticated restaurant. Here you can find contemporary, imaginative 'Japanese tapas' dishes, all made from top-notch ingredients.

## Go Chisou   £-££

📖 *3 Princes Street, W1*
☎ *020 7629 0029*
🚌 *Oxford Circus LU*

Aimed at busy lunchtime diners, this branch of Chisou offers take-away sushi rolls, salads and a selection of hot dishes. Seating is available, but limited at lunchtimes.

## Kyoto   ££

📖 *26 Romilly Street, W1*
☎ *020 7734 7622*
🚌 *Leicester Square,*
   *Tottenham Court Road LU*

A cosy informal restaurant offering a range of reasonably-priced, classic Japanese dishes, from sushi and sashimi to tempura soba and chicken teriyaki.

## Satsuma   ££

📖 *56 Wardour Street, W1*
☎ *020 7437 8338*
✎ *www.osatsuma.com*
🚌 *Leicester Square LU,*
   *Piccadilly Circus LU*

From the Wagamama school of refectory-style dining: a sleek, streamlined affair with long wooden tables and benches. Staff are lively and the food, ranging from chicken Teriyaki to sushi, is well-presented and tasty.

## Yoshino   ££-£££

📖 *3 Piccadilly Place, W1*
☎ *020 7287 6622*
✎ *www.yoshino.net*
🚌 *Piccadilly Circus LU*

In a side-street off Piccadilly, this restaurant is noted for the quality of its fresh fish, which can be enjoyed in dishes such as sashimi and sushi platters. The set menus are excellent value and beautifully presented.

## Delicatessen Yoshino   £

*59 Shaftesbury Avenue, W1*

☎ *020 7434 3610*

🚇 *Piccadilly Circus*

In the heart of theatreland, this narrow 'shop' offers Yoshino's excellent, freshly-made and reasonably-priced sushi to go.  The toppings and fillings ranging from eel to avocado.

# North

## Asakusa   ££-£££

*265 Eversholt Street, NW1*

☎ *020 7388 8533*

🚇 *Mornington Crescent*

Warmly recommended by Japanese friends, this shabby-looking restaurant offers evening diners some superb Japanese food at bargain prices. Such is its popularity that booking a table is strongly recommended.

## Café Japan   ££-£££

*626 Finchley Road, NW11*

☎ *020 8455 6854*

🚇 *Golders Green LU*

Small and cramped, this Japanese restaurant has a loyal local following for its reasonably-priced sushi.

## Jin Kichi   £££

*73 Heath Street, NW3*

☎ *020 7794 6158*

✍ *www.jinkichi.com*

🚇 *Hampstead LU*

A friendly, long-established restaurant, specialising in yakitori dishes and so offering a large range of tasty salty-sweet skewered foods including chicken and prawns.

## Sushi-Say   ££££

*33B Walm Lane, NW2*

☎ *020 8459 2971*

🚇 *Willesden Green LU*

In deepest Willesden, Sushi-Say, with its pretty, rustic décor is something of an oasis. It has a considerable regular clientele, drawn back by the delicious, freshly prepared Japanese food and the pleasantly relaxed and convivial atmosphere.

## Tosa   £££-££££

*152 High Road, N2*

☎ *020 8883 8850*

🚇 *East Finchley*

This small, cosy restaurant, a branch of the Hammersmith restaurant (see below) serves up an appetizing range of Japanese dishes, specialising in skewers of ingredients such as chicken liver, quail's eggs and shiitake mushrooms, freshly grilled to order over charcoal.

# West

## Sushi-Hiro  ££
🖼 *1 Station Parade, Uxbridge Road, W5*
☎ *020 8896 3175*
🚌 *Ealing Common LU*

Handily situated just across the road from
the tube station is this spick and span sushi
restaurant, discreetly hidden behind a frosted
glass façade, offering excellent value sushi
either to eat in or take-away.

## Tosa
🖼 *332 King Street W6*
☎ *020 8748 0002)*
🚌 *Ravenscourt Park LU*

A small, friendly restaurant offering sushi,
sashimi and noodles, but particularly noted
for its extensive range of tasty, freshly grilled
skewers of ingredients from offal to fish.

# Cookbooks

## Food of Japan
Shirley Booth
An illuminating look at Japanese cuisine
with recipes and detailed ingredient
information.

## Step-by-Step Japanese Cooking
*Leslie Downer and Minoru Yoneda*
A clear and well written introduction to
Japanese cuisine.

## Easy Sushi
*Emi Kazuko*
An illustrated, accessible guide to the
joys of home-made sushi.

## Harumi's Japanese Cooking
*Harumi Kurihara*
Aimed at demystifying Japanese
cuisine, this is an attractive, appetising
introduction to Japanese cuisine.

## The Heart of Zen Cookery
*Soei Yoneda*
A guide to the centuries-old vegetarian
cuisine of the Zen temples.

*Platters*

The Jewish presence in England dates back to the eleventh century when French Jews followed William the Conqueror and settled here. They were legally restricted to certain trades and professions but moneylending, forbidden to Christians, was allowed, indeed encouraged, and became the basis for a prosperous and established community. Persecution of the Jews grew, however, and in 1290 all Jews were expelled from England by Edward I.

Following the expulsion of Jews from Spain in 1492, some Sephardi Jews (Mediterranean Jews) accepted the Christian faith but continued to practise Judaism in secret. They became known as Marranos and a small community of them settled in London. In 1655 Rabbi Menassah ben Israel, resident in Holland, appealed to Oliver Cromwell to permit Jewish resettlement. In June of the following year Cromwell declared that Judaism would again be permitted in England and a small community of Sephardi merchants, bankers, bullion dealers and gem importers settled in London. The Sephardi community's first synagogue was in a house at Creechurch Lane in the East End. In 1701, when this had become too small, the Bevis Marks synagogue was built – and continues in use to this day.

The Jewish community was also expanded by the immigration of Ashkenazi Jews from Eastern Europe, who followed a different liturgy. In general they were artisans, peasants, tailors and shoemakers. By 1690, they had established their own synagogue in Dukes Place. George I encouraged German Jews to come to England and by the middle of the eighteenth century the Ashkenazi community outnumbered the Sephardi.

Aldgate and Houndsditch were popular Jewish areas, although in the first half of the nineteenth century a move took place among the established and prosperous Jewish families, such as the Rothschilds and Montefiores, who left St Swithins Lane for the fashionable West End. In 1858, a special parliamentary resolution enabled Lionel de Rothschild to take his seat in the House of Commons, which marked a watershed in Jewish emancipation in Britain. During the late nineteenth century middle-class Jews moved into the new suburbs and by 1882, the St John's Wood synagogue was in operation.

For the poorer Jewish immigrants, however, the East End remained the focus. As Stephen Brook puts it in his fascinating book, 'The Club', 'Jews tend to live in enclaves not out of natural

Jewish London

gregariousness but because they want to be close to institutions vital to the life of the community. Religious Jews will not ride or drive on the Sabbath so they wish to live within easy walking distance of a synagogue. They also needed convenient access to Jewish schools (there were seven in existence in 1851) and kosher butchers. Naturally new arrivals tended to join fellow Jews in the areas favoured by those who had arrived before them.'

Following the assassination of the liberal Russian Tsar Alexander II in 1881, a series of pogroms was unleashed in Russia and Poland, which continued into the early twentieth century. Thousands of Jews fled westwards, many aiming for and reaching America, but some staying in Britain instead of continuing their journey. Between 1881 and 1914 the Jewish population of the East End swelled by well over 100,000 people. These were Orthodox, Yiddish-speaking, semi-skilled or unskilled Jews; and the already established Anglo-Jews felt ambivalent about the influx, fearing an anti-Semitic backlash.

The Ashkenazi immigrants moved into the East End, especially around Whitechapel. Food shops sold the herrings and pickles of their homelands and the number of chevras (small synagogues) grew. The United Synagogues established dispersal committees to encourage Jewish immigrants to move out of the East End into the expanding suburbs of Dalston, Stoke Newington and Hackney. In the 1920s there was a move northwards from the East End into Stamford Hill and then into the newly established suburbs of Golders Green, Edgware and Ilford. The rise of anti-Semitism in the 1930s brought in around 70,000 Jews from Central Europe, with the influx increasing sharply after the 1938 Anschluss (unification) with Austria and the Kristallnacht pogrom. These were prosperous middle-class refugees who settled in north-west London in areas such as Hampstead, St John's Wood and Swiss Cottage. The decline of the Jewish East End community was hastened by the war, bombing destroying both families and property. Instead of returning after service or evacuation, many East End Jews opted for the suburbs with their by now well-established Jewish communities. By the 1970s the population of the East End Jewish community had shrunk to less than 5,000; today, around a third of Britain's Jewish population lives in north-west London.

# Jewish Cuisine

Jewish cuisine reflects the widely dispersed Jewish community by containing a range of dishes and styles of cooking from around the world. Two broad and diverse strands stem from the culinary traditions of the Ashkenazi and the Sephardi. The former, influenced by long, cold winters, features preserved and pickled dishes such as rollmop herrings and smoked salmon; while the latter delights in aromatic spices and Mediterranean produce such as aubergines, peppers and olive oil. Common to all Jewish food, however, are the Kashrut, the strict dietary laws governing the preparation and consumption of food, which stem from biblical injunctions. They have been adhered to over the centuries.

Leviticus permits certain fish and meat: 'Any animal that has true hoofs, with clefts through the hoofs, and that chews the cud such you may eat' and 'Anything in water, whether in the seas or in the streams, that has fins and scales these you may eat'.

Cattle, sheep and most fish, therefore, are permitted, but pigs, rabbits and shellfish are not, neither certain birds nor anything that crawls or swarms. Permitted animals and birds must be ritually slaughtered in a way that allows as much blood as possible to drain from the carcass. As the consumption of blood is forbidden, raw meat must be 'koshered' by being soaked in water, treated with salt, drained and then rinsed.

The injunction 'Thou shalt not boil a kid in its mother's milk' has been interpreted to mean that meat and dairy products may not be consumed together. Food containing dairy products may not be eaten after meat until at least three hours have passed. This extends to separating kitchen equipment used for meat products from that for dairy products. 'Pareve' means neutral and refers to foods that may be eaten with either meat or dairy products.

The commandment that 'On the seventh day thou shalt do no

work, neither thy maidservant nor thy manservant' has produced a range of characteristically Jewish dishes that are prepared the day before they are eaten. Cholent is one of the most famous of these dishes: a Sabbath stew traditionally cooked slowly overnight. Harry Blacker, in his book of East End reminiscences Just Like It Was, writes of the cholent being 'carried to the nearest bakehouse, where for a small consideration (about 2 pence), the baker would put the pan in the oven to cook until the following midday'.

Religious festivals also influence Jewish cuisine. At Pesach (Passover), when wheat flour is banned, dishes are made with ground nuts, matzo meal or potato flour. Certain symbolic foods and dishes are eaten both during the weekly Shabbat (Sabbath) and the festivals. During Pesach, which celebrates the Jewish delivery from slavery to the Egyptians, a 'Seder' plate is assembled made up of symbolic ingredients such as haroset, a sweet fruit paste representing the mortar used by Jewish slaves when they worked on the Pharoah's cities, and a bitter herb, such as endive, representing the bitterness endured during slavery. Matzos, the unleavened bread used during Pesach, represents the bread which didn't have time to rise as the Jews fled.

Another element common to Jewish cookery across the continents is its ingenuity, born out of the poverty and lack of ingredients which Jewish communities often suffered. Meat, in particular, was eked out in resouceful dishes such as helzel, stuffed chicken neck skin, and koureven, stewed chicken gizzards.

# Glossary

**Bagels:** circular bread rolls with a distinctive, chewy texture which comes from being first boiled then baked. Increasingly available both plain and flavoured.

*Bagels*

**Bulka:** the 'everyday' cholla loaf, made from the same dough as bagels but shaped differently.

**Cholla:** a symbolic plaited loaf made from an egg-rich dough, and with a brown glaze. It plays a prominent part in most Jewish festivals and is especially associated with Shabbat, the weekly Sabbath.

**Chopped liver:** a tasty mixture of finely chopped liver, onion and hard-boiled egg.

**Falafel:** small, savoury chickpea croquettes, now regarded as an Israeli national dish.

*Herring*

**Gefilte fish:** minced fish balls, either poached or fried.

**Herrings:** a staple fish, preserved by salting or pickling. Chopped herring, a sweet-sour mixture of herrings, onions, apple, sugar and vinegar; rollmops or Bismarcks, pickled herrings rolled around onion rings; schmaltz herrings or matjes, smoked young herrings, often ready-filleted.

**Kreplach:** triangular dumplings with a meat or cheese filling. The three corners symbolise the three patriarchs: Abraham, Isaac and Jacob. These can be found ready-made in freezer sections.

**Latkes:** shredded potato fritters associated with Chanucah.

*Latkes*

**Lokshen:** egg noodles, used in soups and also to make lokshen kugel, a rich baked pudding, traditionally baked overnight for Shabbat.

**Mandlen**: from Yiddish for 'almonds', these are fried or baked dough 'soup nuts', used like croutons as a garnish.

**Matzos**: a flat unleavened bread, similar in texture and taste to a water biscuit. It is the main element in Passover cookery, which forbids the use of leavened grain. The entire process of matzo-making must take no longer than 18 minutes, otherwise fermentation may start.

*Matzos*

**Matzo balls (knaidlach)**: walnut-sized, matzo-meal dumplings.

**Matzo meal**: a binding element made from finely ground matzos.

**Rye bread**: bread made from rye, with a distinctively rich flavour.

**Salt beef**: boiled and pickled beef, usually brisket. Available freshly-made or in packets.

**Smoked salmon (lox)**: smoked salmon has its origins in London's nineteenth-century Jewish community, who brought the tradition of smoking fish to preserve it with them from Poland and Russia. Until the 1970s and the advent of salmon farming, wild Scottish salmon was used, with this luxurious food finding an appreciative audience both within and outside London'Jewish community. Today, smoked salmon continues to be popular within the Jewish community, with smoked salmon bagels a bakery bestseller.

# Food Shops

The food shop has always been important in Jewish life, both to satisfy religious dietary needs and as a focus of identity. The food that we find in Jewish shops in Britain is predominantly Ashkenazi rather than Sephardi. In 'East End Story', A. B. Levy remembers the aromas that 'wafted through the open fronts of delicatessen shops, from smoked salmon and roe, barrelled cucumbers and sauerkraut, and herrings in various guises, kippered, schmaltz, chopped and pickled.' These items continue to be familiar Jewish deli fare but nearly all the East End shops have gone and the delicatessens are now found in the North London suburbs.

Perhaps what is most baffling for a non-Jew are the varying degrees of kosherness. The Kashrut are strict dietary laws which govern the preparation and consumption of foods. Certain food shops display certificates to show that they are supervised or licensed by authorities such as the Kedassia, the Joint Kashrus Committee of the Union of Orthodox Hebrew Congregations, the Adam Yisroel Synagogue and the Golders Green Beth Hamedrash Congregation. These are the shops and eating places that I have called 'kosher' in my guide, but readers should satisfy themselves as to the standards of Kashrut observed. Some shops have a large range of kosher foodstuffs without being supervised while others carry a range of non-kosher Jewish foods. Kosher food, nowadays, is an increasingly sophisticated business and the range of kosher items available has increased enormously, from tandoori chicken to champagne.

# North

## Adafina

- 67 Abbey Road
- 020 7624 2013
- www.adafina.co.uk
- St John's Wood LU
- Mon-Thur 8.30am-7pm,
  Fri 8.30am-3 hours before Shabbat

Pleasantly light and airy, contemporary kosher food shop. It does a popular range of smartly-packaged in-house traiteur dishes, including the eponymous adafina (a Sephardi stew of slow-cooked beef and potatoes) and fish tagine. There is also an extensive stock of good quality deli items and groceries.

## La Boucherie (Kosher) Ltd

- 4 Cat Hill, East Barnet, EN4
- 020 8449 9215
- NewBarnet rail
- Mon 8.30am-2.30pm, Tue-Thur
  8.30am-5pm, Fri 8am-1pm, Sun
  8.30am-1.30pm and 3.30pm-7.30pm

This vast, scrupulously clean shop is one of London's leading kosher butchers and always bustles with customers. There are 40 staff altogether, including six chefs working behind the scenes on ready-made dishes such as Beef Wellington and the kofte kebabs for which La Boucherie is famous.

## Carmelli Bakeries

- 128 Golders Green Road, NW11
- 020 8455 3063
- Golders Green LU
- Mon-Wed 7am-1am, Thur all night,
  Fri 7am-2pm, Sat all night through to
  Sun 11pm

Smart and glitzy, this famous kosher bakery continues to attract crowds of customers. Noted for its bagels, it also offers a host of breads, cakes, pastries, quiches and biscuits. It is divided into a Pareve or 'non-milky' counter and a 'milky' counter. Visitors get a glimpse behind the scenes which bustles with bakers producing the goods.

## J. A. Corney Ltd

- 9 Hallswelle Parade
  Finchley Road, NW11
- 020 8455 9588
- Golders Green LU
- Tue-Thur 7.30am-5pm, Fri 7.30am-4pm,
  Sat-Sun 7.30am-1pm

This well-established fishmonger's has been in the Corney family for decades. It stocks a large range of fish, such as St Peter's fish and carp and Jewish specialities such as minced fish (a mix of haddock, whiting and bream). They will also mince more expensive fish minced on request. Staff are friendly and knowledgeable.

Jewish Food Shops

## Daniel's Bagel Bakery

⌖ *13 Halleswelle Parade*
*Finchley Road, NW11*
☎ *020 8455 5826*
🚌 *Golders Green LU*
🕐 *Sun-Wed 7am-9pm, Thur 7am-10pm,*
*Fri 7am-1½ hours before Shabbat*

A busy kosher bakery noted for its top-notch bagels as well as its good range of cholla, rye bread, pitta breads and pastries.

## The Grapevine

⌖ *94 Brent Street, NW4*
☎ *020 8202 2631*
🚌 *Hendon Central LU*
🕐 *Mon-Wed 9am-6pm, Thur 9am-8pm*
*Fri 9am-4pm Sun 10am-2pm*

This well-stocked kosher off-licence sells kosher wines from all over the world. They stock Kiddush, the sweet red wine used for sacramental purposes and Israeli wines.

## Greenspans

⌖ *9-11 Lyttelton Road, N2*
☎ *020 8455 7709*
🚌 *East Finchley LU*
🕐 *Mon-Thur & Sun 8.30am-5.15pm*
*Fri 8.30am-1pm*

This roomy kosher butchers offers a fresh meat counter and a range of frozen ready meals. It's particularly noted for its own-cooked meats, including salt beef.

## Hendon Bagel Bakery

⌖ *35-37 Church Road, NW4*
☎ *020 8203 6919*
🚌 *Hendon Central LU*
🕐 *Mon-Thur 7am-11pm, Fri 8am-3pm*
*Sat 7pm until Sun 11pm*

A well-established and popular kosher bakery, selling bulka, dark and light rye breads, pretzels and a wide choice of bagels.

## Panzer's

⌖ *13-19 Circus Road, NW8*
☎ *020 7722 8162/8596*
✎ *www.panzers.co.uk*
🚌 *St John's Wood LU*
🕐 *Mon-Fri 8am-7pm, Sat 8am-6pm,*
*Sun 8am-2pm*

Warmly recommended by Evelyn Rose, the doyenne of Jewish cookery, this large bustling delicatessen has been established since 1955. Peter Vogel now carries on the family tradition. In its range and depth of stock, Panzer's is more like a supermarket than a deli, stocking everything from Swiss Miss chocolate mallows (for the area's ex-pat American community) to Israeli wine. Although not supervised, there is a large selection of kosher lines plus traditional Jewish foodstuffs. The large deli-counter offers six types of herring and four grades of smoked salmon among its delicacies. Panzer's smoked salmon bagels are a must.

## Platters

🏠 *10 Halleswelle Parade*
   *Finchley Road, NW11*
☎ *020 8455 7345*
🚌 *Golders Green LU*
   *then bus 82, 102, 260*
🕐 *Mon-Sat 8.30am-4.30pm,*
   *Sun 8.30am-2pm*

This friendly shop is still run by the Platters family. It offers a range of fresh, own-made, classic Jewish deli fare, from moreish fried gefilte fish to chopped liver. A highlight is the hand-carved smoked salmon, skillfully sliced by octigenarian Len.

# North-West

## Ivor Silverman

🏠 *4-5 Canons Corner*
   *London Road, Stanmore, Middlesex*
☎ *020 8958 8682/2692*
🚌 *Stanmore LU*
🕐 *Mon 8am-3pm, Tue-Wed 7,30am-6pm,*
   *Thur 7.30am-7pm, Fri 8am-1pm,*
   *Sun 8am-3pm.*

An elegant and upmarket kosher butcher-cum-deli. The butcher part of the shop offers freshly-cut meat and poultry and a large range of prepared meat dishes. Next door at the deli is a range of Jewish specialities such as chopped liver, latkes and delicious salt beef

# East

## Brick Lane Beigel Bake

🏠 *159 Brick Lane, E1*
☎ *020 7729 0616*
🚌 *Liverpool Street LU/Rail*
🕐 *Daily 24 hours*

This small, down-to-earth bakery is a reminder of the East End's Jewish history. Piled high with bagels and chollas, it remains popular with trendy shoppers and London cabbies alike.

# MAIL ORDER

## Forman & Field

🏠 *30a Marshgate Lane, E15*
☎ *020 85252 352*
✏ *www.formanandfield.com*

Founded in 1905, H. Forman is the last surviving East End smokery. Very much an artisanal business, with the fish hand rather than machine-filleted. Forman's is noted for the quality and freshness of its smoked salmon and famous for its luxurious wild smoked salmon.

# Eating Places

## Central

### Bevis Marks Restaurant  £££-££££

🏠 *4 Heneage Lane, EC3*
☎ *020 7283 2220*
🖊 *www.bevismarkstherestaurant.com*
🚌 *Aldgate, Liverpool Street LU*

An elegant kosher establishment, next to the historic Bevis Marks synagogue. It offers a stylish modern take on classic Jewish foods such as salt beef and chicken soup.

### Nosh Bar  £

🏠 *39 Great Windmill Street, W1*
☎ *020 7734 5638*
🚌 *Piccadilly Circus LU*

In the heart of theatreland, on the site of Phil Rabin's original, much-loved Nosh Bar, this retro-style bar has revived the tradition, serving hot salt beef sandwiches.

## North

### Aviv  £££

🏠 *87 High Street, HA8*
☎ *020 8952 2484*
🚌 *Edgware LU*

A well-established kosher restaurant that specialises in Israeli food. For this reason there is a definite Middle Eastern flavour to the menu which offers mezze (including excellent houmous) and grilled meats.

### Blooms  £££

🏠 *130 Golders Green Road, NW11*
☎ *020 8455 1338*
🚌 *Golders Green LU*

Opened in 1965, this Golders Green institution has survived its better-known Whitechapel counterpart and continues to serve traditional kosher Jewish food. The salt beef is famous and the portions are generous. A great place to enjoy the comfort of homely Jewish food.

### Dizengoff  £££

🏠 118 Golders Green Road, NW11
☎ 020 8458 7003
🚌 Golders Green LU

This popular eaterie offers Sephardi food, such as Israeli grills and fresh salads.

### Harry Morgan's  £££

🏠 *31 St John's Wood High Street, NW8*
☎ *020 7722 1869*
🚌 *St John's Wood LU*

Dapper, well-established restaurant offering all the classics including chicken noodle soup with dumplings, salt beef and latkes.

# Cookbooks

## Jewish Cooking from Around the World
*Josephine Bacon*
A lively and accessible cookbook exploring both Sephardi and Ashkenazi cooking.

## The Jewish Holiday Cookbook
*Gloria Kaufner Greene*
An informative look at Jewish festival and holiday dishes.

## The Book of Jewish Food
*Claudia Roden*
A fascinating and absorbing study of Jewish food around the world, taking in both Sephardi and Ashkenazi traditions.

## The Complete International Jewish Cookbook
*Evelyn Rose*
An excellent basic and reliable cookbook by a doyenne of Jewish cookery.

## New Jewish Cuisine
*Evelyn Rose*
A straightforward book of Jewish recipes.

## The Jewish Heritage Cookbook
*Marlena Spieler*
A well-illustrated cookbook filled with appetising recipes, including classics like gefilte fish, hamantashen and chopped eggs and onion.

Middle Eastern London

*Persepolis*

The Middle Eastern community in London comprises several nationalities, drawn here at different times and for varying reasons. The Egyptians came to Britain in the 1940s and 1950s, both for education and work. The oil boom in the 1970s and the discovery by Arab countries of new sources of wealth and power resulted in an increasingly wealthy Arab presence in London, mainly focused around Mayfair and Kensington. A series of political disturbances has also contributed considerably to the Middle Eastern presence here. The overthrow of the Shah and the Iranian revolution brought in an influx of wealthy Iranian families who were able to use their money and connections to escape, many to America but some to London. They were followed by political opponents of the Ayatollah, seeking refuge. The civil war in Lebanon resulted in a substantial Lebanese presence in London. Edgware Road, Bayswater, Mayfair, Knightsbridge and Kensington together form the heartland of the Middle Eastern community, served by a splendid assortment of restaurants, fruit juice bars, cafés, banks, shops and clubs.

The Turkish community (which is included in this chapter because of the Ottoman Empire's culinary influence on Middle Eastern cuisine) is predominantly Turkish-Cypriot; many came to Britain because they were displaced following the Turkish invasion of Cyprus in 1974. For some time the community was largely based in Islington, Hackney and Haringey, with the Stoke Newington end of Green Lanes being a particular focal point. Many of the cafés and kebab houses remain male preserves, with the sound of backgammon being played behind the scenes.

# Middle Eastern Cuisine

This is an ancient cuisine, whose recipes can be traced back hundreds of years. An Egyptian recipe for melokhia soup, for example, dates from the time of the Pharoahs. The former spice routes which passed through the Middle East have left a fragrant legacy in the region's cooking.

Claudia Roden, an authoritative and knowledgeable writer on Middle Eastern cookery, identifies four main strands: Iranian or Persian, Arab, Ottoman Turkish and North African. Iranian cuisine is subtle and refined, a product of ancient Persia. Rice forms the heart of the cuisine and is carefully cooked and exquisitely garnished. The combination of meat with fruit or nuts is a hallmark of the Persian kitchen, shown in dishes such as koresh-e-fesenjan, chicken in walnut and pomegranate sauce. Arab cuisine is very flavourful, using strong-tasting herbs such as mint and coriander and fragrant spices such as cardamom, cinnamon and allspice. Grilled meats are popular, served with rice, burghul or flat breads.

During the Ottoman Empire, Turkish cuisine reached luxurious heights. Cooking at the Topkapi Palace in Istanbul followed rules, still followed by chefs today. Ottoman food was spread through the Empire by the army, with shish kebab said to date back to when Turkish soldiers cooked over their camp fires. This culinary legacy includes stuffed vegetables, such as imam bayaldi (an aubergine dish named after a priest who swooned with delight upon trying it); and layered nutty pastries in sweet syrups, beloved throughout the Middle East. North African cooking, in contrast, has a fiery element, produced by hot sauces such as harissa. It is also a cuisine of subtle and delicate spicing.

The influence of Islam means that certain dietary laws are observed throughout the Middle East. Pork is forbidden and meat must be ritually slaughtered. Lamb is the most highly-prized meat throughout the region. Yoghurt is widely used: as a refreshing drink, in hot and cold soups, and in salads and marinades.

# Glossary

**Allspice:** round berry, similar to peppercorns, with a flavour of nutmeg, cinnamon and cloves.

*Apricot paste sheets*

**Apricot paste sheets (amretin):** translucent orange sheets made from apricots which, when diluted with water, make a refreshing drink. Especially popular during the fasting month of Ramadan.

**Arab bread (khoubz):** flat round bread

**Barberries (zerezhk):** small, tart, red berries, used dried in Iranian cooking to add colour and flavour.

*Barberries*

**Burghul (bulgar):** parboiled, cracked grains of wheat, available both coarse or finely ground.

**Coriander:** a flat-leafed green herb, similar in appearance to flat-leafed parsley but with a distinctive sharp taste.

**Couscous:** fine yellow cereal made from semolina.

**Dibbis:** thick, dark brown syrup made from dates.

**Dill:** a caraway-scented herb with fine, feathery green fronds.

*Dried limes*

**Dried limes (limoo):** hard, brown, dried limes, used to add a distinctive flavour to Iranian and Iraqi soups and stews.

**Dried mulberries:** mulberries are prized in Iranian cuisine, with sweet-tasting, honey-coloured. dried mulberries sold loose or packaged.

**Filo:** paper-thin fine pastry usually found frozen but occasionally available fresh.

**Freekeh:** roasted green wheat.

**Golpar:** Persian hogwart, available in seed form or ground. Valued for its anti-flatulence properties, the seeds are used in pickling while golpar powder is sprinkled over pulses.

**Harissa:** a fiery, red pimento paste.

*Dried mulberries*

**Kashk:** stony lumps of pungent dried buttermilk, used in soups and stews. Also available in powdered form.

**Konafa (kadaif):** a vermicelli-like dough, white in its raw state but resembling shredded wheat once cooked.

**Labne (lebne):** thick, strained concentrated yoghurt (usually sold bottled) which has been shaped into balls, and floats in oil.

**Mahlab:** small, pale brown seeds which are the kernels of blackcherry stones, with a spicy fragrance.

**Melokhia:** a green, leafy vegetable, similar in appearance to mallow, used in making a famous eponymous Egyptian soup. Fresh melokhia is sometimes found, while dried is readily available.

**Merguez:** a spicy sausage from North Africa.

**Okra:** tapering, ridged green pods, available fresh, dried, tinned or frozen.

**Onion seeds (sharmar):** small, black teardrop-shaped seeds, not related to onions!

**Orange–flower water**: a fragrant flavouring made from orange flower essence, used in sweets, drinks and desserts.

**Orange peel:** fine strips of dried orange peel, traditionally from sour (Seville) oranges.

**Pine nuts:** small, ivory-coloured kernels, with the fine, long Lebanese pine nuts being particularly prized.

**Pistachio:** a small, green-coloured nut, indigenous to Iran.

*Nibbed pistachios*

*Pomegranate*

**Pomegranate syrup (pomegranate molasses):** made from the concentrated juice of sour pomegranates and used in Iranian cooking.

**Pulses:** black-eyed beans, with characteristic black markings; chickpeas, rounded yellow peas; Egyptian brown beans (ful), small brown broad beans.

**Quince:** a hard yellow-skinned fruit, resembling a large, craggy pear. Usually cooked, whereupon its flesh turns pink.

**Rice:** long-grain rice is a Middle Eastern staple. Fine quality Iranian rice is hard to get over here, with Basmati rice being the closest substitute.

**Rose water:** an essential scented flavouring made from rose essence and used in sweets and desserts.

*Quince*

**Saffron:** a costly spice made from the stigmas of a particular crocus variety, sold in thread or powdered form.

**Salep:** a thickening agent made from dried, crushed orchid roots, used in Iran to thicken ice cream.

**Sumac:** a dark red powdery spice, made from crushed berries, with a tangy flavour. Sometimes diluted and used as a lemon juice equivalent.

**Tahini:** sesame seed paste.

**Tamarind:** a brown pod with sour, dark brown, pulpy flesh and seeds. Available in de-seeded pulp form or as a paste. Also used to make a syrup, which is then diluted into a refreshing drink.

**Turmeric:** an orange-fleshed root, usually sold in its ground form as a yellow-orange powder. It has a harsh, flat taste and is used to add flavour and a distinctive yellow colour to dishes.

**Vine leaves:** large, distinctively shaped leaves of the vine. Occasionally found fresh, but more usually sold in packets, preserved in brine, when they require soaking in water.

**Yoghurt:** tangy sheep's and goat's yoghurt as well as cow's yoghurt is widely used in Middle Eastern cooking.

**Zahtar:** a spice mix made from thyme, salt, sumac and sometimes roasted sesame seeds, often baked on the top of breads.

# Food Shops

Attractive greengrocers-cum-delis selling everything from bunches of fresh herbs to pretty pastries, as well as bakers and halal butchers – all serve the Middle Eastern community in London. Bustling Edgware Road is lined with Middle Eastern grocers, cafés and restaurants and is well worth exploring if you're at all interested in Middle Eastern food. Drive along the road late at night and you'll observe a lively, metropolitan scene with drivers pulling in to get a take-away kebab and people sitting on pavement tables watching the world go by.

## Central

### Comptoir Libanais
🖼 *66 Wigmore Street, W1*
☎ *020 7935 1110*
🚌 *Marble Arch LU*
🕐 *Mon-Fri 8am-8pm, Sat-Sun 10am-8pm*
This attractive, funky café comes complete with a deli section. On offer are a mouthwatering range of Middle Eastern goodies such as rose syrup, pomegranate molasses and harissa. The café counter also offers freshly baked breads, such as green and black olive bread and a delectable rage of pastries.

### Green Valley
🖼 *36 Upper Berkeley Street, W1*
☎ *020 7402 7385*
🚌 *Marble Arch LU*
🕐 *Daily 8am-10pm*
Warmly recommended by cookery writer Claudia Roden, this spacious Lebanese shop, just off the Edgware Road, has an eye-catching array of pastries. Stock is impressively comprehensive: fresh produce, groceries, a halal meat counter notably strong on offal and an in-house bakery with a baker industriously producing freshly-baked flat-breads and a traiteur counter offering superb mezze to take-away. Customers with a sweet tooth are well-catered for by the ice-cream counter, pastry counter and a huge assortment of sweet meats.

## North

### Antepliler
🖼 *47 Grand Parade, Green Lanes, N4*
☎ *020 8809 1004*
🚌 *Manor House LU*
🕐 *Daily 8am-10pm*
Bright and cheery, this bakery and café is famous for its high quality Turkish pastries. Truly luxurious nut-filled, syrup-laden con-coctions, delicious with coffee or mint tea.
*Branch: 33A Newington Green, N16 (020 7226 9409)*

## Fio's Food Centre

🗋 *1338-1340 High Road, N20*

☎ *020 8445 4155*

🕘 *Daily 6am-11pm*

This huge, spacious store offers a range of Mediterranean and Middle Eastern ingredients. Stock ranges from fresh vegetables and fruit and halal lamb to an extensive range of pulses, store-cupboard ingredients and spices.

## Hormuz

🗋 *5 Ashbourne Parade*
   *Temple Fortune, Finchley Road, NW11*

☎ *020 8455 8184*

🚌 *Golders Green LU, then bus 82, 102, 260*

🕘 *Daily 9am-9pm*

Next door to an Iranian bookshop of the same name, this neatly arranged Iranian grocery is recommended by Claudia Roden as having "a lot of good things". Inside there is a pleasing cross-section of Iranian foodstuffs: jams (including barberry), teas, pulses, flower waters and syrups, pastries, pickles and dairy products.

## Phoenicia

🗋 *186-188 Kentish Town Road, NW5*

☎ *020 7267 1267*

🚌 *Kentish Town LU/Rail*

🕘 *Mon-Sat 9am-8pm, Sun 11am-4pm*

This large, bright, halal food hall was deliberately named Phoenicia by its owner Ghassan to reflect its Mediterranean stock. Foodstuffs here range comprehensively across the Mediterranean, so Italian pasta can be found beside couscous and Bulghur wheat, assorted Lebanese and Iraqi flatbreads nestle alongside ciabatta. One side of Phoenicia is a café, with a counter laden with Lebanese pastries (baklava and mamoul), a nut counter and Italian ice creams as well as a sandwich bar. Customers stock up on everything from halal meat from the butcher's counter to fruit syrups and juices. Shopping here is helped by the customer car park behind the shop.

## Sahand

🗋 *74 Ballards Lane, N3*

☎ *020 8343 3279*

🚌 *Finchley Central LU*

🕘 *Mon-Sat 8am-10.30pm, Sun 9am-9pm*

This small, neatly arranged Iranian food shop offers a useful cross-section of Iranian ingredients: packets of tea, bottles of scented waters and syrups, pulses and an array of pastries. The courteous manager is happy to offer advice.

## Super Persia

⌨ *621 Holloway Road, N19*

☎ *020 7272 2665*

🕐 *Mon-Sat 7am-11pm, Sun 10am-4pm*

Adding a touch of colour to Holloway Road, this bright shop is cheerfully decked out with plastic fruits and Astroturf by the fresh fruit and veg outside. Inside the shop is full of Iranian foodstuffs, from fresh cakes and pastries to frozen vegetables. Iranian music is played and staff are friendly.

## Turkish Food Centre

⌨ *363 Fore Street, N9*

☎ *020 8807 6766*

🚌 *Edmonton Green rail*

🕐 *Daily 8am-10pm*

A branch of the established Turkish supermarket chain

## Turkish Food Centre

⌨ *678-682 High Road, N17*

☎ *020 8808 6664*

🚌 *Seven Sisters LU*

🕐 *Daily 8am-10pm*

A branch of the established Turkish supermarket chain.

## Turkish Food Centre

⌨ *542-544 Lordship Lane, N22*

☎ *020 8365 8846*

🚌 *Wood Green LU*

🕐 *Daily 8am-10pm*

A branch of the established Turkish supermarket chain.

## Yasar Halim

⌨ *493-495 Green Lanes, N4*

☎ *020 8340 8090*

🚌 *Manor House LU*

🕐 *Mon 8am-9.30pm, Tue-Sun 8am-10pm*

A veteran establishment. This bustling Turkish food store usefully combines a bakery, greengrocer's, deli and halal meat counter. Here one can find anything from fresh green almonds and spanking fresh flat-leafed parsley to tubs of sheep's yoghurt and jars of quince jam. The bakery here remains a bustling focal point, with customers queueing up for the freshly baked, round loaves of village bread. The sweet and savoury pastries such as guzleme, baked on the premises and sold still warm from the oven are also very popular.

## Yasar Halim

⌨ *2A Hedge Lane, N13*

☎ *020 8882 3100*

🚌 *Palmers Green Rail*

🕐 *Mon-Sat 8am-10pm, Sun 10am-4pm*

This Palmers Green branch of the established Green Lanes store offers an extensive range of stock, from keenly-priced fresh fruit and vegetables to an impressive array of olives.

Middle Eastern Food Shops

# West

## Bahar Patisserie

🏠 *349 Kensington High Street, W8*
☎ *020 7603 5083*
🚌 *High Street Kensington LU*
🕐 *Daily 8.30am-9pm*

A bright, cheery Iranian food shop, with stock ranging from fresh fruit and vegetables to sweet pastries.

## Damas Gate

🏠 *81 Uxbridge Road, W12*
☎ *020 8743 5116*
🚌 *Shepherd's Bush*
🕐 *Daily 9am-9.30pm*

This bustling, down-to-earth, Middle Eastern store offers an impressive range of ingredients. Outside is an eye-catching display of fruit and vegetables, from apricots and peaches to aubergines and peppers. Inside stock includes halal meat, grains, pulses, nuts and sweetmeats and an extensive range of breads – including flatbreads and injeera.

## Lebanese Food Centre

🏠 *153 The Vale, W3*
☎ *020 8740 7365*
🚌 *Acton Central Rail*
🕐 *Daily 8am-10pm*

A large friendly shop resembling a small supermarket, complete with a halal meat counter and an adjoining kebab restaurant. The stock is strong on basics such as pulses, spices and dried herbs with a small selection of fresh fruit and vegetables outside on the pavement.

## Le Marrakech

🏠 *64 Golborne Road, W10*
☎ *020 8964 8307*
🚌 *Ladbroke Grove LU*
🕐 *Mon-Sat 8.30am-7.30pm*
   *Sun 10am-4pm*

An attractive front-of-shop display of earthenware tagines indicates this food shop's Moroccan roots. Inside, there are delights such as olives with kumquats, pomegranate molasses and pickled lemons. Cookware includes couscoussiers and gilded tea-glasses. Lanterns, chandeliers and wall-hangings create something of a bazaar atmosphere – compounded on my visit by one of the staff pulling out a box of Moroccan leather slippers and offering them to an interested punter.

## Reza Patisserie

📠 *345 Kensington High Street, W14*
☎ *020 7602 3674*
🚌 *Kensington High Street LU*
🕐 *Daily 8.30am-9pm*

This long-established shop, reputedly the first Iranian food shop in London, is still going strong. A tempting assortment of freshly-baked pastries are on offer here, including both Arabic pastries, characterised by nuts and syrup, and Iranian pastries, which are simpler and more subtle. The freezer contains Iranian ice creams, flavoured with rose water and saffron, while the shelves carry an array of nuts, sweetmeats and dried fruit, such as Iranian sour cherries.

## Sara Super Market

📠 *7 Hereford Road, W2*
☎ *020 7229 2243*
🚌 *Bayswater LU, Notting Hill Gate LU, Queensway LU*
🕐 *Daily 8am-11pm*

Tucked away down a side-street, Massooud's small, neat, friendly shop offers fresh fruit and vegetables such as pomegranates and sour cherries and a selection of Iranian basics including nuts, cheeses, pickles and syrups. In addition, the shop is famous within Britain's Iranian community for its stock of Iranian music (both classical and popular) and films.

Persepolis

## Zaman

🖵 *347-349 High Street Kensington, W8*
☎ *020 7603 8909*
🚎 *Kensington High Street LU*
🕒 *Daily 9am-10pm*

'Iranian Caviar' says the awning on this attractive shop, signalling one of the many delicacies to be found within. A colourful fresh fruit and vegetable display in front of the shop, includes seasonal treats such as hand-picked pomegranate kernels, mild-flavoured, fresh pistachios and sweet lemons. Stock includes an eye-catching self-service counter of nuts, seeds and dried fruit such as mulberries and figs, a chilled cabinet with labne and yoghurt drinks and an assortment of pickles with their characteristic sour scent. Non-edible items on sale include inlaid backgammon boards, splendid Iranian teapots and tea-glasses and a basement room of CDs and tapes. Popular Iranian music is played in the store adding to the atmosphere of the place.

## Super Masoud

🖵 *9A Hammersmith Road, W14*
☎ *020 7602 1090*
🚎 *Olympia LU*
🕒 *Daily 10am-10pm*

This down-to-earth Iranian food shop offers fresh produce at the front and range of basic foodstuffs inside.

# South

## Tas EV

- 97-99 Isabella Street, SE1
- ☎ 020 7620 6191
- 🚌 Waterloo LU/Rail
- 🕐 Mon-Fri 7.30am-10pm,
  Sat 8.30am-10pm, Sun 8.30am-8.30pm

Spectacularly housed in a railway arch, this stylish delicatessen and café stocks a huge range of Turkish foodstuffs. The in-house bakery produces a range of breads, including traditional' pide' – a flatbread.

# South-East

## Persepolis

- 28-30 Peckham High Street. SE15
- ☎ 020 7639 8007
- 🚌 Peckham Rye Rail
- 🕐 Mon-Sun 10.33am-9.59pm

A jaunty yellow façade signals this cheerful Iranian delicatessen, run with exuberance and panache by Sally Butcher, who, together with her Iranian husband Jamshid, also runs a business importing Iranian food. The stock here is impressive, from Iranian pastries, flavoured with rosewater, and smoked sturgeon to pomegranate molasses and dried soured cherries. This is a wonderfully personal shop, with Sally's humorous handwritten notes about ingredients, Persian customs and advice adorning the shelves. In addition to the food stock, there's a tempting display of Persian homewares, films and music. Sally herself is the author of a great Persian cookbook, Persia in Persepolis, and is happy to answer give advice.

## Turkish Food Centre

- 163-165 Bromley Road, SE6
- ☎ 020 8698 9880
- 🚌 Catford Bridge Rail
- 🕐 Daily 8am-10pm

A spacious branch of the well-established Turkish supermarket.

# South-West

## Del' Aziz

- 24-28 Vanston Place, SW6
- ☎ 020 7386 0086
- 🚌 Fulham Broadway Rail
- 🕐 Mon-Sat 7am-8pm, Sun 8am-6pm

Dominating a Fulham side-street, Del'Aziz is an eye-catching operation with colourful displays of Moroccan ceramic tableware and an appetising range of patisserie and sweets. Inside, Del'Aziz operates as a deli and café, with a central dining area and a long counter, offering own-cooked dishes. Diners sit surrounded by a picturesque assortment of foodstuffs, including confectionery, preserves and oils.

## Mediterranean Food Centre

- 45 A & B Streatham Hill, SW2
- 020 8678 1385
- Streatham Hill Rail
- Daily 6am-1am

This large corner store serves the local community by offering, as its sign declares, 'English, Turkish, Greek, West Indian Food'. Fresh fruit and vegetables include quinces and pumpkins alongside chow-chows and yams. The comprehensive stock also features pulses, dairy products, dried fruit, nuts and spices. Next door is the bakery, selling freshly baked pide and they also have a halal butcher's counter.

# East

## Turkish Food Centre

- 89 Ridley Road, E8
- 020 7254 6754
- Dalston Junction Rail
- Daily 8am-10pm Summer; 8am-9pm Winter

A large, down-to-earth, competitively-priced Turkish supermarket. Stock ranges from an ample selection of fresh fruit and vegetables to an impressive assortment of nuts.

## Turkish Food Centre

- 647-66 High Road, E11
- 020 8558 8149
- Leytonstone LU
- Daily 8am-10pm Summer; 8am-9pm Winter

A large branch of the Turkish supermarket chain, which carries an extensive, keenly-priced range of foodstuffs.

# Eating Places

London's thriving Middle Eastern restaurants cater very much for the ex-pat community and therefore standards are generally high. The range is such that you can enjoy simple but good street food, such as a tasty lamb kebab washed down with freshly squeezed fruit juice, or a leisurely meal of sophisticated Lebanese mezze in elegant surroundings.

## Central

### Al–Hamra   ££££
📠 *31-33 Shepherd Market, W1*
☎ *020 7493 1954*
🚌 *Green Park LU*

Elegant décor, efficient service and fine Lebanese food combine in one of London's best-known Lebanese restaurants, with prices reflecting the affluent location. The mezze are superb (including delights such as walnut-stuffed baby aubergines). Unfortunately the atmosphere and service can be on the chilly side.

### Al Sultan   ££££
📠 *51-52 Hertford Street, W1*
☎ *020 7408 1155*
🚌 *Green Park LU*

This intimate, upmarket Lebanese restaurant is an excellent place in which to sample quality mezze. Among the dishes is as smooth-as-silk hummus Shawarma, topped with pine nuts and tender pieces of lamb.

### Ali Baba   ££
📠 *32 Ivor Place, NW1*
☎ *020 7723 5805*
🚌 *Baker Street LU*

This modest café, with its bargain-priced food, is recommended by Claudia Roden for its 'real Egyptian' food. The melokhia and falafel are particular recommended.

### Comptoir Libanais   £-££
📠 *66 Wigmore Street, W1*
☎ *020 7935 1110*
🚌 *Marble Arch LU*

In the heart of the West End, this wittily stylish café, adorned with striking murals, offers both sweet and savoury treats. Among the treats are prawn falafel wraps and rosewater-flavoured macaroons.

## Levant £££-££££

- Jason Court
  76 Wigmore Street, W1
- 020 7224 1111
- Bond Street LU

Hidden in a basement, this glamorous Lebanese bar and restaurant, with its over-the-top décor is a splendid setting in which to enjoy a fine mezze.

## Original Tagines ££

- 7A Dorset Street, W1
- 020 7935 1545
- Baker Street LU

A small and charming restaurant, serving carefully cooked tagines. Dishes include chicken with preserved lemon and lamb with caramelised pear.

## Patogh ££

- 8 Crawford Place, W1
- 020 7262 4015
- Edgware Road LU

A down-to-earth Iranian restaurant, noted for its kebabs and bustling with diners.

## Ranoush Juice Bar £-££

- 43 Edgware Road, W2
- 020 7723 5929
- Marble Arch LU

Gleamingly glitzy with its black marble interior, this take-away bar serves fresh fruit juices and tasty Lebanese snacks. Dishes include succulent lamb shawarma for which you pay first, then order your food.

## Sofra ££

- 36 Tavistock Street, WC2
- 020 7240 3773
- Covent Garden LU

This spacious Turkish restaurant offers good, simple Turkish food. The staff are polite and the food is great value.

## Tas ££

- 33 The Cut, SE1
- 020 7928 2111
- Waterloo LU/Rail

This large, contemporary Turkish restaurant offers reasonably-priced, tasty Turkish food.

## Yalla Yalla £-££

- 1 Green Court, W1
- 020 7287 7663
- Piccadilly Circus LU

Hidden down a Soho alleyway, this small, pretty Lebanese café offers mezze such as fried chicken livers with pomegranate molasses as well as grilled meats and filled wraps to take away.

# North

## Mangal II  £-££
- 4 Stoke Newington Road, N16
- ☎ 020 7254 7888
- 🚌 Stoke Newington Rail

A relaxed, friendly atmosphere and seriously flavourful Turkish food at bargain prices.

## Yayla  £
- 429 Green Lanes, N4
- ☎ 020 8348 9515
- 🚌 Manor House LU

Small, cheery corner café serving tasty Turkish food, from kebabs to pide.

# West

## Abu Zaad  ££
- 29 Uxbridge Road, W12
- ☎ 020 8749 5107
- 🚌 Shepherds Bush LU

A friendly, relaxed Syrian restaurant, offering generous portions of homely food.

## Adams Café  ££-£££
- 77 Askew Road, W12
- ☎ 020 8743 0572
- 🚌 Hammersmith LU, then bus 266

An established restaurant with a loyal following, it offers good-value, tasty Tunisian food. Freshly fried brik make an excellent starter and there are many couscous dishes.

## Alounak  ££
- 10 Russell Gardens, W14
- ☎ 020 7603 7645
- 🚌 Kensington Olympia LU/Rail

Originally housed in a portacabin in an Olympia car park, Alounak has expanded into more conventional premises. Still on offer, however, is gutsy Persian food – excellent lamb kebabs and flavourful stews. *Branch: 44 Westbourne Grove, W2 (020 7229 0416)*

## Fresco  ££
- 25 Westbourne Grove, W2
- ☎ 020 7221 2355
- 🚌 Bayswater LU

A colourful, down-to-earth Lebanese café serving freshly-made fruit juices and a range of Lebanese-inspired snacks including delicious wraps.

## Hafez  ££
- 5 Hereford Road, W2
- ☎ 020 7221 3167 or 020 7229 9398
- 🚌 Bayswater or Notting Hill Gate or Queensway LU

A pleasantly laid-back Iranian restaurant offering classic dishes such as Persian bread with dips, grilled meats and Persian stews.

## Maroush   ££££

*21 Edgware Road, W2*

*020 7723 0773 or 020 7262 1090*

*Marble Arch LU*

Very much an Edgware Road institution, this smart Lebanese restaurant serves high-quality food, complete with live entertainment at weekends.

## Mohsen   ££

*152 Warwick Road, W14*

*020 7602 9888*

*Earls Court LU*

*Kensington Olympia LU/Rail*

Despite an unprepossessing location opposite a huge Homebase, this small Iranian restaurant, with its outside courtyard area, is warmly recommended by food writer Margaret Shaida. Diners here can enjoy Persian dishes, including kebabs and stews, at their flavourful best.

## Moroccan Tagine   ££

*95 Golborne Road, W10*

*020 8968 8055*

*Ladbroke Grove LU*

A small, relaxed North African restaurant noted for its excellent, reasonably-priced tagines.

## Mr Falafel   £

*New Shepherd's Bush Market*
*Uxbridge Road, W12*

*Shepherds Bush LU*

'The Best Palestinian falafel' proclaims the sign above the doorway of Ahmed Yassine's small, jaunty green-and-yellow café. It does a roaring trade in take-away falafel-filled wraps, with customers choosing from extras such as ful medames, avocado or pickled baby aubergines.

## Yas   ££-£££

*7 Hammersmith Road, W14*

*020 7603 9148*

*Kensington Olympia LU/Rail*

Bright and cheerful, this friendly, well-established Iranian restaurant serves freshly baked Iranian breads, dips, kebabs and Persian stews. Business is brisk, especially in the early hours of the morning.

# East

## Mangal Ocakbasi   £-££

*10 Arcola Street E8*

*020 7275 8981*

*Dalston Kingsland Rail*

A hugely popular, down-to-earth Turkish restaurant, noted for its flavourful grilled meat and delicious mezze.

# Cookbooks

## A Season in Morocco
*Meera Freeman*
A gorgeously-illustrated taste of Morocco, written with affection and knowledge.

## The Lebanese Cookbook
*Hussein Dekmak*
Classic Lebanese recipes from an acclaimed Lebanese chef.

## Lebanese Cuisine
*Anissa Helou*
An appetising cookbook offering an insight into the glories of Lebanese cuisine.

## The Legendary Cuisine of Persia
*Margaret Shaida*
An elegant and well written book charting the history of Persian cuisine and filled with excellent recipes.

## Moroccan Cuisine
Paula Wolfert
A seminal and delicious collection of Moroccan recipes.

## The New Book of Middle Eastern Food
*Claudia Roden*
An invaluable and classic book on Middle Eastern cookery. It is evocatively and authoritatively written, with tempting recipes.

## Persia in Peckham
*Sally Butcher*
A lively and engaging cookbooks, written with zest by Sally Butcher, who runs Persepolis, a Persian delicatessen in Peckham.

Middle Eastern Cookbooks

Polish London

*Polsmak*

From the eighteenth century onwards, Poland's history of partition, invasion and resistance, created a Polish presence in London – a self-contained, close-knit community, with a military bias. Following the collapse of communism in Poland, however, business opportunities for British-born Poles have increased, and the former sense of exile which marked the ex-pat Polish community has gone. London's Polish community, however, retains and cherishes a very strong awareness of its Polish roots.

In 1765, Poland was divided up between Austria, Prussia and Russia. Many Polish émigrés fled to France and a few to England, so starting a pattern of political exile. A succession of failed insurrections in 1830-31, 1848 and 1863-64 brought more exiles to Britain. In Highgate Cemetery, White Eagle Hill is the resting place of the leaders of the failed 1863-64 uprising. The author Joseph Conrad emigrated first to France and then to Britain after his father's arrest in the period prior to that rebellion. Some Poles came to Britain for purely economic reasons, taking on jobs as artisans or labourers. By the late nineteenth century, a Polish Christian community in London was centred around the Polish Catholic church on Devonia Road in Islington, Our Lady of Czestochowa. Large numbers of Polish Jews entered Britain during this period but they became assimilated into the Jewish community.

A real increase in Britain's Polish community – swelling its numbers from 5,000 to tens of thousands – came with the Second World War. Following the German invasion in September 1939, over 30,000 Poles from the government and the military came to Britain and a Polish Government-in-Exile under Prime Minister Sikorski was declared. Operational headquarters were set up around South Kensington and the Polish Air Force fought alongside the RAF. Their contribution was extensive: during the Battle of Britain one in seven of the German planes shot down was dispatched by Polish airmen. A memorial to the 1,241 Polish airmen who died stands on the edge of Northolt Airport.

The Soviet occupation of Poland and the Treaty of Yalta dispossessed thousands of Poles by handing over Eastern Poland to the Soviet Union, so many Poles who had come to Britain to fight in the war stayed on. The British government offered free domicile to the 250,000 Poles (and their families) who had fought under British command, and over 150,000 accepted. Offers of British nationality were usually refused by Poles on patriotic grounds, in an effort to keep the political situation in Poland a 'live' issue.

Post World War II, high property prices created a move west from Kensington to Earls Court, with Cromwell Road becoming known as the 'Polish Corridor'. Polish clubs founded during the war, such as the magnificent White Eagle Club in Knightsbridge and the aristocratic Ognisko on Exhibition Road, had provided community focal points, but again rising costs edged the Polish community out into Balham, Chiswick and Ealing. Many of the upper and middle-class Poles (who constituted the majority of the community) had to adapt to difficult circumstances following the war.

The completion in 1982 of POSK, the Polish Social and Cultural Centre, at considerable expense, was a source of pride to London's ex-pat Polish community. The Catholic Church, too, played an important part in London's Polish community, with around 12 Polish Catholic centres and churches in London. Following the collapse of Communism and the opening up of borders in 2004, London's Polish community has grown substantially. One estimate numbers London's current Polish community as being at least 120,000 people.

# Polish Cuisine

The bitter Polish winters mean that many of the essential ingredients are those that can be stored or preserved: grains, root vegetables, sauerkraut, dried mushrooms, and salted and pickled herrings. Stews and soups are popular, with krupnik (barley soup) and yellow-pea soup dating back to the Middle Ages.

Polish food is often described as Russian-influenced and the cuisines do share many dishes and ingredients. Other influences on Polish food, include Italian cuisine (traceable back to the 1518 marriage of King Sigismund to Bona Sforza) and French cuisine, with one of the earliest Polish cookbooks translated from the French.

Meat has always been highly valued in Polish cookery. Every bit is used, producing the famous sausages, hams, black puddings, tongues and brawn. The Poles also enjoy game. Bigos, or huntsman's stew, is made from game, sauerkraut and sausages. When Bona Sforza and her Italian retinue came to live in Poland, they introduced salads and certain vegetables. Even today 'wloscyzna', the word for basic green vegetables, means 'things Italian'.

Grains and cereals have always been important crops for the Poles, and rye bread is a staple. In her fascinating book 'Old Polish Traditions in the Kitchen and at the Table', Maria Lemnis writes, 'The popularity of bread in Poland is manifested in the numerous old sayings, e.g. 'bread unites the strongest'... or, sharper in tone, 'whomever bread harms, a stick can cure'. Cereals such as millet and buckwheat are used widely in dishes from soups to kasha, a purée of cooked grains.

The Catholic Church has had a marked influence on Polish cooking. Catholic festivals are celebrated with a host of special dishes and cakes. Catholic fasts are also an influence, with fish and mushroom dishes replacing meat at certain times of the year. Christmas Eve, for example, is traditionally celebrated with a feast including carp or pike.

Polish cookery remained frozen in time after the Second World War but following the collapse of Communism with increased travel and trading opportunities, Polish cuisine is developing and changing.

# Glossary

**Buckwheat:** a triangular brown-green grain. Buckwheat flour is used in blinis.

*Buckwheat*

**Cakes:** Cakes and pastries are an important feature of Polish life, and a huge variety are made, with some traditionally eaten at Christmas and Easter. Babka, a famous Easter yeast cake with a distinctive fluted shape; cheesecake, traditionally baked and not oversweet; makowiec, poppy-seed roll; mazurek, flat, traditionally rectangular cakes eaten at Easter; and paczki, Polish doughnuts, often filled with plum jam.

**Caraway seeds:** tiny, ridged brown seeds, with an aniseed flavour.

*Kohlrabi*

**Curd cheese:** a slightly tangy soft cheese made from curds, used in pierogi and cheesecake.

**Dill:** a caraway flavoured herb with delicate, feathery fronds.

**Dried mushrooms:** hunting for wild mushrooms is a national pastime in Poland. Fresh wild mushrooms are rarely found in the shops, but both dried and pickled mushrooms are widely available.

**Juniper berries:** aromatic, blue-black berries, used with game.

**Kohlrabi:** a plump, rounded vegetable, either pale green or deep purple, called a 'cabbage-turnip' by Jane Grigson.

**Pierogi:** filled pasta pouches, often called Polish ravioli.

**Pinhead barley:** fine-grained barley.

**Polish pure spirit:** a powerful spirit – 168 proof – used to make vodka.

**Poppy seeds:** tiny white or purple-blue seeds, used in vast quantities in Polish baking.

**Rye bread:** a Polish fundamental. Rich-flavoured, dark brown Ukranian rye is distinctive.

**Sauerkraut:** pickled, shredded cabbage with a sharp flavour, available fresh or bottled.

**Sausages:** boiling ring, loops of spicy sausages; kabanos, long, thin pork sausages; kielbasa, pork and beef sausage flavoured with garlic; krakowska, garlic sausage, eaten as a salami.

*Polish Sausage*

**Vodka:** flavoured vodkas in Poland include: honey, lemon, sliwowica (prune), winiak (matured in wine barrels), wisniak (cherry), and zubrowska (bison-grass, easily identifiable because of the blades of long grass in the bottle).

# Food Shops

Twenty years ago there were just a handful of Polish food shops in London, playing an important part as a meeting place for London's small, self-contained Polish community. Today, with a far larger Polish community in London, the phrase 'Polski sklep' (Polish Shop) crops up all over the capital and the original food shops have been joined by many new businesses.

## North

### Beetroot

🏠 *92 Fleet Road, NW3*
☎ *020 7424 8544*
🚌 *Hampstead Heath rail*
🕐 *Mon-Fri 8am-7pm, Sat 9am-5pm*

Bartek Fabianski's friendly deli-cum-café offers North Londoners a taste of Poland, from home-made pierogi or Polish pastries and cakes, either to take away or to sit and sample. Strategically positioned near St Dominic's church with its Polish congregation, Bartek has built up a loyal local following of both Poles and the British.

## Fortune Foods

🏠 *387-389 Hendon Way, NW4*
☎ *020 8203 9325*
🚌 *Hendon Central LU*
🕐 *Daily 10am-10pm*

This roomy shop stocks an extensive range of East European foodstuffs from Lithuania, Poland, Russia and Slovakia.

## Polish Delicatessen

🏠 *32 Crouch Hill, N4*
☎ *07970 112 489*
🚌 *Finsbury Park LU/Rail*
🕐 *Mon-Sat 9.30am-8pm*
   *Sun 9.30am-4pm*

This small, basic shop, despite space constraints, offers a large range of Polish foodstuffs, all imported directly from Poland. These include sausages, rye breads, cakes, smoked fish (including eel and halibut), fresh pierogi, dairy products and even Polish eggs.

# North-West

## Morawski

- 157 High Street, NW10
- 020 8965 5340
- Willesden Junction LU
- Mon-Sat 9am-6pm

A veteran delicatessen, this friendly, old-fashioned offers a good range of Polish foodstuffs, from storecupboard ingredients to deli items such as pierogi.

# West

## Polanka

- 258 King Street, W6
- 020 8741 8268
- www.polanka-rest.com
- Ravenscourt Park LU
- Mon-Sat 10am-10pm, Sun 11am-8pm

A firm favourite among London's Polish community, this deli and restaurant has an extensive stock of Polish foodstuffs. Stock includes Polish sausages and cured meats, sweets, cakes, Krakus jams and pickles.

## Enca Foods

- 2 Salisbury Pavement Dawes Road, SW6
- 020 7385 5762
- Fulham Broadway LU
- Mon-Fri 7am-6pm, Sat 8am-5pm

Hidden away among Fulham's backstreets is this well-established, family-run Polish food supplier. It is famous for the 30 types of sausages and cooked and cured meats made on the premises – an appetising, savoury smell permeates the shop. Raw carcasses are delivered to the back door to be transformed into specialities such as pork brawn or roasted pork poledwica. There is also a basic grocery stock of Central European foodstuffs: rye breads, cakes, pickles and jams.

## Parade Delicatessen

- 8 Central Buildings, The Broadway, W5
- 020 8567 9066
- Ealing Broadway LU/Rail
- Mon-Fri 9.15am-6pm, Sat 9.15am-5pm

There's been a Polish food shop on these premises for well over 50 years now. This appetising delicatessen carries an excellent range of Polish foods, from sausages and cured meats, plus a variety of herrings, curd cheese and pierogi. Also on offer is a good choice of groceries, from biscuits and sweets to packet soups and Polish jams.

## Polish Specialities

- 📇 *226-8 King Street, W6*
- ☎ *020 8741 8686*
- 🕐 *Mon-Sat 9.30am-7.30am,*
  *Sun 11am-6pm*
- 🚌 *Hammersmith LU*

One of a chain of retail shops showcasing products from a successful importer of Polish foods. It carries an extensive range of Polish foodstuffs.

## Polish Specialities

- 📇 *55, New Broadway, W5*
- ☎ *020 8840 8016*
- 🕐 *Mon-Sun 8am-9pm*
- 🚌 *Ealing Broadway LU, rail*

A branch of a chain of retail shops it carries an extensive range of Polish foodstuffs.

## Prima Delicatessen

- 📇 *192 North End Road, W14*
- ☎ *020 7385 2070*
- 🚌 *West Kensington LU*
- 🕐 *Mon-Thur and Sat 9.30am-6pm,*
  *Fri 9.30am-7pm*

Founded in 1948, this old-fashioned corner shop is warmly recommended by Polish friends. It has an excellent stock of Polish ingredients including sausages and smoked meats, rye breads, cakes and pastries as well as dried goods and a selection of chilled foods such as pickled mushrooms.

# South-West

## Fat Jack

- 📇 *265 Balham High Street, SW17*
- ☎ *0753 3070614*
- 🚌 *Balham LU/Rail*
- 🕐 *Mon-Fri 9am-7pm, Sat 10-6pm,*
  *Sun 10am-4pm*

A small pretty café-cum-deli. Polish foodstuffs range from fruit juices to pre-packed Polish sausages while the café serves Polish cakes and savouries.

## Korona Delicatessen

- 📇 *30 Streatham High Road, SW16*
- ☎ *020 8769 6647*
- 🚌 *Streatham Hill Rail;*
  *Bus 159, 109 or 133*
- 🕐 *Mon-Sat 9.30am-7pm,*
  *Sun 10.30am-3.30pm*

This well-established food shop, now run by Katarzyna Ciesielska, offers a fine, neatly-arranged selection of Polish and continental foodstuffs and has a loyal local following. The long chilled counter offers an extensive range of Polish, German, Hungarian and Italian sausages, salamis and cured meats and deli items such as fresh sauerkraut and cheeses. On the shelves are Polish jams, pickles, packet soups and biscuits. Fresh carp are stocked at Christmas.

## Panadam Delicatessen

🏠 *2 Marius Road, SW17*
☎ *020 8673 4062*
🚌 *Balham LU/Rail*
🕐 *Mon 9.30am-6pm,*
*Tue-Fri 9.30am-6.30pm,*
*Sat 9.30am-6pm,*
*Sun 9am-1.30pm*

This veteran delicatessen has been serving Balham's large Polish community for many years and is now run with friendly hospitality by Magda. The deli-counter offers a good selection of Polish sausages, meats and herrings, and there is a range of rye breads and cakes. The Sunday opening is explained by the presence round the corner of the Polish church of Christ the King.

## Polish Specialities

🏠 *73 Stockwell Road, SW9*
☎ *020 7733 3526*
🚌 *Stockwell LU*
🕐 *Mon-Sat 10am-8pm,*
*Sun 10am-6pm*

A branch of the Polish chain of retails this store carries an extensive range of Polish foodstuffs.

## Polish Specialities

🏠 *258 Streatham High Road, SW6*
☎ *020 8696 7660*
🚌 *Streatham raill*
🕐 *Mon-Sat 10am-8pm,*
*Sun 10am-5pm*

A south London branch of the Polish chain of retails this store carries an extensive range of Polish foodstuffs.

# East

## Polsmak

🏠 *39 Balls Pond Road, N1*
☎ *020 7275 7045*
🚌 *Dalston Kingsland Rail*
🕐 *Mon-Fri 9am-8pm,*
*Sat-Sun 9am-6pm*

A cheerful, friendly shop, Polsmak is full of an extensive array of Polish and East European foods. There is a fine assortment of sausages and cured meats such as boczek (Polish bacon), kielbasa Polska and baked pate, chilled goods such as large cartons of buttermilk, sieved cottage cheese and ready-made pierogi and Polish beers. Seasonal specialities include Easter cakes and pre-ordered Christmas carps. A steady stream of customers visit for coffee and fresh Polish pastries and tasty sandwiches – all freshly made to order.

# Eating Places

Some of London's best-known Polish eating places continue to be housed in veteran clubs or institutions, characteristic of the close-knit Polish community.

## Central

### Daquise   £-£££
- 20 Thurloe Street, SW7
- 020 7589 6117
- South Kensington LU

This pleasantly old-fashioned restaurant founded in 1947. Now run by the Gesslers, restaurateurs from Poland, Daquise continues to offer a chance to sample coffee and cakes or freshly cooked Polish dishes such as pierogi or bigos at reasonable prices. A real gem of a restaurant.

## West

### Café Grove   £
- 65 The Grove, W5
- 020 8810 0364
- Ealing Broadway LU/Rail

A pretty café serving Ealing's Polish community and offering a tempting range of savoury dishes and classic Polish cakes.

### Ognisko Polskie   £££
- Polish Hearth Club,
  55 Princes Gate, Exhibition Road SW7
- 020 7589 4635
- www.ognisko.com
- South Kensington LU

Housed in an elegant room, the restaurant at this famous Polish club is a bastion of first-rate Polish food. The menu offers a chance to sample upmarket renditions of classic Polish dishes such as bigos, beetroot soup and pierogi. There is also a good choice of flavoured vodkas to compliment your meal. Summertime sees diners enjoying alfresco meals on the attractive terrace.

### Patio   ££-£££
- 5 Goldhawk Road, W12
- 020 8743 5194
- Goldhawk Road LU
  Shepherd's Bush LU

This intimate, unpretentious restaurant attracts a loyal following for its generous helpings of tasty Polish food and convivial atmosphere.

Polish Eating Places

## Polanka

⌨ *258 King Street, W6*
☎ *020 8741 8268*
🖱 *www.polanka-rest.com*
🚌 *Ravenscourt Park LU*

This homely restaurant offers diners a chance to sample a range of Polish foods, from snacks such as poppy seed cake to more substantial dishes such as golabki (stuffed cabbage leaves), bigos and goulash.

## Wodka   ££££

⌨ *12 St Albans Grove, W8*
☎ *020 7937 6513*
🚌 *High Street Kensington LU*

A sleek, contemporary Polish restaurant serving distinctly upmarket food at corresponding prices. As the name implies, a huge range of flavoured vodkas is also available to accompany your meal.

# South

## Baltic   £££££-£££££

⌨ *74 Blackfriars Road, SE1*
☎ *020 7928 1111*
🚌 *Southwark LU/Rail*

A smart, contemporary East European restaurant and vodka bar. It serves elegant, East European food and a spectacular range of vodkas.

# South-West

## Polish White Eagle Club   ££-£££

⌨ *211 Balham High Road, SW17*
☎ *020 8672 1723*
🖱 *www.whiteeagleclub.co.uk*
🚌 *Balham LU/rail*

Housed in a veteran Polish club, the restaurant here serves huge portions of reasonably-priced, traditional Polish food.

# Cookbooks

## The Food and Cooking of Eastern Europe
*Lesley Chamberlain*
A clearly written, overall look at East European cookery.

## The Polish Kitchen
*Mary Pininska*
A well-written, knowledgeable book on Polish cookery, with appetising recipes.

South-East Asian

*New Loon Moon*

The South-East Asian community in London is widespread and diverse, reflecting the variety of its national origins. The term 'South-East Asia' encompasses Indonesia, Malaysia, the Philippines, Singapore, Thailand and Vietnam. There is no obvious centre for London's South-East Asian community, no equivalent, for example, to Gerrard Street for the Chinese community, but Peckham and Dalston are focal points for the Vietnamese, while Earls Court is a centre for the Filipino community. Wat Buddhapadipa in Wimbledon, the UK's first Buddhist temple, is an important focal point for the Thai community. April sees Thai New Year celebrations at the temple, a characteristically friendly affair offering a chance to sample street-style Thai food from assorted stalls.

# South-East Asian Cuisine

The term 'South-East Asian cuisine' is the blanket term used to describe the cuisines of Indonesia, Malaysia, the Philippines, Singapore, Thailand and Vietnam – a simple way to describe a complex set of overlapping national cuisines. Seemingly no dish has a single recipe in South-East Asia: variations abound from country to country, region to region and family to family. Satay in Thailand may be served with toast and a sweet chilli-based dipping sauce, whereas the Malaysian version comes with a spicy peanut sauce, cucumber and cubes of compressed rice. Differences stem from race and religion with, for example, pork avoided by the Muslim Malays but enjoyed by the Chinese. These variations help create a rich and diverse set of cuisines, but there are certain shared characteristics across the region.

Both Chinese and Indian cuisines have influenced South-East Asian food in cooking techniques and ingredients. From China comes the balancing of five flavours: sweet, sour, hot, salty and bitter, and from India, the use of spices and curry pastes. Like both Chinese and Indian cuisine, South-East Asian cuisine is mainly rice-based.

Certain ingredients provide unique flavours that distinguish South-East Asian cooking. Coconut milk, extracted from the flesh of the versatile coconut, is a key ingredient. It is widely used in both savoury and sweet dishes as a marinade, a stock, a curry base and a dairy equivalent. Fragrant aromatics have a citrus quality: lemon grass, lime juice, kaffir lime leaves and rind. To the Asian trinity of onion, garlic and ginger are added the more subtle rhizomes: galangal and krachai. Chillies, introduced by the Portuguese and Spanish in the sixteenth century, provide a chracteristic South-East Asian 'hot' kick.

Seafood is important in South-East Asian cooking and found in abundance. In its dried and fermented forms, seafood is used to add saltiness to food. Fish sauce often replaces soy sauce in Thailand, the Philippines and Vietnam, while pungent dried paste is used throughout South-East Asia.

Indonesian and Malay cooking

are often grouped together, as the dominant religion in both countries is Islam. Singapore is distinguished culinarily by Nonya or Straits Chinese cuisine, a unique blend of heavily spiced dishes combining Chinese and Malay ingredients and techniques. Thai cooking, with its emphasis on aesthetic presentation, is marked by its use of aromatic herbs such as coriander, Thai mint and several varieties of basil. Filipino cuisine stands out from the rest of South-East Asia, as it was influenced by the Spanish colonization of the country from 1521 to 1898 and subsequent American occupation until 1946. The Spanish influence is apparent in Filipino dishes such as adobo and paella while American influences crop up in a predeliction for condensed milk and apple pie. Brightly coloured rice cakes and desserts are also popular in the Philippines, made with ingredients such as makapuno, soft-fleshed coconut. Vietnamese cuisine, influenced by Chinese and French cuisines, is noted for its subtlety and characterised by the generous use of fresh herbs, including basil, coriander and mint.

# Glossary

**Agar agar**: a vegetarian setting agent obtained from seaweed which does not require refrigeration to set. Available in either powdered form or translucent strands. Filipino agar agar *(gulaman)* comes in bright pink and yellow to add colour to desserts.

**Annatto (achuete)**: small red seeds which impart an orange colour.

**Banana leaves:** used to wrap foods in the way that kitchen foil is used, with the added virtue of also adding flavour to whatever is cooked within.

**Basil**: a herb used in Indonesian, Thai and Vietnamese cuisines. In Thailand one finds bai horapa (similar to European sweet basil), bai mangluk, and bai garapo or holy basil.

**Bean curd (tahu, tokua)**: a nutritious soya-bean product. Fresh ivory-coloured bean curd has a firm, custard texture and bland flavour and is sold packed in water. Deep-fried bean curd has a

*Thai Basil*

golden colour and spongy texture. Both are found in the chilled section.

**Betel leaves (La lot)**: the large, heart-shaped, dark green leaves of a climbing pepper plant. With a distinctive flavour, these are used as an edible packaging in South-East Asian cooking. Wipe the leaves with a damp cloth before using them.

**Candlenuts (kemiri, buah keras)**: large, white, waxy nuts, used to thicken curry pastes, sold unshelled. Raw macadamia nuts are the closest substitute.

**Chilli paste (nam prik pow)**: a thick sauce made from chillies, onions and sugar.

**Chillies (prik, cabe, sili labuyo)**: introduced from South America by the Portuguese and Spanish in the sixteenth century, chillies are an essential ingredient in South-East Asian cookery. Generally the smallest are the hottest, for instance, the tiny Thai bird's eye chillies.

**Coconut milk (santen)**: this thick white 'milk' is made from the grated flesh of the coconut and not from the cloudy water found inside the coconut. In South-East Asia freshly-made coconut milk is sold in markets;

270

here, tinned coconut milk is the best option widely available. Creamed coconut and coconut milk powder, both of which need mixing with hot water, are the other options.

*Coconut Milk*

**Coriander (cilantro, Chinese parsley, daun ketumbar, pak chee)**: this green flat-leafed herb, similar in appearance to continental parsley, has a distinctive sharp flavour. Both the seeds and the leaves are used throughout South-East Asia.

**Custard apple (sweet-sop)**: an apple-shaped, green-skinned fruit with creamy flesh and plentiful small seeds.

*Duku*

**Duku (llangsat, ong kong)**: a fawn-skinned tropical fruit, related to the lychee, which grows in clumps and contains small, separate, juicy segments with a delicate, pomelo-like flavour.

**Durian**: a notorious large, spiky, green-skinned fruit, prized as a delicacy throughout South-East Asia. It is notable for its pungent smell, described as a cross between

Camembert and turpentine and, as a result, is banned on airlines.

**Fish sauce (nam pla, nuoc mam, patis)**: a thin, brown salty liquid, produced from compressed shrimps or small fish, and used similarly to soy sauce as a salty flavouring.

*Fish sauce*

**Galangal (Siamese ginger, kenguas, languas, ka)**: a fleshy rhizome, resembling a creamy-coloured root ginger with pink nodules, and a sharp, medicinal aroma. Available fresh, dried, or in powder form (Laos powder).

*Galangal*

**Ginger**: a brown-skinned rhizome, noted for its aromatic flavour and digestive qualities. Lesser ginger (krachai in Thai) is a milder relation and, while similarly-coloured, comes in clusters of small 'fingers'.

**Jackfruit**: bulky, football-sized fruit with a thick green skin covered in prickles, similar in appearance to durian. Yellow jackfruit flesh is available tinned.

**Kaffir lime (jeruk purut, makrut)**: large limes with a bumpy, dark-green skin. The glossy lime leaves, sold in bunches or packets of loose leaves, are used in South-East Asian cooking and add a distinctive citrus flavour.

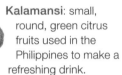

**Kalamansi**: small, round, green citrus fruits used in the Philippines to make a refreshing drink.

*Kaffir Lime*

**Kangkong**: water-convolvulus leaves, eaten as a green vegetable.

**Lemon grass (serai, sereh, takrai)**: a fibrous grey-green grass with a white bulbous base and subtle citrus flavour.

**Long coriander (ngo gai, saw leaf herb)**: a herb with a fragrance similar to that of coriander, used particularly in Vietnamese cookery.

**Macapuno**: a type of coconut with soft, slightly sticky flesh, used in Filipino desserts.

**Mango**: an orange fleshed, fragrant fruit, eaten fresh and used in desserts. Pale orange Thai mangoes are particularly prized for their delicate flavour and scoopable flesh.

**Mangosteen**: an apple-sized fruit with thick purple skin which, despite its name, is no relation to the mango. Inside, it contains white pulpy segments with a delicate, perfumed flavour.

*Mangosteen*

**Milkfish (bangus)**: a bony, white-fleshed fish, cultivated and eaten extensively in the Philippines.

**Mooli (daikon):** a large, long white radish with crisp flesh.

**Noodles:** *cellophane noodles* (also known as beanthread, glass or transparent noodles) are fine threadlike noodles made from mung beans, which need soaking before they can be easily cut; *yellow egg noodles* (available fresh and dried); *dried white rice noodles* and *vermicelli; river rice* or *sarhor noodles*, made from ground rice and water. Fresh river rice noodles are sold in clear packets, usually stored near the chilled section.

**Palm sugar (gula melaka):** a caramel-flavoured, dark brown sugar made from the coconut palm flower, sold in small, hard cylinderical blocks.

**Pandan leaves**: long, thin, dark green screwpine leaves, sold fresh in bunches. They add a unique, slightly nutty flavour and green colouring to desserts.

**Pawpaw (papaya):** a gourd-like fruit, which comes in varying sizes and colours from deep green to orange. Green pawpaw is used in salads by the Thais.

**Pea aubergine:** tiny pea-sized aubergines with a sharp, bitter taste, used especially in Thai cooking.

*Pea Aubergine*

**Pomelo (shaddock):** the largest of the citrus fruits, resembling a huge grapefruit with a flattened end; used in Thai salads.

**Prawn crackers (krupuk):** flat wafers which puff up when fried. Emping are a slightly bitter Indonesian version, made with melinjo nuts, and used to garnish gado gado salad.

**Rambutan**: a fruit resembling a hairy, red egg – the name comes from 'rambut', Malay for 'hair'. Inside is a translucent, juicy egg-shaped fruit, prized for its refreshing qualities.

**Rice**: long-grain rice is commonly used, with the best coming from Thailand. The phrase 'perfumed rice' is an indicator of quality. Short-grained white and black glutinous rice is also used in both savoury and sweet dishes.

**Rice paper wrappers**: round, triangular or square rice flour wrappers, sold dried. Dip them in hot water for just a few seconds before using them as a wrapping.

**Shrimps, dried**: small, shelled, dried pink shrimps, with a strong salty flavour.

**Shrimp paste (blachan, terasi, bagoong, kapee, mam tan)**: a paste made from fermented shrimps, available in many forms, from solid brown blocks to bottled pink-grey liquid. It has an extremely pungent smell, so store in an airtight container.

**Soy sauce**: a dark brown, salty liquid made from fermented soya beans, available as thin, salty Light Soy Sauce or as thicker, sweeter Dark Soy Sauce. Kecap manis is a thick, sweet Indonesian soy sauce.

**Starfruit (carambola)**: a ridged, fleshy fruit which produces star-shaped slices.

*Shrimp paste*

273

**Straw mushrooms:** cone-shaped mushrooms, usually available canned.

**Tamarind (asam, mak kum):** a bean-like fruit from the tamarind tree, available in lumps of de-seeded pulp, and used to add tartness to dishes. Tamarind sauce, although slightly salty, is a convenient version. 'Tamarind slices', from a different fruit with similar qualities, is also available.

**Tempe:** a pressed fermented soya bean product, with a nutty taste.

**Turmeric:** a slender, brown-skinned rhizome, with a deep orange flesh. Widely available in dried powdered form, or occasionally found fresh.

**Ube:** a bright purple, sweet yam used in Filipino cookery.

*Yam bean*

**Yam bean:** a brown-skinned, turnip-shaped tuber, with dense white, slightly sweet crunchy flesh, a traditional ingredient in rojak salads.

**Yard-long beans:** as the name implies, these are long green beans, commonly cut into short lengths before cooking.

# Food Shops

While British supermarkets increasingly carry South-East Asian store cupboard basics such as coconut milk or rice noodles, many of the more specialist ingredients can only be found at South-East Asian food shops. Traditionally, too, the more established Chinese supermarkets have acted as umbrella suppliers, carrying a range of South-East Asian ingredients.

## Central

### New Loon Moon Supermarket
🏠 *9a Gerrard Street, W1*
☎ *020 7734 9940*
🚌 *Leicester Square LU*
🕐 *Daily 10.30am-8pm*

This busy Chinese food shop is well known for the range and quality of its Thai ingredients. When in season, fresh fruits on display outside range from durians to mangosteens. A separate room inside the shop stocks a striking range of fresh Thai produce, including pandan leaves, petai beans, and green mangoes for Thai salads. The grocery section, spread out over a number of rooms, includes a good range of South-East Asian ingredients, including gula melaka, curry pastes and tapioca pearls.

## See Woo

🏠 *19 Lisle Street, WC2*
☎ *020 7439 8325*
🚌 *Leicester Square LU*
🕐 *Daily 10am-8pm*

This veteran Chinese supermarket is also a reliable stockist of South-East Asian ingredients, including fresh flavourings such as kaffir lime leaves and galangal.

# North

## Kmart

🏠 *869 Finchley Road, NW11*
☎ *020 8209 0760*
🚌 *Golders Green LU*
🕐 *Mon-Sat 9.30am-9pm; Sun 11am-9pm*

Korean, Japanese and Filipino ingredients are on offer here. The stock consists primarily of dried, frozen, tinned or bottled ingredients, including an eye-catching range of tinned tropical fruits.

## Taste of Siam

🏠 *45-47 Camden High Street, NW1*
☎ *020 7383 5002*
🚌 *Camden Town / Mornington Crescent LU*
🕐 *Mon-Sun 10am-10pm*

This small, neat shop is run by the same people as the Thai restaurant next door. It has a good range of South-East Asian foodstuff, from very reasonably priced fresh Thai herbs to store-cupboard staples such as rice noodles and sauces.

## Wing Yip (London) Ltd

🏠 *395 Edgware Road, NW2*
☎ *020 8450 0422*
🚌 *Colindale LU*
🕐 *Mon-Sat 9.30am-8pm, Sun 11am-5pm*

This huge Chinese supermarket, located just off Staples Corner, contains an impressive range of South-East Asian ingredients. It is particularly strong on bottled, tinned, dried and frozen foods. Fresh food includes seafood such as clams, lobster and pomfret and produce ranges from lemon grass to mangoes.

South-East Asian Food Shops

# North-West

## Pacific Plaza

⌖ *Wembley Retail Park,*
*Engineers Way, Wembley, HA9*
☎ *020 7409 7747*
🚇 *Wembley Park LU*
✍ *www.pacificplaza.co.uk*
🕐 *Daily 10am-10pm*

For those who lament the loss of Colindale's Oriental City, the arrival of Pacific Plaza is a very welcome development. A number of Oriental City traders have now re-located to Pacific Plaza. The Pacific Plaza features a food court (offering reasonably-priced Japanese, Korean, Malaysian and Singaporean dishes) a supermarket and a number of specialist food shops.

# West

## Impress Food Oriental Supermarket

⌖ *169-171 Queensway*
☎ *020 7792 8887*
🚇 *Queensway LU*
🕐 *Mon-Thur 10am-10pm,*
*Fri-Sat 10am-11pm, Sun 11am-10pm*

This roomy food shop offers a range of Chinese and South-East Asian ingredients, with the emphasis on tinned,

canned, bottled and frozen foodstuffs, from sauces to frozen seafood.

## Manila Supermarket

⌖ *11-12 Hogarth Place, SW5*
☎ *020 7373 8305*
🚇 *Earls Court LU*
🕐 *Daily 9am-9pm*

As the name and the stacks of The Filipino newspaper near the door suggest, this friendly store specialises in Filipino foodstuffs such as purple yam jam, coconut spread and pork sausages. However, it also stocks an excellent range of general South-East Asian ingredients. One room contains freezers of grated cassava, fresh coconut milk, sweet potato leaves and a variety of fish and seafood. Among the Greengrocery items are chillies, galangal and banana leaves.

## Muay

⌖ *8A Hogarth Place, SW5*
☎ *020 7341 3599*
🚇 *Earls Court LU*
🕐 *Mon-Sat 8am-8pm, Sun 10am-8pm*

This long, narrow Thai food shop (above a basement hairdressers) sells an excellent selection of fresh Thai vegetables and herbs. The produce ranges from green mangoes for Thai salads to bundles of lemon grass. Store cupboard stock includes tubs of curry pastes, rice noodles and wrappers.

## Sri Thai

- 56 Shepherd's Bush Road, W6
- ☎ 020 7602 0621
- Shepherd's Bush LU
- 🕐 Daily 9am-7pm

This veteran Thai shop, run with friendly courtesy by Mr and Mrs Threpprasits, has a great stock of Thai ingredients, with the excellent selection of fresh Thai produce being a particular forte. Tuesday is the best day to visit for fresh vegetables and herbs jetted in from Thailand, such as bitter melon, fresh Thai basil and galangal.

## Tawana

- 16-20 Chepstow Road, W2
- ☎ 020 7221 6316
- Bayswater LU
- 🕐 Daily 9.30am-8pm

"There were only two Thai restaurants in London when we started," muses owner Mr Farooqi. Today, Thai cuisine is popular and his roomy, well-stocked shop does a roaring trade in Thai staples such as kaffir lime leaves, coconut milk and lemon grass. Wednesdays and Saturdays are the best days for fresh produce flown in from Thailand, including pea aubergines, banana leaves and holy basil. Next door, the 'Oriental Delicatessen' offers take-away Thai dishes including fishcakes, noodles and a wide choice of dainty Thai cakes.
Branch: 243-245 Plaistow Road, E15

# South-East

## See Woo Cash and Carry

- Furlong House
  Horn Lane, SE10
- ☎ 020 8293 9393
- Westcombe Park Rail
- 🕐 Mon-Sun 9.30am-7pm

This huge, cavernous cash-and-carry store carries an extensive range of Thai and Vietnamese foodstuffs.

# South-West

## Amaranth

- 346-348 Garrett Lane, SW18
- ☎ 020 8871 3466 / 8874 9036
- Earlsfield Rail
- 🕐 Mon-Sat 11am-9pm

An extension of the popular Thai restaurant next door, this small food shop stocks basic Thai ingredients, including home-made curry pastes. Deliveries from Thailand arrive on Monday evening, so Tuesday is the best day for fresh Thai produce, such as holy basil or lime leaves. The shop's particular forte is its home-made, frozen ready-to-cook savouries, such as dainty spring rolls or red duck curry. Staff are friendly and and happy to offer cooking advice.

## Talad Thai

🏠 *320 Upper Richmond Road, SW15*
☎ *020 8789 8084*
🚌 *Putney Rail*
🕐 *Daily 9am-8pm*

Upstairs functions as a Thai take-away while downstairs is a basement supermarket with a small back room of fresh vegetables, herbs and fruits such as Thai basil and pea aubergines. The large freezer section contains meat and seafood while the shelves are lined with noodles, condiments, tinned vegetables and coconut milk. The manageress is friendly and helpful and there are Thai cookery demonstrations every Sunday morning.

## Paya Thai

🏠 *101-103 Kew Road, TW9*
☎ *020 8332 2959*
🚌 *Richmond LU/Rail*
🕐 *Daily 10am-7pm*

This large store has every thing you could want for Thai cooking, from fresh pea aubergines and fragrant Thai basil to bottles of fish sauce and tins of coconut milk.

## Wing Thai Supermarket

🏠 *13 Electric Avenue, SW9*
☎ *020 7738 5898*
🚌 *Brixton LU/Rail*
🕐 *Mon-Sat 10am-7pm*

Tucked away behind the bustling fruit and veg market stalls outside, this roomy store has a small fresh produce section. It is particularly strong on bottled, tinned and frozen goods with a selection of Vietnamese products such as dried rice wrappers.

# East

## Hoang-Nam

🏠 *185 Mare Street, E8*
☎ *020 8985 9050*
🚌 *London Fields Rail*
🕐 *Daily 9am-9pm*

A large, well-established Vietnamese supermarket offering hard-to-find Vietnamese herbs and vegetables. Stock ranges from store-cupboard staples (rice, noodles, condiments) to frozen seafood. The store also stocks a selection of Vietnamese homeware from jade jewellery to underware.

# Eating Places

Authentic South-East Asian food in London is pretty scarce. The majority of food on offer is pleasant but lacks the depth of flavour and gutsiness of the genuine article. The places listed below are some of the best places to find authentic South-East Asian food from simple, reasonably-priced cafés to sophisticated, elegant restaurants.

## Central

### Bonda Café  £-££
📷 *190 Sussex Gardens, W2*
☎ *020 7402 5111*
🚌 *Paddington LU*

Tucked away in a basement, this small unassuming restaurant offers an authentic taste of Malaysia. It serves excellent renditions of classic dishes such as nasi lemak, char kway teow and roti canai and has found an appreciative audience of homesick Malaysian ex-pats. Reasonable prices adds to the appeal.

### C & R Café  £-££
📷 *4-5 Rupert Court, W1*
☎ *020 7434 1128*
🚌 *Leicester Square LU*

This bright, cheerful café, hidden down a Soho back-alley, does a roaring business in bargain Singaporean and Malaysian dishes, including Hainanese chicken rice, laksa and ice kacang.

### Jom Makan  £-££
📷 *5-7 Pall Mall East, SW1*
☎ *020 7925 2402*
🚌 *Charing Cross LU*

Just off Trafalgar Square, this spacious, airy restaurant offers a chance to sample Malay dishes, from stir-fried noodles to rich, slow-simmered curries.

### Malaysia Kopi Tiam  £-££
📷 *67 Charing Cross Road, WC2*
☎ *020 7287 1113*
🚌 *Leicester Square LU*

This down-to-earth café serves up generous portions of tasty Malay food such as char kway teow all at bargain prices.

South-East Asian Eating Places

## Nahm   ££££

🏠 *The Halkin, Halkin Street, SW1*
☎ *020 7333 1234*
🚌 *Hyde Park Corner LU*

In smart, subdued surroundings acclaimed Australian chef David Thompson creates a series authentically flavoured Thai dishes, offering a gourmet glimpse into this richly varied cuisine.

## Pho   £-££

🏠 *3 Great Titchfield Street, W1*
☎ *020 7436 0111*
🚌 *Oxford Circus LU*

A bright, airy café – one of a mini-chain – offering reasonably-priced Vietnamese food. The eponymous pho (noodles in broth), arrive accompanied by fragrant Vietnamese herbs.

## Thai Square   £££-££££

🏠 *166 Shaftesbury Avenue, WC2*
☎ *020 7836 7600*
🚌 *Leicester Square LU*

This smart, spacious branch of an established restaurant chain offers a range of classic Thai dishes, from fragrant curries to well-executed salads.

# North

## Khoai Cafe   ££

🏠 *6 Topsfield Parade, Middle Lane, N8*
☎ *020 8341 2120*
🚌 *Finsbury Park LU/Rail, then the W7 bus*

Simple surroundings, combined with polite, friendly service, make this Crouch End restaurant a pleasantly unpretentious place to sample traditional Vietnamese dishes.  Special favourites include betel leaf-wrapped beef and pho, in flavourful stock.
*Branch: 362 Ballards Lane, N12 (020 8445 2039)*

## O's Thai Café   ££

🏠 *10 Topsfield Parade, N8*
☎ *020 8348 6898*
🚌 *Finsbury Park LU/Rail, then the W7 bus*

Bright, light and funky, O's offers the chance to try tasty Thai dishes (such as green chicken curry) at very reasonable prices.  It has a loyal following among Crouch End diners who enjoy authentic Thai food.

## Singapore Garden   £££

   83-83a Fairfax Road, NW6

☎ 020 7328 5314

⌨ www. singaporegarden.co.uk

🚌 Swiss Cottage LU

A loyal multi-cultural clientele testifies to this long-established restaurant's commitment to admirably authentic Singaporean food. The menu offers predominantly Chinese food, but includes a selection of South-East Asian delicacies such as mouth-watering and gloriously messy chilli crab and excellent satay and oyster omelette. This place also serves the best chendol (a coconut milk drink) in town.

# West

## Satay House   £££

   13 Sale Place, W2

☎ 020 7723 6763

⌨ www.satay-house.co.uk

🚌 Edgware Road LU, Paddington LU/Rail

Tucked away in a quiet side street, this smart restaurant offers a chance to enjoy tasty Malaysian dishes such as murtabak (mince-stuffed flat bread) and nasi lemak (coconut rice). Desserts include such treats pulot hitam (black rice in coconut milk).

## Tawana   ££

   3 Westbourne Grove, W2

☎ 020 7229 3785

🚌 Bayswater LU

Run by the owners of Tawana Supermarket, this friendly, unpretentious Thai restaurant has built up a loyal local following.

# South

## Champor-Champor   £££-££££

   62-64 Weston Street, SE1

☎ 020 7403 4600

⌨ www. champor-champor.com

🚌 London Bridge LU/Rail

With its gloriously idiosyncratic, vibrant décor, Champor-Champor stands out from the crowd. The menu, too, is similarly creative, offering chef Amran Hassan's own creative Asian-inspired fusion food. The menu ranges from exquisite salads to indulgent desserts such as smoked banana ice cream.

# South-West

## Blue Elephant £££-££££

*4-6 Fulham Broadway, SW6*
*020 7385 6595*
*www.blueelephant.com*
*Fulham Broadway LU*

A veteran Thai restaurant, the Blue Elephant comes complete with lavish tropical-inspired décor and attentive staff. The cooking is above average, with the set-price Sunday buffet lunch a popular family occasion.

# East

## Song Que Café £

*134 Kingsland Road E2*
*020 76133 222*
*Old Street LU/Rail*

Highly recommended by pho-loving friends, this down-to-earth café serves flavourful Vietnamese food, including splendid pho, at rock-bottom prices.

# Cookbooks

### Modern Thai Food
*Martin Boetz*
A stylish contemporary cookbook, combining mouth-watering photographs with appetising recipes.

### Thai Cooking
*Jennifer Brennan*
A classic book on Thai cuisine, lovingly and authoritatively written.

### South-East Asian Food
*Rosemary Brissenden*
An absolutely indispensable book on the cuisine of South-East Asia. The book is a mine of delicious recipes from throughout the region.

### The Flavours of Vietnam
*Meera Freeman*
A clearly written, appetising Vietnamese cookbook.

### Food and Travels Asia
*Alastair Hendy*
A spectacular book with evocative photographs.

### Far Eastern Cookery
*Madhur Jaffrey*
An appetising regional journey, with clear, useable recipes.

### Indonesian Food and Cookery
*Sri Owen*
An authoritative and in-depth book about Indonesian food.

### New Wave Asian
*Sri Owen*
A handsome book with cutting edge Asian recipes.

### The Complete Asian Cookbook
*Charmaine Solomon*
A comprehensive cookbook.

Spanish & Portuguese

*Brindisa, Borough Market*

Although a Spanish presence in London can be traced back to the Middle Ages, the real growth in the capital's Spanish and Portuguese communities came in the twentieth century. Following the Spanish Civil War (1936-39), many Spanish refugees and political exiles came to Britain. Republican exiles set up El Hogar Español (The Spanish House) in Bayswater: a cultural, social and political focal point. In addition to political reasons for coming to Britain, economic ones also played their part. During the 1950s and 1960s, millions of working-class Spaniards were forced to leave Spain and look for work abroad because of the lack of opportunities at home. The area around Ladbroke Grove was a focal point for the Spanish community. Many of the Spanish in Britain were traditonally from Galicia, the north-west coastal region of Spain which has a seafaring and travelling tradition and which suffered in the post-war depression.

Despite the fact that Portugal is Britain's oldest ally (a tie dating back to the Treaty of Windsor in 1386) the Portuguese community in London is small. It was the decades after the Second World War which saw an influx of Portuguese arriving in London, largely as a result of a lack of economic opportunities in Portugal.

One focal point for the city's Iberian community is the area around Golborne Road and Portobello. On these roads, the community is served by a Spanish school, Spanish and Portuguese delicatessens, and cafés and bars in which to meet other members of the community. Camden Town, Stockwell and Vauxhall, too, are home to a number of Portuguese food shops, cafés and restaurants.

# Spanish & Portuguese Cuisine

**B**oth Spanish and Portuguese cookery share many characteristic ingredients: salted cod, paprika sausages, rice, beans, garlic and olive oil. The Moorish occupation of the Iberian Peninsula from AD 711 has left its mark on the sweets of both countries, with ground almonds and egg yolks used in desserts and cakes such as the Portuguese touchino de ceu or Spanish tarta de naranja.

Seafood is important in both cuisines, with an extensive range fished on the countries' long coastlines. Many of the famous regional dishes are seafood-based, such as zarzuela (Catalan seafood stew), marmitako (Basque bonito soup) and Northern-Portuguese caldeirada. There is no squeamishness when it comes to seafood. Lampreys are eaten in Northern Portugal in a famous dish, lapreia a moda do Minho; while Spanish calamares en su tinta, calls for squid to be cooked in its own black ink. Absolute freshness is demanded and one traditional Spanish fish dish is nicknamed mato mulo (mule killer) because the fish used in it had to be rushed by mule from the coast to Madrid.

There are some obvious differences between the cuisines and national dishes. From Portugal's former colonies come spices and flavourings such as spicy piri piri sauce – used in both Brazil and East Africa. Tapas, however, are quintessentially Spanish. The term means 'little lid' and is thought to come from the bar tradition of covering glasses with a saucer of olives or nuts. Bars vie with each other to offer good tapas and the discerning Spanish, who both enjoy their food and take it seriously, hunt out their favourites with a passion.

Both Spain and Portugal retain a strong sense of regionalism, with traditional dishes still cherished. Many recipes feature a place name, such as de salmao a Lisboeta, or fabada Asturiana. As in Italian cuisine, certain areas or towns are known for the quality of their food, with the best Spanish seafood coming from Cadiz or Galicia and the best Portugese caldo verde from the Minho.

# Glossary

**Aguardiente (orujo):** a potent Spanish spirit, distilled from the left-over grapes and pips after wine has been made.

**Anchovies (boquerones, biqueiros):** tiny cured fish, usually filleted, with a strong, salty flavour.

*Anchovies*

**Capers (alcaparras):** the unopened buds of a Mediterranean shrub, sold and used in their pickled form. Spain is the world's largest producer of capers.

**Cava:** sparkling Spanish wine made using the champagne method, with Cordoniu and Frexenet among the best producers.

**Charcuterie:** *butifarra*, a white Spanish sausage, spiced with cinnamon, cloves and nutmeg; *chorizo* or *chourico*, paprika sausages, used in cooked dishes, to which they add a distinctive colour and flavour, or eaten as a salami; *jamon de Serrano*, a highly prized, salt-cured Spanish ham, the best of which is made from the acorn-fed

pigs of the Estremadura region; *lomo*, cured pork loin from Spain; *presunto*, a fine salt-cured ham from Portugal, traditionally made from acorn-fed pigs from Tras-os-Montes.

**Cheese:** *azeitaio*, small Portuguese sheep's milk cream cheeses; *cabrales*, a famous Spanish blue-veined cheese, made from cow's milk but sometimes with sheep's or goat's milk added; *evora*, a creamy, strong, salty sheep's milk cheese from Portugal; *idiazabal*, a much-prized, semi-soft cheese with a dark rind made from sheep's milk in the Basque region of Spain; *ilha*, a Portuguese Cheddar-like cheese made from cow's milk; *mahon*, a flavourful Spanish semi-soft cow's milk cheese; *manchego*, one of Spain's best-known cheeses, made with sheep's milk and sold in three grades depending on age; *roncal*, a hard, Spanish, sheep's milk cheese; *serra*, a soft, Portuguese, sheep's milk cheese.

**Chickpeas (garbanzos, grado):** hazelnut-shaped, yellow peas.

**Coriander (coentros):** a sharp-flavoured green herb, similar in appearance to continental parsley, widely used in Portuguese cookery.

Madeira: a famous Portuguese fortified wine,             from the island of Madeira.

Madelenas: small, sweet, golden-brown cakes, eaten for breakfast in Spain.

Muscatel raisins: dried muscatel grapes, with a distinctive flavour.

*Muscatel raisins*

Olive oil: olive oil is produced in both Spain and Portugal and is the main cooking oil in both countries. Carbonell, with its elegant Art Nouveau labels, is one of Spain's famous brands.

Olives: green olives stuffed with anchovies are particularly popular in Spain.

Paprika: a bright red powder, made from ground sweet or spicy peppers and used as a spice.

*Pimenton*

Pimenton: Spanish paprika, made from ground Spanish paprika peppers, has a distinctive flavour and is available sweet, medium hot or hot. It is a popular Spanish spice, adding, for example, flavour and colour to chorizo sausages. It has a distinctive is available and is available sweet, medium hot and hot.

Pimientos de padron: slightly piquant, small peppers, delicious pan-fried and sprinkled with sea salt.

Pine kernels (pinon, pinhao): small, ivory-coloured stone pine kernels, used in both sweet and savoury dishes.

Piri piri: a hot Portuguese sauce made from chillies, a culinary legacy from Portugal's colonial past.

Port: a fortified wine from the Douro valley in North-West Portugal. Its creation can be traced back to the early seventeenth century when, due to Anglo-French hostilities, Portuguese wine rather than French claret was exported to England.

*Piri- piri*

**Quince paste (membrillo, marmelo):** a thick, golden, jelly-like paste made from quinces, eaten as a sweetmeat or as a classic accompaniment to cheese.

**Rice:** introduced by the Moors to Spain and Portugal in AD 711. Short-grain rice is used for Spanish paella.

**Saffron:** a costly spice made from the stigmas of a type of crocus, sold in either thread or powdered form.

*Saffron*

**Salt cod (bacalao, bacalhau):** dried, salted cod traditionally eaten on Fridays for religious reasons. In Portugal it is regarded as a national delicacy and there is said to be a different bacalhau recipe for every day of the year. It should be soaked for 24–36 hours before cooking to remove excess salt.

**Sherry:** a classic Spanish wine named after the town of Jerez and imported by the British since the fifteenth century.

**Tiger nut (chufa):** a small, wrinkled rhizome from which horchata, a refreshing almond-flavoured drink thought to have been introduced by the Moors, is made.

**Turron:** Spanish nougat, available in two forms: *alicante*, crisp and textured with chopped nuts, or *jijona*, soft and crumbly, made from ground nuts. Traditionally this is a Christmas treat but it is now available all the year round.

**Vinho verde:** delicate effervescent wines, both white and red, which form around a quarter of Portugal's wine production.

# Food Shops

As with London's Italian food stores, the older food shops began as corner shops, selling everyday ingredients to their community. Brindisa, which started as an importer of top-notch Spanish foodstuffs, has done a huge amount to raise the profile of Spanish cuisine in the UK through its foodshop at Borough Market and its tapas bars.

# Central

## Brindisa Shop

- Stoney Street, Borough Market, SE1
- 020 7407 1036
- Borough LU
- www.brindisashops.com
- Tue-Wed 10am-5.30pm,
  Thur 10am-5.30pm, Fri 10am-6pm,
  Sat 8.30am-5pm

Brindisa have been one of the pioneers of Iberian cuisine in London. Their permanent stall is one of the highlights of a visit to Borough Market, where you can source the finest hand-carved ham and other Spanish store cupboard essentials.

## Caleya Iberica

- 195 Great Portland St, W1
- 020 76368650
- Great Portland Street LU
- www.ibericalondon.co.uk
- Mon-Sat 11am-6pm

This handsome, spacious delicatessen, housed under the same roof as a flourishing tapas bar and Spanish restaurant, is the retail arm of an experienced Spanish exporters, specializing in gourmet foods. As one might expect, therefore, the emphasis is on both quality and breadth, from mouthwatering Serrano and Iberico hams on the bone to the cheese room, which houses an impressive range of cheeses. The extensive stock includes some interesting Spanish wines.

## Delicias de Portugal

- 43 Warwick Way, SW1
- 020 7630 5597
- Pimlico LU, Victoria LU/Rail
- Mon-Sat 8am-8pm, Sun 9am-2pm

This pretty delicatessen caters to hungry office workers, offering pasteis de bacalhau and a selection of Portuguese cakes and pastries as well as sandwiches. There is a large range of deli goods, including huge slabs of bacalhau (cut on demand), packets of 'flan' and a choice of goat's cheeses.

Spanish & Portuguese Food Shops

## Madeira Delicatessen

🏠 *46C Albert Embankment, SE1*
☎ *020 7820 1117*
🚌 *Vauxhall LU/Rail*
🕐 *020 7820 0314*

Under the railway arches at Vauxhall, Madeira Delicatessen is a cavernous, down-to-earth shop. It offers an impressive range of Portuguese foodstuffs, from everyday basics to treats including Portuguese pastries and a large selection of wines.

# North

## Delicias de Portugal

🏠 *1008 Harrow Road, NW10*
☎ *020 8960 7933*
🚌 *Kensal Green LU*
🕐 *Mon-Sat 8.30am-7.30pm,
Sun 9am-2pm*

A well-stocked Portuguese food shop.

## Ferreira

🏠 *40 Delancey Street, NW1*
☎ *020 7485 2351*
🚌 *Camden Town LU*
🕐 *Mon-Sat 8am-9pm, Sun 8am-8pm*

A friendly Portuguese corner store. There is a selection of cakes, Portuguese cheeses and sausages. In addition, there is a selection of tinned and bottled groceries, wines and slabs of bacalhau.

## Lisboa

🏠 *4 Plender Street, NW1*
☎ *020 7387 1782*
🚌 *Camden Town LU*
🕐 *Tue-Fri 9.30am-6.30pm, Sat
9am-7pm, Sun 10am-2pm*

A branch of the established Portuguese delicatessen (see opposite page for further details).

## Villa Franca

🏠 *3 Plender Street, NW1*
☎ *020 7387 8236*
🚌 *Camden Town LU*
🕐 *Mon-Sat 7am-8pm, Sun 9am-7pm*

A small down-to-earth shop and café selling a mixture of Portuguese and English patisserie plus a range of foodstuffs including bacalhau (stored beneath the counter), cured meats, soft drinks and cheeses. Downstairs is a smoking room from which blares the sound of Portuguese satellite TV.

## The Wine Cellar

🏠 *193 Kentish Town Road, NW5*
☎ *020 7267 9501*
🚌 *Kentish Town LU/Rail*
🕐 *Mon-Fri 8am-8pm, Sat 9am-8pm*

This narrow, homely Portuguese food shop and café stocks basic foodstuffs including cheeses, pancetta, pig's trotters, chourico as well as tinned seafood, pulses and packets of 'pudim'. Downstairs, the reason for the shop's name becomes clear: the entire basement is stocked with a wide variety of Portuguese wines plus port and Madeira.

## Rias Altas
⌖ *97 Frampton Street, NW8*
☎ *020 7262 4340*
🚌 *Edgware Road LU*
🕐 *Mon-Sat 9am-7.30pm*
A long, narrow Spanish delicatessen, well-stocked with foodstuffs such as Spanish cheeses, cured meats, bacalao and fine Spanish wines.

# West

## Garcia R. & Sons
⌖ *248 Portobello Road, W11*
☎ *020 7221 6119*
🚌 *Ladbroke Road LU, Notting Hill Gate LU*
🕐 *Mon-Sun 9am-6pm*
Founded in 1957, this spacious food shop is still run by the Garcia family. There is an extensive range of groceries and store cupboard basics, from pimenton and saffron to pulses, paella rice and a huge range of tinned seafood. The deli counter does a roaring trade in anchovy-stuffed olives, chorizo sausages and costly Jamon Iberico (from acorn-fed black-footed pigs). Turrons are kept throughout the year, with the range expanding at Christmas time.

## Lisboa
⌖ *6 World's End Place, SW10*
☎ *020 7376 3639*
🚌 *Fulham Broadway LU*
🚌 *Mon-Sat 8am-6pm*
A branch of the well-established Golborne Road emporium.

## Lisboa Delicatessen
⌖ *54 Golborne Road, W10*
☎ *020 8969 1052*
🚌 *Westbourne Park LU*
🕐 *Mon-Sat 9.30am-7.30pm,*
*Sun 10am-1pm*
When Carlos Gomes opened this shop over 20 years ago, it was the first Portuguese delicatessen in London and he and his partners 'imported' their own stock in suitcases from Portugal. All the essential ingredients for Portuguese cooking can be found in this characterful shop: pungent bacalhau, pulses including Brazilian black beans, sausages and trays full of pickled and salted pig's trotters, snouts, tails and ears. A back room contains a selection of Portuguese wines and spirits.

Spanish & Portuguese Food Shops

## Lisboa Patisserie

🏠 *57 Golborne Road, W10*

☎ *020 8968 5242*

🚌 *Westbourne Park LU*

🕐 *Daily 8am-8pm*

Across the road from the delicatessen, this small, popular patisserie supplies a constant stream of customers with delicious Portuguese pastries freshly baked on the premises. Delicacies include pasteis de nata (custard tarts) and bolo arroz (rice cakes).

# South-West

## A & C Continental Groceries

🏠 *3 Atlantic Road, SW9*

☎ *020 7733 3766*

🚌 *Brixton LU/Rail*

🕐 *Mon-Sat 8am-8pm*

Under the arches, this friendly neighbourhood shop has an excellent range of basics, from fresh fruit, vegetables and herbs outside, to loaves of bread inside. Portuguese chourico, morcela (black pudding) and cheeses can be found at the deli counter. Pasties de nata and baccalau rissoles are delivered daily.

## Delicias de Portugal

🏠 *280 Wandsworth Road, SW8*

☎ *020 7622 9811*

🚌 *Wandsworth Road Rail*

🕐 *Mon-Fri 9am-8pm, Sat 9am-7pm, Sun 10am-7pm*

A down-to-earth, friendly food shop, filled with a good selection of Portuguese staples.

## Sintra Delicatessen

🏠 *146-48 Stockwell Road, SW9*

☎ *020 7733 9402*

🚌 *Stockwell LU*

🕐 *Daily 9am-8pm*

The scent of bacalhau and the hum of conversation evoke Portugal as you enter this homely shop, which is attached to a down-to-earth café and restaurant. There is a good selection of foodstuffs including chourico, presunto and morcela as well as Portuguese cakes and bread. The shelves are lined with all kinds of Portuguese groceries including cereals, olive oil, Portuguese wines and boxes of Ancora crochet yarn.

# Eating Places

Recent years have seen a heightened awareness in Britain of the quality of Spanish foodstuffs. With tapas fitting perfectly into the current dining trend for small dishes and 'grazing' menus. London's Spanish dining out scene has experienced a 'tapas boom' and now features a number of outstanding newcomers. London's Portuguese eateries range from simple cafés in which to enjoy bacalhau fritters, pastries and coffee to restaurants offering hearty dishes such as caldeirada or caldo verde.

## Central

### Barrafina £££-££££

🖃 *54 Frith Street, W1*
☎ *020 7440 1463*
🖲 *www.barrafina.co.uk*
🚌 *Tottenham Court Road LU*

This busy, narrow bar has made a name for itself with its outstanding tapas. A no-booking policy together with this tapas bar's popularity means that finding a seat can be an issue, so come prepared to queue.

### Casa Brindisa £££

🖃 *7-9 Exhibition Road, SW7*
☎ *020 7590 0008*
🚌 *South Kensington LU*

This attractive tapas bar from noted Spanish food importers, Brindisa, offers an appetising showcase for their fine Spanish foods. Happy diners tuck into superb Spanish charcuterie from the Jamoneria, a fine range of Spanish cheeses and piquant padron peppers.

### Fino £££-££££

🖃 *33 Charlotte Street, W1*
☎ *020 7813 8010*
🚌 *Goodge Street / Tottenham Court Road LU*

A stylish, spacious Fitzrovia basement eaterie, serving creative, contemporary tapas, plus an excellent range of sherries and wines.

### Iberica Food & Culture £££

🖃 *195 Great Portland Street, W1*
☎ *020 7636 8650*
🖲 *www.ibericalondon.com*
🚌 *Great Portland Street LU*

This spacious Spanish establishment combines a handsome, airy ground floor tapas bar and delicatessen area with a small, intimate upstairs restaurant. Tapas dishes to look out for include gloriously flavourful black rice with cuttlefish, prawns and alioli and the exemplary ham croquetes Casa Marcial. An extensive Spanish wine list ranges from refreshing whites to elegant reds.

## Moro   £££-££££

⌨ *34-36 Exmouth Market, EC1*

☎ *020 7833 8336*

🖥 *www.moro.co.uk*

🚌 *Farringdon LU/Rail*

Run by creative culinary husband-and-wife team Sam and Samantha Clark, this is a relaxed, convivial restaurant. Moro's draws on Spanish and North African cuisines to create an inventive and richly flavourful menu. The extensive range of Spanish wines and sherries is another draw.

## Navarros   £££

⌨ *67 Charlotte Street, W1*

☎ *020 7637 7713*

🚌 *Goodge Street LU*

A prettily decorated, traditional tapas bar, with a loyal following. It serves a consistently tasty classic tapas, from simple tortilla to prawns in garlic.

## O Fado   £££-££££

⌨ *50 Beauchamp Place, SW3*

☎ *020 7589 3002*

🚌 *Knightsbridge, South Kensington LU*

This long-established, cosy basement restaurant offers a chance not only to sample classic Portuguese food but to listen to night-time performances of haunting fado music.

## Salt Yard   £££

⌨ *54 Goodge Street, W1*

☎ *020 7637 0657*

🚌 *Goodge Street LU*

🖥 *www.saltyard.co.uk*

This popular, relaxed tapas bar draws its inspiration from both Spanish and Italian cuisines. It offers classic Italian charcuterie such as Prosciutto di Parma alongside Jamon Serrano and wines from both countries. Dishes range from stylish bar snacks such as quails' eggs with paprika salt to salt cod fritters with orange alioli or Old Spot pork belly confit.

## Tapas Brindisa   £££

⌨ *Borough Market*
   *8-20 Southwark Street, SE1*

☎ *020 7357 8880*

🚌 *London Bridge LU/Rail*

On the corner of Borough Market, this pleasantly informal, contemporary tapas bar, housed in an old potato warehouse, was set up by Brindisa, the noted Spanish food importers, to showcase their ingredients including their famous Joselito hams. Tapas range from old favourites such as potato tortilla or croquetas to more modish offerings, such as deep-fried Monte enebro goat's cheese with fragrant honey. All the tapas can be washed down with a glass of fine sherry, cava or good Spanish wine.

# North

## La Bota   £££

⌨ *31 Broadway Parade*
*Tottenham Lane, N8*
☎ *020 8340 3082*
🚌 *Finsbury Park LU/Rail, then the W7 bus*

A modest, traditional tapas bar which has a loyal local following.

## El Parador   £££

⌨ *245 Eversholt Street, NW1*
☎ *020 7387 3789*
🚌 *Camden Town LU*

This well-established tapas bar comes into its own in the summer, when you can sit in the garden at the back and sample a variety of tapas accompanied with Spanish wines and beers.

# West

## Café Garcia   £-££

⌨ *246 Portobello Road, W11*
☎ *020 7221 6119*
🚌 *Ladbroke Road LU, Notting Hill Gate LU*

Owned by the Spanish food shop next door, this contemporary café serves up 'proper' Spanish hot chocolate with churros, own-made horchata (the almond-flavoured drink made from tigers nuts), and assorted tapas.

## Café Oporto   £

⌨ *62A Golborne Road, W10*
☎ *020 8968 8839*
🚌 *Ladbroke Grove LU*

Small, friendly Portuguese café in which to enjoy savoury croquettes, sandwiches or delicious, freshly made, coffee.

## Galicia   £££

⌨ *323 Portobello Road, SW10*
☎ *020 8969 3539*
🚌 *Ladbroke Grove LU*
*Notting Hill Gate LU*

This atmospheric tapas bar and restaurant, is popular with the local Spanish community. It specialises in food from Galicia, hence the large number of fish and seafood dishes.

Spanish & Portuguese Eating Places

## Lisboa Patisserie   £

🗒 *57 Golborne Road, W10*
☎ *020 8968 5242*
🚌 *Ladbroke Grove / Notting Hill Gate LU*

This delightful Portuguese patisserie, with its excellent cakes (including delectable pasteis de nata custard tarts), is usually full of regulars sampling coffee and pastries.

# South-East

## Lola Rojo   £££-££££

🗒 *78 Northcote Road, SW11*
☎ *020 7350 2262*
🖱 *www.lolarojo.net*
🚌 *Clapham Junction Rail*

This diminutive tapas bar restaurant is perpetually buzzing with contented diners and drinkers enjoying a delicious selection of classy tapas and quality wines.

# South-West

## Funchal Bakery   £

🗒 *141-143 Stockwell Road, SW9*
☎ *020 7733 3134*
🚌 *Stockwell LU*

In addition to the bakery and deli, Funchal offers a relaxed café area in which to enjoy delicious Portuguese cakes and pastries. The pasteis de nata and coffee are both to be recommended.

## The Gallery   ££-£££

🗒 *256A Brixton Hill, SW2*
☎ *020 8671 8311*
🚌 *Brixton LU*

Come hungry and head past the take-away at the front to the dining room at the back. Excellent value, seriously tasty portions of grilled chickens and meat are the speciality at this restaurant which is only open in the evenings.

## Rebatos   £££-££££

🗒 *169 South Lambeth Road, SW8*
☎ *020 7735 6388*
🚌 *Stockwell LU*
🖱 *www.rebatos.com*

A veteran of London's tapas bar scene, Rebatos is run with jovial professionalism and remains hugely popular. The front bar area is the place in which to enjoy tapas, while the roomy, tiled restaurant at the back offers an extensive a la carte Spanish menu, with fish and seafood a speciality..

# Cookbooks

## The Spanish Kitchen
*Nicholas Butcher*
A knowledgeable book conveying the regional diversity of Spanish cooking.

## The Foods and Wines of Spain
*Penelope Casas*
A comprehensive and appetising survey of Spanish cuisine.

## Casa Moro
*Sam & Sam Clark*
Guaranteed to make you want to cook, with gutsy flavourful Spanish and Arabic-inspired food ranging from tapas dishes to partridge with oloroso sherry.

## Moro: the Cookbook
*Sam & Sam Clark*
A wonderful resource from the chef-owners of Moro restaurant. It offers simple recipes, drawing on Spanish and Arabic cuisine.

## The Food of Spain & Portugal
*Elizabeth Luard*
An attractive guide to Iberian cuisine, with accessible recipes.

## 1080 Recipes
*Simone and Ines Ortega*
A huge, comprehensive cookbook, including regional recipes from all over Spain.

## The Food of Spain and Portugal
*Elizabeth Lambert Ortiz*
An authoratitive look at Iberian cooking, with accessible recipes.

## Seasonal Spanish Food
*Jose Pizarro*
Written by the talented Head Chef at Tapas Brindisa, this is a delicious collection of recipes and evocative anecdotes.

## The Taste of Portugal
*Edite Vieira*
A wonderfully evocative and appetising cookbook, offering a considerable insight into Portuguese cuisine.

Miscellaneous

Scandinavian Kitchen

Afghan
American
Argentinian
Austrian
Belgian
Brazilian
Burmese
Colombian
Czech
Georgian
German
Hungarian
Korean
Mexican
New Zealand
Russian
Scandinavian
South African
Taiwanese

# Afghan

## Afghan Kitchen   £-££
🏠 *35 Islington Green, N1*
☎ *020 7359 8019*
🚌 *Angel LU*
This tiny, restaurant offers simple, tasty home-style Afghani food at very reasonable prices and with friendly service.

## Masa £-£££
🏠 *24-26 Headstone Drive, HA3*
☎ *020 8861 6213*
🚌 *Harrow & Wealdstone LU*
This smart restaurant has a loyal following among London's Afghan community.  Dishes include impeccably-cooked kebabs and mantoo (filled pasta).

# American

## Hummingbird Bakery
🏠 *133 Portobello Road, W11*
☎ *020 7229 6446*
🚌 *Notting Hill Gate LU*
A small American-style bakery selling treats such as eye-catching, brightly frosted cupcakes, pecan pie and lemon meringue pie.  Hummingbird is proving really popular with the locals and visitors to the market.

## Panzer's

🏠 *13-19 Circus Road, NW8*

☎ *020 7722 8596*

🚌 *St John's Wood LU*

🕐 *Mon-Fri 8am-7pm*
   *Sat 8am-6pm, Sun 8am-2pm*

St John's Wood affluent American ex-pat community is shrewdly catered for by this large Jewish delicatessen. Panzer's makes a point of stocking American favourites such as grape jelly, flour tortillas and mini-marshmallows.

## Partridges

🏠 *2-5 Duke of York Square*
   *King's Road, SW*

☎ *020 7730 0651*

🖮 *www.partridges.co.uk*

🚌 *Sloane Square LU*

🕐 *daily 8am-10pm*

This upmarket grocers stocks a range of American foodstuffs.

## Partridges

🏠 *17-21 Gloucester Road, SW7*

☎ *020 7581 0535*

🖮 *www.partridges.co.uk*

🚌 *Gloucester Road LU*

🕐 *Daily 8am-11pm*

A smaller branch of the King's Road establishment, with a particular focus on American foodstuffs.

## Rosslyn Delicatessen

🏠 *56 Rosslyn Hill, NW3*

☎ *020 7794 9210*

🚌 *Hampstead LU*

🕐 *Mon-Sat 8.30an-9.30pm*
   *Sun 8.30am-8pm*

This well-established delicatessen offers North London's American community an entire section devoted to American foodstuffs imported from the USA. Expect to find classics like Betty Crocker cake mixes, Froot Loops cereal and Aunt Jemima's pancake mix.

# Argentinian

## Buen Ayre

🏠 *50 Broadway Market, E8*

☎ *020 7275 9900*

🚌 *London Fields LU*

This friendly, intimate restaurant does a roaring trade in Argentinian beef dishes, including hearty grill-cooked meat selections.

## Freggo

🏠 *27-29 Swallow Street, W1*

☎ *020 7287 9506*

🚌 *Piccadilly Circus*

🕐 *Mon-Thur 8am-11pm, Fri 8am-2am,*
   *Sat 10am-2am, Sun 10am-11pm*

An off-shoot of the Gaucho restaurant chain, specialising in Argentinian cuisine, this smart ice cream parlour offers luxurious ice cream – in flavours including Malbec and Berries and Dulce de Leche.

## Gaucho Piccadilly
🖃 *25 Swallow Street, W1*
☎ *020 7734 4040*
🚌 *Piccadilly Circus LU*

This smart restaurant is famous for its prime Argentinian beef. It also has classic dishes on the menu such as empanadas and ceviches.

# Austrian

## Kipferl
🖃 *70 Long Lane, EC1*
☎ *020 7796 2229*
🚌 *Farringdon/St Paul's LU*
🕑 *Mon-Fri 8am-5pm, Sat 9am-5pm*

A delicious taste of Austria is on offer here at this small, austerely stylish Austrian delicatessen and café, run by the courteous Christian Malnig. A carefully sourced selection of Austrian foodstuffs includes pumpkin seed oil, kren (horseradish sauce), top-notch jams and fine Austrian wines, such as Biegler's Zweigelt. Kipferls is also noted for its own-baked Austrian cakes and pastries, such as the famous Sacher torte and topfentorte. Customers sit and enjoy excellent coffee or tuck into sausages such as kaesekrainer or debreziner served with rye bread and mustard.

# Belgian

## Belgo Noord   ££
🖃 *72 Chalk Farm Road, NW1*
☎ *020 7267 0718*
✒ *www.belgo-restaurants.co.uk*
🚌 *Chalk Farm LU*

Mussels and frites washed down with flavourful Belgian beers are the house speciality at this popular restaurant, with its minimalist décor and bustling atmosphere. *Branches: 50 Earlham Street, WC2, 67 Kingsway WC2,  48 Clapham High Street, SW4,  173 Upper Street, N1*

# Brazilian

## Casa Brasil
🖃 *289 Regent's Park Road, N3*
☎ *020 8371 1999*
🚌 *Finchley Central LU*

This small, friendly café and deli offers a taste of Brazil, with its owner happy to answer any enquiries about Brazilian food.

# Burmese

## Mandalay   ££-£££
- 444 Edgware Road, W2
- ☎ 020 7258 3696
- 🚇 Edgware Road LU

This relaxed, friendly restaurant offers a rare chance to sample Burmese cuisine. A fascinating blend of Asian, Chinese and Thai ingredients and cooking techniques. The owners are happy to offer menu advice.

# Colombian

## Brixton Market
- Brixton Station Rd, Pope's Rd, Atlantic Rd, Electric Rd & Electric Av, SW9
- 🚇 Brixton LU/Rail
- 🕐 Mon, Tue & Thur-Sat 8am-5.30pm, Wed 8am-1pm

These days Brixton Market houses a number of Colombian businesses, ranging from cafés and bars to several food shops, including butchers and fishmongers.

## Nardo Coffee
- ✎ www.café-ita.co.uk

A website-based business offering organic and biodynamic coffee from its own farm in north-east Brazil.

# Czech

## Czechoslovak Restaurant
- 74 West End Lane. NW6
- ☎ 020 7372 1193

Housed in Czechoslovak National House, this old-fashioned restaurant serves up large portions of classic Czech-Slovak dishes such as halusky, brawn, roast goose and goulash. Desserts – such as apricot dumplings - are similarly substantial.

# Georgian

## Tbilisi
- 91 Holloway Road, N7
- ☎ 020 7607 2536
- 🚇 Highbury & Islington LU

A hospitably-run restaurant offering a chance to sample Georgian cuisine, from soups and hearty stews as well as some fine Georgian wines.

# German

## Backhaus
- 175 Ashburnham Road, TW10
- ☏ 020 8048 6040
- 🚌 Richmond LU/Rail, then bus 371
- 🕐 Mon-Fri 8am-6pm, Sat 8am-4pm

This neatly arranged delicatessen stocks a wide range of products imported from Germany, including frozen ready-meals and a huge choice of hams and sausages, such as bratwurst and leberwurst. Just down the road is the shop's bakery which produces an impressive array of German baked goods, including rye breads, pretzel and caraway sticks. At Christmas, lovingly prepared stollen, made in September and matured for eight weeks, is available.

## German Deli
- 3 Park Street, SE1
- ☏ 020 7378 0000
- ✎ www.germandeli.co.uk
- 🚌 London Bridge LU/Rail
- 🕐 Mon-Fri 9am-7pm, Sat 9am-5pm

This small orderly shop is one of the few places in London selling an extensive range of German foodstuffs and has a predominantly German clientele. Customers can choose from sausages and cured meats, such as leberkase, the shop's own-baked sourdough breads and fresh pretzel rolls. They also stock an array of tinned, jarred and packaged goods, including salty liquorice. Christmas sees the stock increase to include seasonal treats such as ebkuchen, stollen and marzipan.

## K & S Bakery
- 247 Old Brompton Road, SW5
- ☏ 020 7373 8338
- ✎ www.ksbakery.co.uk
- 🚌 Earl's Court LU
- 🕐 Mon-Sat 7am-7pm, Sun 10am-5pm

This neat bakery offers Londoners a rare chance to sample freshly baked German breads, cakes and pastries. Offerings range from rye bread, multigrain bread and pretzels to classic Apple Strudel.

# Hungarian

## The Gay Hussar   £££-££££
- 2 Greek Street, W1
- ☏ 020 7437 0973
- 🚌 Leicester Square / Tottenham Court Road LU

A venerable Soho restaurant, noted for its literary and political clientele as well as its generous portions of authentic Hungarian food. Renowned dishes include chilled cherry soup and Transylvanian stuffed cabbage.

## Louis Patisserie   £

- 🏠 *32 Heath Street, NW3*
- ☎ *020 7435 9908*
- 🚌 *Hampstead LU*
- 🕐 *Daily 9.30am-6pm*

Set up by Mr Louis over 30 years ago, this charmingly old-fashioned patisserie sells Hungarian cakes and pastries such as dobos (caramel cake) and makos (poppyseed slice). There is also a tearoom.

# Korean

## Centre Point Food Store

- 🏠 *20-21 St Giles High Street, WC2*
- ☎ *020 7836 9860*
- 🚌 *Tottenham Court Road LU*
- 🕐 *Mon-Sat 10am-10.30pm,*
  *Sun 12noon-8pm*

In the shadow of Centre Point's looming tower, the Centre Point Food Store is a large, well-stocked food shop. Around half the shop is given over to a comprehensive selection of Korean foodstuffs.

## Hanna

- 🏠 *41 Store Street, WC1*
- ☎ *020 7636 4118*
- 🚌 *Goodge St LU*
- 🕐 *Mon-Sat 10am-6pm*

Hidden down a peaceful Bloomsbury side-street, this tidy shop stocks a good range of Korean foodstuffs, from rice to pickles.

## Nippon & Korea Centre

- 🏠 *9 Wardour Street, W1*
- ☎ *020 7434 1777*
- 🚌 *Leicester Square, Piccadilly Circus, LU*
- 🕐 *Daily 10am-7pm*

In the heart of Soho, this shop offers a range of gaudy, packaged Korean and Japanese foodstuffs.

## Song's Supermarket

- 🏠 *76-78 Burlington Road,*
  *New Malden, Surrey, KT3*
- ☎ *020 8942 8471*
- 🚌 *New Malden Rail*
- 🕐 *Daily 9am-8.30pm*

New Malden's substantial Korean community is served by a number of restaurants and shops. Song's is next to Jie's Café, an informal Korean café from where the most appetising, savoury aromas waft. Neatly arranged, Song's has an impressive range of stock: fresh meat and fish counters, fresh fruit, vegetables and herbs and a huge array of groceries. Particularly tempting is the extensive range of chilled, ready-made dishes such as spinach with garlic and chilli.

# Mauritian

## Chez Liline   ££-££
101 Stroud Green Road, N4
020 7263 6550
Finsbury Park LU/Rail

Laid-back and unpretentious, this is a place to enjoy large portions of Mauritian seafood, combining both tropical and French flavours.

# Mexican

## Cool Chile
www.coolchile.co.uk

Founded by Dodie Miller, Cool Chile have been promoting authentic Mexican food in the UK long before it became fashionable. Visitors to the website can stock up with an awesome range of Mexican chilles as well as ingredients such as fresh tomatillos, pulses, mole poblano paste and Mexican drinking chocolate. These are also on offer at Cool Chile's restaurant, Taqueria (see opposite for details), and their stall at Borough Market on Fridays and Saturdays.

## Mestizo
103 Hampstead Road, NW1
020 7387 4064
www.mestizomx.com

A firm favourite of Mexican friends, this roomy, informal Mexican restaurant offers substantial portions of tasty Mexican food, with the molcajete especially recommended.

## Taqueria
139-143 Westbourne Grove, W11
020 7229 4734
www.taqueria.co.uk

A relaxed Mexican restaurant specialising in tacos made from fresh corn tortillas, baked on the premises. Fillings and toppings range from grilled jalapeno peppers to shredded slow-cooked pork.

## Wahaca
66 Chandos Place, WC2
020 7240 1883
www.wahaca.co.uk

Founded by Masterchef winner Thomasina Miers, this trendy basement restaurant is a lively affair, buzzing with customers. The wide-ranging, seasonally-varying menu takes its inspiration from Mexican market food, offering dishes such as huitlacoche quesadilla and chicken pibil burrito.

Mauritian/ Mexican

# New Zealand

## Kiwifruits

⊞ 6-7 Royal Opera Arcade, Pall Mall, SW1
☎ 020 7930 4587
✎ www.kiwifruitsnzshop.com
🚌 Piccadilly Circus LU
🕐 Mon-Fri 9am,-5.30pm, Sat 10am-4pm

In the heart of a smart West End shopping arcade, this shop caters to ex-pat Kiwis. Stock includes books, music, clothing, jewellery and a range of foodstuffs.

# Russian

## Kalinka

⊞ 35 Queensway, W2
☎ 020 7243 6125
🚌 Bayswater LU, Queensway LU
🕐 Mon-Sat 11am-8pm,
    Sun 12noon-6.30pm

Behind its window proudly decorated with a Moscow scene, this long narrow shop is well-stocked with Russian and Ukranian foodstuffs, catering to the nearby Russian and Ukranian embassies. Food ranges from basics such as savoury salted fish and sausages to condiments, biscuits, cakes and a colourful display of confectionery.

New Zealand/ Russian

## Russkij Bazar

🏠 276 Cambridge Heath Road, E2
☎ 020 8980 6964
🚇 Cambridge Heath LU
🕐 Daily 10am-10pm

A down-to-earth shop, specializing in Latvian, Lithuanian, Polish and Russian foodstuffs.

# Scandinavian

## Garbo's

🏠 42 Crawford Street, W1
☎ 020 7262 6587
🚇 Baker Street LU

This Swedish restaurant is a long-established institution, complete with a stuffed moose. The menu offers traditional Swedish fare including meatballs, herrings and salads.

## Harcourt Arms

🏠 32 Harcourt Street, W1H 4HX
☎ 020 7723 6634
🚇 Edgware Road LU, Marylebone LU

Known to London's Swedish community as 'the Swedish pub'. This pub pulls in an ex-pat Swedish crowd who meet to socialize and watch Swedish sport on TV.

## Ikea

🏠 2 Drury Way
  North Circular Road, NW10
☎ 020 8451 5611
🕐 Mon-Fri 10am-8pm, Sat 9am-6pm,
  Sun 11am-5pm

Situated on the North Circular, this cavernous Swedish furniture store has a small food outlet. Stock includes essentials such as huge circular crispbreads, gravadlax, lingonberries and frozen Swedish meatballs.

## Scandinavian Kitchen

🏠 61 Great Titchfield Street, W1
☎ 020 7580 7161
🖱 www.scandikitchen.co.uk
🚇 Oxford Circus LU
🕐 Mon-Fri 8am-7pm, Sat 10am-6pm

Husband-and-wife team Jonas Aurell (Swedish), and Bronte Aurell (Danish), run this bright and cheery café-cum-deli with warm hospitality. The grocery and deli section here stocks an impressive 600 different foodstuffs from Denmark, Norway, Sweden and Finland. Scandinvian ex-pats can stock up on confectionary, crispbreads, mustards and jams such as lingonberry. Seasonal treats include frozen Swedish crayfish and saffron buns in December. On offer in the café area are an array of smorrebrod (open sandwiches), freshly made in the kitchen, and own-baked sweet treats.

## Totally Swedish

- 32 Crawford Street, W1
- 020 7224 9300
- Baker Street LU
- Mon-Fri 10am-6pm, Sat 10am-5pm

Patriotically painted in yellow and blue this pretty shop carries a whole range of Swedish edibles, from pickled herrings to treats such as liquorice sweets and aquavit.

During the run-up to Christmas look out for Christmas fairs and bazaars at the following Scandinavian churches and also at the Danish YWCA which offer a chance to buy and sample a host of Danish, Finnish, Norwegian and Swedish seasonal treats.

## Danish YWCA

- 43 Maresfield Gardens, NW3

## The Danish Church

- 4 St Katherine's Precinct Regent's Park, NW1
- www.danskekirke.org

## The Finnish Church in London

- 33, Albion Sreet, SE16
- www.finnishchurch.org.uk

## St Olav's (the Norwegian church)

- 1 St Olav's Square, SE16
- www.sjomannskirken.no/london

## Ulrika Eleonora Church (the Swedish church)

- 6-11 Harcourt Street, W1
- www.swedishchurch.com

# South African

## St Marcus

- 1 Rockingham Close, Priory Lane, Roehampton, SW15
- 020 8878 1898
- www.biltongstmarcus.co.uk
- Barnes Rail
- Daily 9am-6pm

Lovers of 'fine South African foods' including biltong and boerewors can satisfy their cravings at this 'mini-market'. The place is run with zest by South African master butcher Emory St Marcus.

# Taiwanese

## Leong's Legends

- 4 Macclesfield Street, W1
- 020 7287 0288
- Leicester Square LU

This pleasant restaurant offers Londoners a chance to sample Taiwanese cuisine, with its soup dumpling particularly popular.

# Kitchenware

Gill Wing Cookshop

# Central

## David Mellor

- 4 Sloane Square, SW1
- 020 7730 4259
- www.davidmellordesign.com
- Sloane Square LU
- Mon-Sat 9.30am-6pm, Sun 11am-5pm

Since its opening in 1969 this elegant shop has consistently championed good design. It stocks a select range of quality kitchenware and tableware that both looks great and works well. Stock here ranges from trademark David Mellor cutlery and ceramic mugs to hand-carved wooden salad and baking tins.

## Denny's

- 55A Dean Street. W1
- 020 7494 2745
- www.dennys.co.uk
- Leicester Square, Piccadilly Circus LU
- Mon-Fri 9.30am-6pm
  Sat 10.30am-4.30pm

A Soho institution, run with down-to-earth, knowledgeable expertise. Denny's has supplied generations of chefs with their kitchen kit, including uniform jackets, footwear and a range of professional knives. Because this is a shop for professionals, all prices are quoted without VAT

## Divertimenti

- 227-229 Brompton Road, SW3
- 020 7581 8065
- www.divertimenti.co.uk
- Knightsbridge, South Kensington LU
- Mon-Tue, Thur-Fri 9.30am-6pm
  Wed 9.30am-7pm, Sun 12noon-5.30pm

This smart, spacious shop – a sister shop to Marylebone's Divertimenti – offers the same tempting mixture of attractive tableware and good quality kitchen equipment, as well as a cookery theatre.

## Divertimenti

- 33-34 Marylebone High Street, W1
- 020 7935 0689
- www.divertimenti.co.uk
- Baker Street LU
- Mon-Wed & Fri 9.30am-6pm,
  Thur 9.30am-7pm, Sat 10am-6pm,
  Sun 10am-5.30pm

This ia an attractive, airy kitchenware store, complete with a café area. It offers a discerning mixture of ceramic tableware – from classic white French porcelain to colourful rustic ware – alongside pots, pans and Magimix and Kitchen Aid gadgets. The downstairs Cookery Theatre hosts a range of cookery classes by well-known food writers and chefs.

Kitchenware

## Leon Jaeggi

🏠 *77 Shaftesbury Avenue, W1*

☎ *020 7580 1974 or 020 7434 4545*

🚌 *Leicester Square LU*
*Piccadilly Circus LU*

🕒 *Mon-Sat 9am-5.30pm*

Trading since 1919, Jaeggi specialises in professional catering equipment and utensils. Highlights include top-notch cook's knives, from brands such as Global and Gustav, and French stainless steel pots and pans. Stock is extensive and the staff are helpful and knowledgeable. Note that prices do not include VAT.

## Pages

🏠 *121 Shaftesbury Avenue, W1*

☎ *0845 373 401*

✎ *www.pagescatering.co.uk*

🚌 *Leicester Square LU*
*Tottenham Court Road LU*

🕒 *Mon-Fri 9am-6pm, Sat 9am-5pm*

Aimed primarily at the catering trade, this large well-stocked shop offers professional kitchen equipment, from ice cream makers to ice sculpture moulds. Useful items for home cooks include superior knives, white ceramic tableware and a range of heavy duty blenders and processors. As with other professional stores, prices in store do not include VAT.

# North

## Gill Wing Cookshop

🏠 *190 Upper Street, N1*
☎ *020 7226 5392*
✑ *www.gillwing.co.uk*
🚌 *Highbury & Islington LU/Rail*
🕐 *Mon-Sat 9.30am-6pm, Sun 10am-6pm*

A friendly, well-stocked kitchen shop with a comprehensive range of kitchenware, ranging from stainless steel saucepans to decorative tableware and baking utensils for home bakers.
*Branch: 45 Park Road, N8 (020 8348 3451)*

## Richard Dare

🏠 *93 Regent's Park Road, NW1*
☎ *020 7722 9428*
🚌 *Chalk Farm LU*
🕐 *Mon-Fri 9.30am-6pm, Sat 10am-4pm*

This established, attractive kitchenware shop offers a tempting mix of stock, including ceramic tableware, wine glasses and knives.

## The Scullery

🏠 *123 Muswell Hill Broadway, N10*
☎ *020 8444 5236*
🚌 *Bus 134*
🕐 *Mon-Sat 9.30am-6pm*

A neat, cheery shop with a wide range of tableware plus kitchen utensils and cookware.

# North-West

## Doki Japanese Tableware

🏠 *Pacific Plaza, Unit 16, The Junction Wembley Retail Park, Engineers Way, Wembley, HA0*
☎ *020-8903 0235*
🚌 *Wembley Park LU*
🕐 *Daily 10am-6.30pm*

Formerly housed at the late, much-missed Oriental City shopping plaza in Colindale, Doki's new shop offers an extensive range of reasonably-priced Japanese tableware, from bowls to lacquerware.

## Popat Stores

🏠 *138 & 156-158 Ealing Road*
☎ *020 8902 2543 / 020 8903 6397*
🚌 *Alperton/Wembley Central LU*
🕐 *Mon-Sat 10am-6.30pm,*
   *Sun 11am-6.30pm*

Mr Popat opened his first shop at No 138 in the early 1970s, one of the first Asian businesses in the area. Today Ealing Road is lined with Asian businesses and the Popat family run both the original shop and its sister shop a few doors away at 156-8. Specialising in Indian kitchenware and household goods, the extensive stock ranges from spice tins and baskets for Indian flat breads to coconut scrapers and stone pestles and mortars.

# South-West

## Dentons
- 2-4 Clapham High Street, SW4
- ☎ 020 7450 0466
- 🖊 www.dentons.co.uk
- 🚌 Clapham Common LU
- 🕐 Mon-Fri 8.30am-5.30pm,
  Sat 8.45am-1pm

This established family-run firm offers an extensive range of catering equipment. All the stock is neatly displayed in this roomy showroom and there is plenty of knowledgeable staff at hand if you need any help or advice.

## Kooks Unlimited
- 2-4 Eton Street, TW10
- ☎ 020 8332 3030
- 🖊 www.kooksunlimited.com
- 🚌 Richmond LU/Rail
- 🕐 Mon-Sat 9.30am-6pm, Sun 11am-5pm

This friendly shop is crammed to the gills with stock, ranging from reputable cookware to gastro-gizmos. Sugarcraft equipment and decorations are a popular element, as are the cake stands for sale and hire.

## La Cuisiniere
- 81-83 Northcote Road, SW11
- ☎ 020 7223 4487
- 🖊 www.la-cuisiniere.co.uk
- 🚌 Clapham Junction Rail
- 🕐 Mon-Sat 9.30am-6pm

A veteran of the kitchenware scene, La Cuisiniere has expanded to three shops on the same road. Pots, pans and kitchen gadgets are stocked here, with friendly staff on hand to proffer advice. Tableware and ceramics are sold at La Cuisiniere Too (91 Northcote Road, SW11, 020 7223 4409) and bakeware can be found at the diminutive shop round the corner (85a Northcote Road, SW11, 020 7228 0325).

# West

## Whisk
- 2 The Green, High Street, Ealing, W5
- ☎ 020 8579 3444
- 🕐 Mon-Fri 10am-5.30pm, Sat 10am-6pm,
  Sun 10.30am-4.30pm

This bright, airy shop offers an excellent range of cookware, from Le Creuset pans and baking tins to tagine dishes and barbecues. Home-bakers are well catered for with a range including cookie cutters, cupcake cases and flavoured icings.
*Branch: 1a Devonshire Road, Chiswick, W4 (020 8995 8900)*

Kitchenware

Mail Order & Websites

T hanks to the Internet, it is now possible to track down and order many specialist foodstuffs, from great meat and organic vegetables to chillies and spices.

# Bacon & Ham

## Emmett's Stores

- *Peasenhall, Saxmundham, Suffolk, IP17 2HJ*
- *01728 660250*
- *www.emmettsham.co.uk*

This remarkable village store is noted for its own-made, traditional Suffolk cured bacon and ham. Emmett's acquired a Royal Warrant from the late Queen Mother.

# British Foods

## Forman & Field

- *30a Marshgate Lane, London, E15 2NH*
- *020 85252 352*
- *www.formanandfield.com*

Top quality British foods are on offer from this mail order business – established by the famous producers of smoked salmon. The emphasis is on fine foods such as caviar, game and goose, as well as seasonal treats.

# Cakes

## Bettys by Post

- *1 Parliament Street, Harrogate, North Yorkshire, HG1 2QU*
- *0845 345 3636*
- *www.bettysbypost.co.uk*

Established in 1919, Bettys Tea Room has become a much-loved Yorkshire institution. Betty's mail order service offers a chance to try her own-baked cakes and specialities including Yorkshire fat rascals, Simnel cakes and parkin without the trek to Yorkshire for the pleasure.

# Chillies

## Cool Chile Company

- *P.O. Box 5702 London, W11 2GS*
- *0870 902 1145*
- *www.coolchile.co.uk*

A must for chilli connoisseurs, Dodie Miller's mail order company sells an extensive range of dried Central American chillies from mild guajillo to intensely hot habaneros. Cool Chile also offers difficult to find Mexican ingredients such as blue Masa Harina.

## Peppers by Post

🏠 *Sea Spring Farm,*
*West Bexington, Dorchester,*
*Dorset, DT2 9DD*
☎ *01308 897892*
🖥 *www.peppersbypost.biz*

Chilli-enthusiasts Michael and Joy Michaud run a mail order service selling fresh chillies and tomatillos grown on their own Dorset farm. On offer are a range of chillies, including Jalapeno, Hungarian Hot Wax and Serrano, all freshly picked and delivered the following day

# Geese

## Goodman's Geese

🏠 *Walsgrove Farm, Great Witley*
*Worcestershire, WR6 6JJ*
☎ *01299 896272*
🖥 *www.goodmansgeese.co.uk*

Judy Goodman's free-range geese are traditionally reared on the Goodman's farm and have won many awards. They are particularly busy in the run-up to Christmas when their quality Geese are much sort after as an alternative to the ubiquitous and often dry turkey.

## Seldom Seen Farm

🏠 *Billesdon, Leicestershire, LE7 9FA*
☎ *0116 259 6742*
🖥 *www.seldomseenfarm.co.uk*

Claire and Robert Symington specialise in free-range geese, carefully reared on their own Leicestershire farm. The geese are slaughtered humanely, dry-plucked and hung for at least 10 days. Very much a seasonal treat, the geese are available in November and December.

# French Ingredients

## Natoora

🖥 *ww.natoora.co.uk*
☎ *020 7627 1600*

Founded in Paris, Natoora specialises in quality French foods.

# Italian Ingredients

## Fratelli Camisa

☎ *01992 763 076*
🖥 *www.camisa.co.uk*

An on-line Italian delicatessen run by Fratelli Camisa. They offer a great range of Camisa Italian foods to your door, from charcuterie to pasta.

## Valvona & Crolla

☎ *0131 556 6066*

✎ *www.valvonacrolla.co.uk*

An on-line shop from Edinburgh's famous Italian delicatessen, run with flair and dedication by the Contini family.

## Machiavelli Foods

✎ *www.machiavellifoods.co.uk*

☎ *020 7498 0880*

Machiavelli Foods are a well-established importers of Italian foodstuffs. They now offer a mail order service, enabling customers to source high-quality, artisanal foods and have them delivered to their door.

# Japanese Ingredients

## Mount Fuji

✎ *www.mountfuji.co.uk*

A useful website offering a range of Japanese ingredients, from noodles to delicious Yuzu Juice.

# Kitchenware

## Lakeland Ltd

🖃 *Alexandra Buildings, Windermere, Cumbria LA 23 1BQ*

☎ *05394 88100*

✎ *www.lakeland.co.uk*

This well-established, efficient Cumbria-based mail order kitchenware company inspires a loyal following across the UK. The range of stock is impressive, from essentials such as baking and icing equipment to specialised gadgets such as strawberry hullers and cherry and olive stoners.

## Squires Kitchens

🖃 *Squires House, 3, Waverley Lane Farnham, Surrey, GU9 8BB*

☎ *0845 225567*

✎ *www.squires-shop.com*

Squires Kitchens specialise in manufacturing and retailing cake decorating and sugarcraft products. Their website offers over 4,000 products, from frivolous cupcake cases to professional food colourings.

# Meat and Game

## Fletchers of Auchtermuchty

- *Reediehill Farm, Auchtermuchty, Fife, Scotland, KY14 7HS*
- *01337 828369*
- *www.seriousgoodvenison.co.uk*

Nicola and John Fletcher sell prime Scottish venison from deer raised on their own farm in Fife. Their mail order business offers numerous cuts of venison from medallions and carpaccio to osso buco or boned and rolled haunch of venison. If you're uncertain how to cook venison, Nicola is only too happy to share her considerable expertise in game cookery.

## Graig Farm Organics

- *Dolau, Llandrindod Wells, Powys, LD1 5TL*
- *01597 851 655*
- *www.graigfarm.co.uk*

This pioneering organic meat company is noted for the quality of its organic meat. Produce ranges from beef and pork to game and goat.

## Heal Farm

- *Kings Nympton, Devon, EX37 9TB*
- *01769 574 341*
- *www.healfarm.co.uk*

Anne Petch's passionate commitment to creating a market for rare breeds has resulted in a flourishing mail order business. She offers traditionally reared beef, lamb, pork and poultry.

## Higher Hacknell Farm

- *Burrington, Umberleigh, Devon, EX37 9LX*
- *01769 560909*
- *www.higherhacknell.co.uk*

This organic meat, mail order business gets all produce from its home farm in North Devon. Higher Hacknell offers prime, organically-reared beef, lamb, pork and chicken with a comprehensive range of cuts and the facility to have meat cut to requirement.

# Mediterranean Foods

## Belazu

✍ www.mybelazu.com

A discriminatingly chosen, high quality range of Mediterranean specialities, including argan oil, rose harissa, good olives and fine olive oils.

# Moroccan Ingredients

## Maroque

✍ www.maroque.co.uk

A mail order site offering an extensive range of Moroccan foodstuffs

# Organic Produce

## Riverford Organic Vegetables

📧 *Wash Barn, Devon, TQ11 0JU*

☎ *0845 600 2311*

✍ *www.riverford.co.uk*

Founded by Guy Watson in Devon, Riverford offers an exemplary organic produce box scheme supplying homes around the country with weekly boxes of organic vegetables, fruit and meat. The food comes from both Riverford and other organic farms.

## Abel & Cole

📧 *www.abelandcole.co.uk*

☎ *08452 626364*

Founded in 1988, Abel & Cole have a large following for their well-organised organic veg box delivery service. They offer an extensive range of organic produce and foodstuffs and a fast and efficient order and delivery system.

# Smoked Fish

## L. Robson & Son

📧 *Craster,*
*Northumberland, NE66 3TR*

☎ *01665 576 223*

✍ *www.kipper.co.uk*

Craster kippers have a distinctive, rich smoky flavour and are the speciality of this Northumbrian smokery. You can order this unique product directly from Robson over the phone or via the website.

## Alex Spink & Sons

📧 *24 Seagate, Arbroath*
*Scotland, DD11 1BJ*

☎ *01241 879 056*

✍ *www.abroathsmokiesonline.co.uk*

Traditionally-produced, tasty Arboath smokies (smoked small haddock) are on offer from Spink & Sons.

## Brown and Forrest

⌨ *Bowden Farm Smokery*
*Hambridge, Somerset, TA10 0BP*

☎ *01458 250 875*

🖰 *www.smokedeel.co.uk*

This family-run smokery, which offers smoked fish and meats, are particularly noted for their succulent smoked eel.

# Thai

## Thai Food

🖰 *www.thai-food-online.co.uk*

A web-based shop offering an extensive range of Thai ingredients, including fresh herbs and vegetables, curry pastes and noodles.

# Miscellaneous

## Verjuice

🖰 www.verjuice.co.uk

Verjuice is a condiment made from the juice of unripe grapes, which was popular in medieval Europe. Today, it is enjoying something of a revival as a flavouring. Jayson Hunter's company offers a mail order service selling verjuice to those eager to try this historic ingredient for themselves.

# Shopping For Cookbooks

## Books For Cooks

⌨ *4 Blenheim Crescent, W11*

☎ *020 7221 1992*

🖰 *www.booksforcooks.com*

🚌 *Ladbroke Grove LU*

🕐 *Tue-Sat 10am-6pm*

This Notting Hill bookshop, crammed with cookbooks from floor to ceiling, is a goldmine for anyone interested in food and cookery. The stock is extensive, covering cuisines from across the world. Staff are knowledgeable and helpful. Appetising cooking smells waft out from the small back kitchen, where recipes from books stocked in the shop are tested daily then sampled in the back-room café area. Books for Cooks also offer a range of cookery courses run from their kitchen upstairs (See page 94 for further details).

# Bibliography

The books used for my research include the cookbooks recommended in each section of the book. The books below are additional sources.

**Across Seven Seas** *Caroline Adams* (Tharp Books 1987)

**The British Museum Cookbook** *Michelle Berriedale-Johnson* (British Museum Publications 1987)

**Just Like It Was** *Harry Blacker* (Vallentine, Mitchell & Co 1974)

**Fruits and Vegetables of the Caribbean** *M.J. Bourne, G.W Lennox, S.A. Seddon* (Macmillan 1988)

**The Club** *Stephen Brook* (Constable 1989)

**Polish Cookbook** *Zofia Czerny* (Panstowowe Wydawnictwo Ekonomiczne 1975)

**The Oxford Companion to Food** *Alan Davidson* (Oxford University Press 1999)

**Galing Galing** *Nora and Mariles Daza* (Daza 1974)

**The Fine Art of Japanese Cooking** *Hideo Dekura* (Bay Books n.d.)

**Inside Soho** *Mark Edmonds* (Robert Nicholson 1988)

**The Streets of East London** *William Fishman* (Duckworth 1979)

**Staying Power** *Peter Fryer* (Pluto Press 1984)

**Jewish Cookbook** *Florence Greenberg* (Hamlyn 1980)

**Jane Grigson's Vegetable Book** *Jane Grigson* (Penguin 1980)

**Exotic Fruits & Vegetables** *Jane Grigson and Charlotte Knox* (Jonathan Cape 1986)

**Singapore Food** *Wendy Hutton* (Times Books International 1989)

**Filipino Cooking Here and Abroad** *Eleanor Laquian and Irene Sobrevinas* (National Book Store Inc 1977)

**Old Polish Traditions in the Kitchen and at the Table** *Maria Lemni and Henryk Vitry* (Interpress Publishers n.d.)

**East End Story** *A.B. Levy* (Vallentine, Mitchell & Co. 1950)

**Guide to Ethnic London** *Ian McAuley* (Michael Haag 1987)

**The Peopling of London** *Nick Merriman* (Museum of London 1993)

**Flavours of Korea** *Marc and Kim Millon* (Andre Deutsch 1991)

**A Popular Guide to Chinese Vegetables** *Karen Phillips and Martha Dahlen* (Frederick Muller 1983)

**Fruits of South-East Asia** *Jacqueline M Piper* (Oxford University Press 1989)

**The Oxford Companion to Italian Food** *Gillian Riley* (Oxford University Press 2007)

**Living London** *George Sims* (Cassell 1904-06)

**The Best of Singapore Cooking** *Mrs Leong Yee Soo* (Times Books International 1988)

**Penang Nonya Cooking** *Cecilia Tan* (Times Books International 1983)

**Sushi Made Easy** *Nobuko Tsuda* (John Weatherhill Inc 1982)

**The London Encyclopaedia** *Ben Weinreb and Christtopher Hibbert* (Papermac 1987)

**Cooking the Polish-Jewish Way** *Eugeniusz Wirkowski* (Interpress Publishers 1988)

**Jewish London** *Linda Zoff* (Piatkus 1986)

# Index

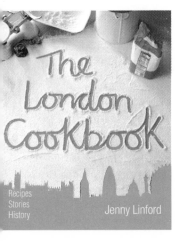

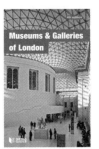

# Acknowledgements

First of all, my thanks to Metro Publications – Andrew and Susi and the team, for all their work on Food Lovers' London. Rosie Kindersley at Books For Cooks was the person who, many years ago, suggested that I contact Metro Publications regarding Food Lovers' London. This is now the fourth edition published with Metro Publications – so many thanks, Rosie. Food Lovers' London simply wouldn't be the book it is without Chris Windsor's great photographs. He deserves special thanks for putting so much time and energy into travelling around London with me on the quest for photos for the book.

Over the years, many people have spared time to talk to me and offer advice, suggestions and recommendations and my grateful thanks go to the following: Yasmin Alibhai-Brown, Jonas Aurell and Bronte Blomhoj, everyone I spoke at the BBC World Service (especially Nina Dekhan), Jon Cannon, Antonio Carluccio, Anna del Conte, Fuchsia Dunlop, Sarah Edington, Richard Ehrlich, Claire Ferguson, Anna Giacon, Wendy Godfrey, Roopa Gulati, Susan Hackett, Pat Howard, Shehzad Husain, The Jewish Chonicle, Sav Kyriacou, Michael Michaud, Ray O'Connor, Sri Owen, David Papp, Laki Pattelis, Sudi Pigott, Mary Pininska, Jackie and Mike Robins, Claudia Roden, the late Evelyn Rose, Polly Russell, the late Margaret Shaida, Siyu magazine, Imogen Smith, the late Yan Kit-So, Marlena Spieler, the late Kate Whiteman, Jan and Dinah Wieliczko. Finally, my thanks go to the shopkeepers themselves who patiently answered my many questions and from whom I learned so much.